LIVE THE dream

BIRMINGHAM
STORIES FROM A CITY OF DREAMERS AND ACHIEVERS

BY BILL CATON AND NIKI SEPSAS • PHOTOGRAPHY BY BEAU GUSTAFSON

Foreword

Two years ago, the Birmingham Regional Chamber of Commerce began a multimedia advertising and promotional campaign designed to celebrate our community. Entitled Birmingham, Live The Dream, the campaign celebrated today's Birmingham with its world-class health care, wonderful neighborhoods, active cultural life and growing business enterprises.

This beautifully written and photographed book is a part of that same spirit of celebration. Readers might notice that unlike many coffee table books that feature communities in photographic essays of buildings and cityscapes, the content of this book is people-centered, focusing on the stories of people who are doing exceptional things in our community and businesses that are thriving through the hard work and brain power of Birminghamians. The pictures and stories in this book capture the humanity and promise of our community far more than architecture or infrastructure can ever express. In these pages we've tried to capture the true heart of our region and the nature of our dreams.

I hope we've succeeded and that you'll enjoy sharing this keepsake book with family, friends and associates the world over. —Dave Adkisson, CEO, Brmingham Regional Chamber of Commerce

---

More than a skyline of buildings or an interconnected market of goods and services, a city is a collection of dreams—dreams realized, dreams derailed, dreams just taking shape in the worlds of business and commerce, science, the arts and music.

In alternating chapters that move between stories of Birmingham's most fascinating dreamers to profiles of successful businesses that call this city home, to an essay and photos that tell the tale of today's Birmingham, this book brings the vast appeal of this region to life.

In order to put this book together, we called upon the writing talents of Bill Caton and Niki Sepsas and the wonderful photography of Beau Gustafson. My thanks to each of them for this terrific work.

—Joe O'Donnell, Editor, Birmingham magazine

Published in 2003 by the Birmingham Regional Chamber of Commerce and *Birmingham* magazine,

505 North 20th Street, Suite 200, Birmingham Alabama 35203

Editorial Photography: Beau Gustafson, Big Swede Photography Copyright 2003

Text: Bill Caton and Niki Sepsas Copyright 2003

Art Direction: Chuck Beveridge, Katie Chipman

Jacket Design: Robin Colter

Editors: Joe O'Donnell, Marietta Urquhart

ISBN: 0-9741374-1-3   Printed in Canada

Contents

Contents

120 Profile: Southwire
One man's desire to be able to offer his grandmother the opportunity to sit under an electric light in her own house led to the foundation of a company that has become one of the world's leading manufacturers of wire and cable.

122 Profile: Alabama Gas Corporation
Alabama Gas Corporation (Alagasco) is the largest natural gas utility in Alabama and a subsidiary of Birmingham-based Energen Corporation.

124 People: Odessa Woolfolk
She's been a catalyst for a great many wonderful Birmingham developments, including the Birmingham Civil Rights Institute.

126 Profile: The Hackney Group
T. Morris Hackney went on a shopping spree in the 1980's, and he hasn't stopped yet.

127 Profile: Children's Health System
Children are the center of our lives.

128 Profile: Southern Natural Gas Company
Southern Natural Gas Company was founded almost eight decades ago through the vision of a group of business leaders in the South seeking to deliver natural gas to the cities of Birmingham and Atlanta.

130 Profile: Elements, Inc.
Elements, Inc. has been pioneering communications solutions for its clients for a half century.

132 Profile: Ogihara America Corporation
The company turned a 110-acre pasture in the Tarrant-Pinson Valley just outside Birmingham into an $85 million plant producing sidewalls, doors, hoods, fenders, and tailgates for the Mercedes M-class vehicles.

133 Profile: Liberty National Life Insurance
A symbol of business success in Birmingham, Liberty National Life established a presence in Alabama back in 1900.

134 People: Steve Yoder
Steve Yoder sat on a concrete bench outside the Birmingham Museum of Art and looked at Vulcan's huge head.

136 People: Eric Essix
He was born a child of the south, a native of Birmingham, Alabma during the turbulent 60's.

138 Profile: Vestavia Hills
In addition to its beautiful neighborhoods and award-winning homes, the city's school system, ranked as one of the best in the state, has served as a major catalyst of the city's growth.

140 Profile: University of Alabama at Birmingham
In just three decades, the University of Alabama at Birmingham has evolved from a promising medical center and urban extension program into the largest single employer in Alabama.

142 Profile: UAB Health System
Medicine that touches the world. UAB is recognized worldwide for its excellent patient care and ground-breaking research.

144 People: Marian McKay
Her back to a window in a small, classy suburban restaurant, Marian McKay Rosato is singing. Night is falling outside.

146 Profile: Imaging Business Machines
From the very beginning, Murphy set out to manufacture and market color scanners that go beyond taking photographs of pieces of paper.

147 Profile: Nelson Brothers Inc.
Almost a half century later, the company two brothers founded has developed a global reach, exporting to 17 countries around the world.

148 Profile: The Banc Corporation
The new look that The Bank brought to Birmingham's financial community also resulted in a new look for the John Hand building.

149 Profile: Eastern Health System, Inc.
Its three hospital facilities offer community platforms for inpatient and outpatient services, and a variety of related programs.

150 People: Dr. Lawrence Pijeaux
This educator, who spent most of his years in schools, says his job as executive director of the Civil Rights Institute "has special meaning in part because I see how far we have come. I can see the growth my people have made.

152 Profile: National Bank of Commerce
National Bank of Commerce is the lead bank of publicly traded Alabama National BanCorporation (ALAB).

153 Profile: Luckie & Company
The roots of Luckie & Company are clearly visible. The vintage Smith Corona manual typewriter that Robert Luckie used when he launched the advertising business in 1953 is prominently displayed.

154 Profile: Hand Arendall
One of the leading providers of legal services in Alabama.

155 Profile: Early Learning Center of Birmingham
In 1995, a unique partnership of business, government and education leaders brought to downtown Birmingham a new concept in early education for children.

156 Profile: American Cast Iron Pipe Company
American Cast Iron Pipe Company (ACIPCO) has been a major player in Birmingham's economy since the company was founded in 1905, helping establish the Magic City's early reputation as the industrial center of the South.

157 Profile: Protective Industrial Insurance Company
One of the oldest African-American owned businesses in Alabama traces its roots to the son of a former slave who saw a need and sought to fill it.

158 Profile: The Metro Grill
The Metro Grill, located in the Brookwood Village complex on Lakeshore Drive, is a gourmet American grill featuring casual fine dining and live entertainment.

159 Profile: Sloss Real Estate Group
Members of the Sloss family have been helping to transform the skyline of Birmingham since the 19th century when Colonel James Withers Sloss founded the giant furnaces on First Avenue North that forged the Magic City's future in iron and steel.

Contents

LIVE THE DREAM

In sports bars on the Southside, in the fellowship halls of churches in the city's west end, in suburban family rooms lit by the blue light of the television screen, a city found its improbable voice.

He was an immense presence on a small screen, at the center of a national obsession with fame. American Idol was a television orgy of hype and money, advertising and ratings points, and something even more extraordinary—the sincerity of a dream pursued, the love of a city called home.

Ruben Studdard brought that to Birmingham in the spring of 2003. He's a good place to start any examination of pursuing a dream. He believed in his dream of singing for a national audience that would find in his voice and stage presence something to love for a night, or a season, or a lifetime.

A big jersey, extraordinary hype, a big love for a place called Birmingham, a place called home.

Television often seems the most powerful of voices—sounds heard around the world, pictures shot clean through a neighborhood, power personified.

In the spring of 2003, television defined Birmingham for a time. Four decades earlier images broadcast over television captured forever a painful time in the city's history. This time the flickering light brought audiences images of a city a young man could really love.

What's not to love?

It's the end of the day. Light fading. The western sky a burning orange. We are discharged from the day.

Here are some of the things that might just happen.

Night falls in Birmingham's City Center.

You walk slowly past the Frank Fleming sculpture in the fountain at Five Points South and the bells of Highlands Methodist church begin to ring. A hymn to the wonders of life—maybe it's "Ode to Joy"— sings out over the noise of the traffic, the din of fleeting five o'clock madness. The music of the city holds us, fascinated, for a time.

At dinner at Chez FonFon, you could easily feel yourself transported to a bistro in France. Wine bottles in cubbyholes on the creamy walls, boiled eggs in a metal tree on the bar. Wonderfully simple, flavorful food waits.

Deep in the leafy suburban neighborhood of Crestline, a child is swinging. Pumping arms, swinging feet, reaching for the treetops and the slowly darkening sky beyond. Playing in the playground is a joy not reserved for Birmingham and its environs. We haven't even perfected it, but the joy is here.

In the chill of an October early morning, hundreds of runners gather in Linn Park downtown for the Susan B. Komen Race for the Cure run. These people are running for women who have lived, women who have died, women not yet born. Here in Linn Park and on the surrounding streets of the city, you can experience the chilliness of a Komen run and the warmth you feel after completing it.

It's the Sunday after Thanksgiving and families are walking up the uneven pavements to Bessemer First United Methodist. Just as they have for more than 50 years, Birmingham Concert Chorale is performing *The Messiah*. Every year. Five decades. Families coming back to this old church, year after year, to hear a story of redemption.

A quiet neighborhood in Homewood.

At the top of Red Mountain, Vulcan has been redeemed, too. Restored. Refurbished. He was falling down, you know. Leaching through his metal skin the concrete that earlier generations had filled him with, in order to withstand the force of the wind. Vulcan, the mythological Roman god of the forge, is arguably the most unusual symbol ever concocted for a city. But he's ours. Quirky. A worker. Been through a lot. When he came back from the St. Louis World's Fair, where he was Birmingham's exhibit of Southern industrial might, they put him at the state fairgrounds, stuck a giant fake ice cream cone in his hand, and made him a shill for summer treats.

He's back on the mountain now. Totally refurbished inside and out, Vulcan was placed back on his pedestal and looks out again over a city that grew like magic 130 some years ago at a railroad crossing in the middle of a Southern nowhere.

From nothing to a smoky, scary city to a place of health and healing in a few generations, the story of Birmingham is probably one of the most unlikely stories in the history of American cities.

And it's a story that continues to fascinate, to intrigue. We're poised on the edge of many great things in the Birmingham region, and we've been working to make them a reality.

It would be hard to imagine a metropolitan area that has been harder at work trying to redefine what makes a city great.

From transportation, which is one of the great challenges facing the region, to core city redevelopment

Through the window of Highland's Bar and Grill at Five Points South.

to arts support and funding, Birmingham is hard at work on finding solutions to problems that bedevil many American cities.

The solutions to some of our challenges are being uncovered.

The Rise of the Creative Class is a best-selling sociology and economic development book written by Richard Florida, a Carnegie Mellon professor in Pittsburgh, Pennsylvania. The book created a sensation by chronicling the changes in society and economics that is driving success in the cities of the 21st century.

Birmingham ranked 47th out of the 286 regions ranked in the creative class indexing completed by Florida. The creativity index for Birmingham is pegged at 722, ranking well in the numbers of the creative class and less impressive in the innovation and diversity categories.

In the arts arena, people who care about the development of the region—from the forces behind Region 2020 to arts group executives and volunteers—have put a lot of effort into developing a cultural master plan. The plan grew out of an effort led by the Massachusetts-based consulting firm, Wolf, Keen & Co., which conducted hundreds of interviews, surveys and focus groups. What they found was an arts community that will have to continue to develop audiences and cooperation among arts groups and organizations in order to both survive and thrive in an increasingly competitive environment.

Exciting examples of cooperative developments include the Birmingham Music Cooperative and the

The Alabama Ballet in performance.

Birmingham Area Theatre Alliance as these groups and others strive to bring to life the spirit of the cultural master plan.

In many ways Birmingham is at a crossroads, a city aware and working on both its assets and liablilities.

Social capital is another way of saying connection, the social networks within a community that bond individuals one to the other, group to group. Harvard professor Robert Putnam wrote about social capital and the community bonds it creates in his landmark book, *Bowling Alone*, published in 2000.

How are we alike and how are we different from other cities? What kind of social capital have we created?

The Community Foundation of Greater Birmingham funded in part the National Social Capital Community Benchmark Survey. How does Birmingham differ from the nation at large?
- 81 percent of us belong to a religious institution, compared to the national average of 65 percent.
- 5 percent of locals interviewed describe religion as unimportant, versus 15 percent nationally.
- 45 percent contribute more than $500 to a religious organization, as opposed to 34 percent in the national sample.

Based on survey norms, the Birmingham region is strongest in the general social trust, formal group involvement and faith-based social capital. The region's lowest scores were realized in the area of

Runners begin the Mercedes Marathon, held each February.

diversity of friendships and the level of interracial trust. In the regional portion of the survey, 478 households were included in Jefferson and Shelby Counties. In the total national survey, 29, 200 were interviewed in 40 communities.

Religious involvement is an important aspect of civic life, particularly in the South and Midwest. While religious involvement seems to make communities stronger particularly in the area of giving and volunteering; it can also lead to low marks in tolerance and social action.

Building social capital in diverse communities is the great challenge of the 21st century. While diversity leads to stronger communities, the more diverse the community the less likely people are to trust others, connect with others, connect across class lines, participate in politics.

Birmingham's community quotients were 103 (social trust), 89 (interracial trust), 90 (conventional politics), 89 (protest politics), 112 (civic leadership), 118 (associational involvement). Atlanta's numbers were 83,91,88,85,89, 104. Charlotte 93,78,91,87, 97, 114. Baton Rouge 99,91,106, 76, 116, 102.

What do the numbers tell us? That we are a city of extraordinary strengths and opportunities and equally daunting challenges. The journey ahead points the way to a future we build day by day.

On a summer Saturday the Pepper Place complex in the Lakeview District of the city, arrayed under white tents bright as summer clouds, dozens of farmers have laid out wonderful Alabama produce, tomatoes, peas, watermelons, set up in a classic market square arrangement. Around the stands, people

Veronique Vanblaere adjusts one of the exhibits at Naked Art gallery downtown.

mingle, leading dogs, children in tow, finding both a sense of community and wonderful healthy food. In one corner of the Pepper Place complex, an O'Henry's coffee stand serves hot coffee, cold smoothies and baked goods. At the other end, one of the city's best chefs, Chris Hastings of Hot and Hot Fish Club, is giving a cooking demonstration and passing out tastes of his singular menu to people.

The air, even this early in the morning, is humid and still, but the spirit is infectious. People are greeting each other; kids are enjoying the wonders of the reddest tomatoes you've ever seen. They are strolling along, eating peaches and getting face and hands sticky in the wonderful way only a kid can get preciously dirty.

The Pepper Place Saturday Market is a city dream fulfilled, one of many that have been given life in the last few years in a region that gives space and fuel to dreams.

In the pages of this book you will follow the stories of people and companies that are living collective dreams in the Birmingham region. A film director once said that he loved the cinema because it was the only place 200 people could gather together and dream the same dream.

In Birmingham we have a million people gathered together and at least a million dreams rising like morning mist from a swiftly flowing river. They can be caught and captured or they can flow away on a current of air. We've captured at least some dreams on this expanse of ink and paper.

But there are more. Always more.

One of the country's original movie palaces, the wonderfully restored Alabama Theatre is the scene of concerts, special events and, of course, movies.

Portfolio

A universe of joy captured in a child's smile.

Art and sunlight at AmSouth Harbert Plaza.

Poet, performing artist and Mojo Mama Laura Secord.

A stone mansion amid a burst of autumn color.

A rope swing punctuates the city's natural treasure, the Cahaba River.

Birminghamian Titus Battle: a tough life lived with grace.

Autumn leaves bring the beauty of four seasons to Birmingham.

Five Points bathed in light.

Portfolio

Looking up.

The interior of the Alabama Theatre.

Pyramids of glass atop the new downtown mid-rise, Concord Center.

A Dart trolley runs along South 20th Street.

Federal Couthouse Building, Birmingham.

Art in public.

Sculpture in the garden at the Birmingham Museum of Art.

Lunch time in the center of the city.

Community art.

Leaves and glass at the Birmingham Public Library.

A heritage of steel.

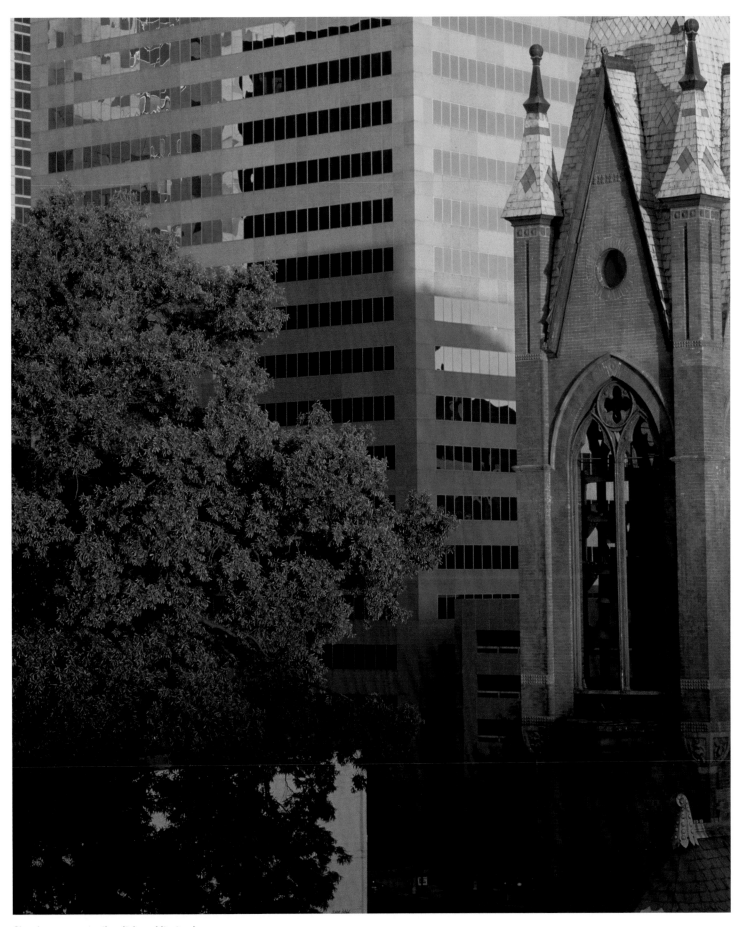

Churches are among the city's architectural gems.

A neighborhood friendship.

A chip shot in the city.

Frank Stitt

The soft light of evening flows through the windows of Chez FonFon, bathing the restaurant in a golden and delicious shade of yellow and brown.

Chef Frank Stitt walks in the back door and stands back by the kitchen, looking out on the room filled with people. He smiles and nods, waves occasionally or visits the table of a customer.

More than just an internationally celebrated chef, Frank Stitt has spent a quarter-century career making his hometown a more stylish, convivial, better place. You can't ask for much more than that.

This is just one of the restaurants that bear Stitt's imprint. Highlands Bar and Grill (right next door to Chez FonFon) has been named the fifth best restaurant in the country by *Gourmet* magazine. Bottega is a very popular Italian restaurant on Highland Avenue. Stitt has also become an author with a cookbook soon to be published and a media chef with regular stint on cable television's Turner South.

Stitt opened Highlands in 1982. "The exciting thing is that I've been able to do foods that were very different—that other people were perhaps afraid to try. And I think that the reason is we developed a trust within the community. People knew we were all about quality, and if something wasn't beautiful and fresh, we weren't going to serve it. If it had to do with oysters or fish or sweetbreads or quail or venison, they knew we were on a mission for quality, and Birmingham responded to that.

"Many people I think were a little bit surprised with a couple of things. One is that we had very ambitious ideas for our food, and two that we called ourselves Highlands Bar and Grill, which is kind of a play on a real casual, simple little restaurant. We wanted to have the relaxed quality of a bar and grill, but with the finesse of a great restaurant. And I think that the juxtaposition of formal but casual, great quality but not stuffy, was something that Birmingham's really taken to."

Tonight at Chez FonFon—seated in wooden chairs at homey tables in a setting reminiscent of a French bistro—people are enjoying themselves, laughing, taking bites of wonderful food and sipping great wine.

"One of the most important things that we are about is allowing a beautiful moment in a person's day. I know that sounds a little hokey, but it's about being at a table with great food and great drink with your friends and family and the people you care about. That is something we provide.

"You've had a tough day. You've had to fight and struggle all day, but you can sit at our table and it can be a very peaceful time—a time of being nurtured, re-energized, slowing down and being thankful for the moment of breaking bread with people you care about.

"And I think in a way that is why Highlands has succeeded. I think that is what the community has seen in us and savors in us. That moment is almost like experiencing a sunset together, of having a beautiful moment of your day.

"I think that one of the goals when you're a businessman is that you want to provide a business that the community needs on many different levels. I think that is how Highlands and Bottega and FonFon are perceived. Birmingham as a community really needed a great restaurant. A restaurant that had the excitement and enthusiasm of a young place, but enough sophistication that you'd feel like dressing up, or you could just come in the bar and meet your friends for oysters and a drink. So Highlands kind of blended some of the excitement of the old New Orleans and San Francisco restaurants, but in a unique, very Southern way."

Chris McNair

It comes as a plain truth from Chris McNair's mouth. It comes without pain, without anger, without self pity. It comes as a simple philosophy from an intelligent, artistic man who has done his share of suffering and celebrating. McNair, at 77, has learned what life can teach.

"I'm not saying I don't have those feelings, but you won't accomplish much if you let that take you over," McNair says of the central tragedy of his life, the death of his 11-year-old daughter Carol Denise in the 16th Street Baptist Church bombing on Sept. 15, 1963. "You have to realize that you aren't the only one to have had problems.

"I've tried to use my energy helping other people when and where I could. But if you let yourself fall prey to anger and disgust ...as a creative person I don't think you can do much while you're in that anger mood.

"Why did I stay here? I was black and I wasn't fixing to change colors and I don't know any place in the nation where I could have gone and not been treated black. I was Southern born and I intended to stay in the South. The South was on fire and I didn't want to go somewhere else and watch it burn. I didn't want to go to California. I'd have been running.

"I like to think I had an impact on changing the South and maybe even the nation."

McNair is a large, solid man. On this sunny day he wears a long-sleeve shirt with an open collar and khaki pants. He sits at a round table in the front of his photography studio and art gallery. The sounds of a business—ringing telephones, intercoms and photo processing machines—meld to a hum behind his deep, experienced voice.

"I was a good photographer, interested in the art," he says. "A lot of people told me then that 'Black folks are not going to buy the kind of pictures you make.'"

This former member of the Alabama House of Representatives and the Jefferson County Commission became interested in photography while earning a degree in Agronomy from what was then called Tuskegee Institute. He moved to Birmingham with his wife and "spent a couple of years here doodling around," before getting a job at White Dairy. His milk route was on the same street where Chris McNair Studios now sits.

McNair always wanted to have a photo studio, so when his sales manager, on a fall day in 1961 asked him, "Mack, you still piddling around out there taking pictures?" he knew it was time to take the leap and follow his passion full time. McNair opened his studio in 1962.

He continued to work through his daughter's murder and in 1972 he ran successfully for the Alabama House.

"If it hadn't been for the business I don't think I could have suffered public service," McNair says. "When I first went to the Alabama Legislature I was the first black ever elected county wide. I felt like I could get elected even though you had to run county wide. May 23, 1973 was my first day there. I was so naïve that I didn't know they paid."

What spurred McNair to run for office?

"I felt like I could get elected. There is no correlation (between the church bombing and his decision to seek public office). In fact I was more reluctant to do it. I didn't want anybody to think that I had gotten into it with that kind of publicity."

The gallery across the hall from the photo shop was still set up from a banquet the previous night. Eighty or so high school juniors and seniors from California had come to McNair's studio to study civil rights history. The program brings students to Atlanta, Montgomery, Selma, several places in Mississippi, Memphis and Little Rock. And they come to Birmingham.

"When they came here we had a dinner for them," McNair says. "We showed them the documentary 'Four Little Girls.' They (participants in the program) have been here 20 times. I speak to them when they come."

He speaks to them in a gallery that has a room dedicated to Carol Denise. Her clothes, toys and some family pictures are displayed in the room along with a letter from a film student named Spike Lee who had an idea about a documentary on the church bombing.

"I'm 77; there aren't a whole lot of us left," McNair says. "We've become important for these young groups. My daughter would have been 51 this November."

BellSouth

BellSouth Corporation is a Fortune 100 communications services company serving more than 44 million customers in the United States and 14 other countries. Birmingham is headquarters for BellSouth's Alabama Operations.

Consistently recognized for customer satisfaction, BellSouth provides a full array of broadband data and e-commerce solutions to business customers, including Web hosting and other Internet services. In the residential market, BellSouth offers DSL high-speed Internet access, advanced voice features, and other services. BellSouth offers long distance service for both business and consumer customers in Georgia, Louisiana, North Carolina, South Carolina, Alabama, Kentucky, Mississippi, Florida and Tennessee.

BellSouth also provides online and directory advertising services, including BellSouth The Real Yellow Pages®.com. BellSouth owns 40 percent of Cingular Wireless®, the nation's second largest wireless company, which provides innovative wireless data and voice services.

TECHNOLOGY

BellSouth was among the first in the industry to embrace the trend in communications away from electrical to optical networking—transmitting signals in pulses of light instead of electrical charges. BellSouth was the nation's first telephone company to offer dedicated, laser-based fiber optic service to meet the needs of individual customers.

Other technological advancements were quick to follow. BellSouth began the decade of the '90s by retiring its last electro-mechanical switch and becoming the first Bell company to complete the transition to an all electronic network. This milestone paved the way for deployment of yet more advanced Custom Calling services to its customers.

The company now boasts one of the most advanced optical networks on the planet, with 4.1 million miles of fiber optics, more than 750 broadband switches, in excess of 21,000 synchronous optical networking (SONET) rings and some 150 dense wave multiplying systems.

BellSouth in 1999 began marketing high speed DSL service to consumers and small businesses in all of the company's top 30 markets in the region. The introduction in 2000 of a self-installing option for its BellSouth FastAccess® DSL Internet service has grown to more than one million subscribers. From homework assignments to music downloads to opening e-mail attachments to on-line shopping, BellSouth customers have discovered the advantages of DSL's speed—up to 50 times faster than dial-up connections.

BROADBAND AND DATA

BellSouth began its systematic transformation of its core network from narrowband analog service to broadband digital data almost two decades ago. In 1990, the company harnessed the incredible power of supercomputers and fiber optics by allowing physicians to remotely access high-resolution medical images. BellSouth also invested more than $300 million in a wireless data venture that opened a whole new market with 10 million potential customers in the U.S. alone. In 1993, BellSouth completed its nationwide wireless data network in the United States.

Today, nearly 90 percent of BellSouth's data revenues come from high speed, high capacity, high reliability digital services for business customers. One of the company's leading products in its fast-growing market is LightGate® service that integrates data, e-business, video, and voice over a fiber-based private line equivalent to 672 dial-up circuits.

LONG DISTANCE

BellSouth entered the long distance market in Alabama in September 2002 with new service options designed to meet customers' personal and business calling needs. "Consumers in Alabama have asked for years for a long distance service that is easy to understand, with one point of contact, one bill, and one call to customer service," said Tom Hamby, president of BellSouth in Alabama. "We're finally able to give Alabama consumers what they want by providing them the value and convenience of having all of their telecommunications services, including local and long distance, from one company and paying one bill. It is also important that BellSouth is a company Alabama consumers have known and trusted for more than 120 years."

INTERNATIONAL MARKETS

BellSouth has focused on providing a comprehensive array of services to customers in markets that are strategically diversified in terms of both geography and products. The company created BellSouth International in 1985 to manage its activities outside the United States. Its first overseas office opened later that year in Hong Kong.

Others were quick to follow. Another overseas office opened in Germany, and wireless data systems were built in Belgium, Germany and Singapore.

BellSouth's wireless expertise was exported to Latin America in 1987. Strategic investments over the years have given the BellSouth Latin America Group the largest wireless footprint in Latin America, with

nationwide licenses in eight of the 11 countries it serves. Together with its wireless partners, the company covers a total population of 224 million people in the region.

BellSouth has also developed a reputation for community service in Latin America through innovative programs such as BellSouth Proniño (BellSouth for Children). The pragmatic initiative extends grants so thousands of kids can attend school rather than have to work to help support their families.

AN EYE TO THE FUTURE

BellSouth employs more than 8,000 people in Alabama, almost 80 percent of them are in the Birmingham area. Each is aware that much of Alabama's economy and security depends on communications

systems and networks that are the best in the world. That understanding will guide BellSouth in the future as the company continues to transform its business for the digital world by maintaining its commitment to service and reliability.

That commitment led to Customer Satisfaction awards from J.D. Power and Associates, and ranking by *Fortune* magazine in its listing of "America's 50 Best Companies for Asians, African-Americans, and Hispanics." That commitment will also be the cornerstone for the company's employees and management team as they continue evolving to the digital future with focused execution.

BellSouth also donates millions of dollars and thousands of hours of employee volunteer time in community service projects across Alabama each year. The BellSouth Pioneers and The BellSouth Foundation have a special emphasis on improving education through special service initiatives and grants to Alabama schools and universities. "Our commitment to Alabama goes beyond our advanced technology," Hamby said. "It also includes an obligation to the values of civic service and improving the quality of life in communities we serve."

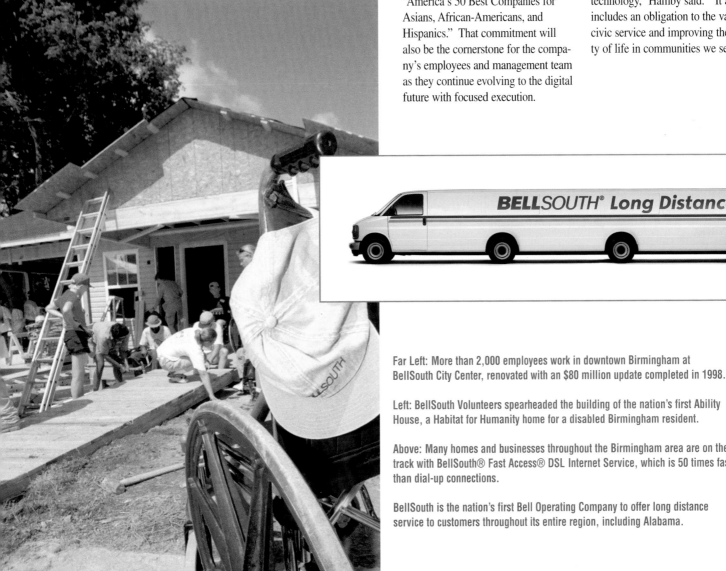

Far Left: More than 2,000 employees work in downtown Birmingham at BellSouth City Center, renovated with an $80 million update completed in 1998.

Left: BellSouth Volunteers spearheaded the building of the nation's first Ability House, a Habitat for Humanity home for a disabled Birmingham resident.

Above: Many homes and businesses throughout the Birmingham area are on the fast track with BellSouth® Fast Access® DSL Internet Service, which is 50 times faster than dial-up connections.

BellSouth is the nation's first Bell Operating Company to offer long distance service to customers throughout its entire region, including Alabama.

REGIONS FINANCIAL CORPORATION

More Than a Bank

ock Solid is a catch phrase that many financial institutions use today, but at Regions Financial Corporation, it is an accurate description of the institution's financial strength. With more than $46 billion in assets, Birmingham-based Regions ranks among the 25 largest financial services companies in the United States. Approximately 16,000

Regions professionals provide traditional commercial and retail banking services from more than 675 offices in Alabama, Arkansas, Florida, Georgia, Louisiana, North Carolina, South Carolina, Tennessee, and Texas. Regions has been ranked as one of the strongest banks in America by nationally known rating services.

The company has spent the past three decades building on its reputation of being 'more than a bank', leading the way with new products, servic-

es, and convenience. Such a responsibility requires offering more than traditional banking services to Regions' customers. Regions underlined that mission in 2001 when it acquired Morgan Keegan & Company, one of the South's largest and most respected investment firms, and Rebsamen Insurance agency, one of the nation's 50 largest insurance brokers.

Founded in 1969, Morgan Keegan has grown to become a premier regional financial services company

providing brokerage, investment banking, trust, and other financial services. An employer of more than 2,000 individuals and listing more than $350 million in equity capital, Morgan Keegan brings to Regions a diversified mix of clients including individual investors in the southern United States, and corporations, government entities, financial institutions, and institutional money managers based throughout the U.S. and abroad.

Regions' leaders feel that combining the bank's strengths and presence with Morgan Keegan & Company and Rebsamen Insurance in the same regional markets will provide its commercial, municipal, retail, and private banking clients with a broader range of financial solutions and advisor services to satisfy their financial needs.

Regions Financial Corporation reached another milestone in 2002 when its common stock began trading on the New York Stock Exchange (NYSE) under the ticker symbol RF. The move from Nasdaq to NYSE offered Regions increased visibility and prestige.

Regions' officers and board of directors are justly proud of the corporation's more than seven decades of service to the Birmingham community, and excited about the opportunity to build long term relationships throughout the South. Now much more than a bank, Regions is ready for new growth and new performance.

Approximately 16,000 Regions professionals provide traditional commercial and retail banking services from more than 675 offices in Alabama, Arkansas, Florida, Georgia, Louisiana, North Carolina, South Carolina, Tennessee, and Texas.

O'NEAL STEEL

Only a few months after the City of Birmingham had celebrated its 50th birthday in the fall of 1921, Kirkman O'Neal founded the steel company that today still bears his name. President Warren Harding had delivered a speech to a crowd of almost 40,000 people at Woodrow Wilson Park at the city's birthday party commenting that Birmingham had truly earned its reputation as the "Magic City". Kirkman O'Neal, who had to borrow $2,000 to launch his business, hoped that his venture would emulate the phenomenal growth that the President said characterized Birmingham.

The son and grandson of two Alabama governors, Kirkman O'Neal began his small steel fabricating business with five employees. Throughout the heady boom times of the 1920's, O'Neal grew the business by focusing on providing high quality products and prompt and effective service to his customers. In a 1926 interview with The Birmingham News, he stated that "We will come along. We hire the best skilled labor we can find, and pay good wages and get good work. We turn out every piece of work and each contract the best that can be done, and we are determined that it shall be satisfactory."

That mission statement by the company's founder was the light by which O'Neal Steel's leadership guided the business over the years. Through the dark days of the Great Depression, the company maintained the strong customer relationships that had established its reputation.

Kirkman O'Neal directed an expansion of the company's focus in the late 1930's. Responding to the demand of its customers, O'Neal Steel became one of the South's first metals service centers. The company focused on serving customers who did not meet the high tonnage purchases required by the mills.

The war years of the 1940's saw additional change and expansion. The company's original headquarters loca-

tion on Birmingham's Westside moved to a new location near the airport to accommodate the deluge of government orders for bombs, gun platforms, and other armament for the war effort. O'Neal Steel became the nation's largest producer of general purpose bombs used in the Pacific Theater of Operations.

Kirkman's son, Emmet, joined the family business in 1946. Together, they opened the company's first satellite district in Jackson, Mississippi six years later. Through corporate planning and acquisitions, O'Neal opened 39 additional districts from Florida to Pennsylvania and Virginia to Arizona. Today, O'Neal Steel is in 22 Southeastern, Midwestern, Southwestern, and Mountain states. Kirkman O'Neal's original workforce of five employees has grown to approximately 2,500 with over 500 working at the Birmingham location. O'Neal Steel now is the largest family-owned metals service center in the United States.

"We would be a Fortune 500 company if we were publicly traded," states Bill Jones, O'Neal's president and CEO. "O'Neal is unique in that we are a family owned business, but I think that gives certain advantages. Our employees are dedicated to making our company grow by providing superior quality and service."

O'Neal's product and services line has also grown far beyond anything that its founder could have envisioned 80 years ago. The company now offers a comprehensive range of metals and processing services including a complete line of carbon, stainless, and alloy steels; aluminum; pipe and tubing; expanded metal; and bar grating. Specialized metals processing services include laser, oxy fuel and plasma cutting, forming, shearing, machining,

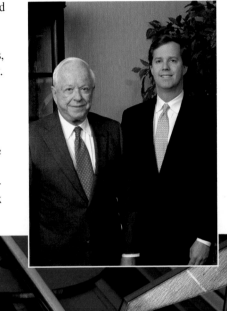

Father and son Emmet and Craft O'Neal exemplify strong relationships at O'Neal Steel.

tube bending, and sawing. Customers include steel fabricators and heavy equipment manufacturers, such as truck trailers, agricultural equipment, construction equipment, and material handling equipment.

Further expansion came in 1997 when O'Neal purchased Metalwest, a light gauge flat rolled service center headquartered near Denver with seven locations in the western United States and Alabama.

The following year, O'Neal Steel received one of its most prestigious awards when it was chosen by H.R. Chally, an independent research organization, as being "World Class". Chally pollsters conducted 23,000 customer interviews at over 7,300 companies nationwide to determine the best sales organizations in America. When

the numbers had been crunched, only 134 companies among the thousands surveyed emerged in that category. O'Neal Steel was one of only two companies in the Birmingham Metropolitan Area to make that list, placing number one in the primary metals category and an impressive 17th in the overall ranking.

"I think that recognition reflects the importance we place on the relationships our company builds with our customers," Bill Jones notes. "Since 1922, we have had excellent employees, a dedicated and involved ownership, and have changed our business as our customers have changed. But we have never forgotten the importance of hard work, integrity, and customer service."

THE TOWN OF MT LAUREL

A Sense of Place

Left: Burnham Street

Above: The Robinson Building in the Town Center

lton B. Stephens, Jr., the Vice-President of EBSCO Industries had long visualized a community built on the concept of the residential areas that characterized America prior to World War II. Those neighborhoods were places where families and friends lived more compact, interactive lives that fostered a sense of togetherness. Stephens gave substance to his dream by establishing the EBSCO Development Company in the late 1990's to spearhead the development of a town. Mt Laurel is a 600-acre community built with a comprehensive planning concept that includes a variety of housing sizes and types, commercial and civic uses and amenities in a defined area.

Nestled among the rolling hills of Dunavant Valley in north Shelby County, Mt Laurel is a classic example of a Traditional Neighborhood Development (TND), part of the New Urbanism movement that integrates environmental, social and economic initiatives in order to offer a timeless way of living.

"We put together a development team dedicated to creating a place where a diverse group of ages and income levels can live, work and play together in an active community of incomparable beauty," Stephens states. "At the heart of the community is the Town Center, a gathering place for residents to shop, work and meet with friends and neighbors. The Town Center will include not only a town hall, library, church and school, but office and shops such as a grocery store, restaurant, hardware store, Fitness Together, soda fountain and apothecary to meet the needs that are part of our daily patterns."

Stephens' team of professionals is bringing the dream to reality. A town director of design, landscape architect and builder worked closely together to fit the homes to the land rather than reshape land to accommodate the architecture. Spacious front porches, extra-wide meandering walkways, and an 11-acre lake surrounded by a park designed for all to enjoy have resulted in a 'walkable community' that encourages interaction among the residents. A variety of cottages, town houses, side yard homes, live/work residences and larger single family homes starting in the low $200,000's have produced an enchanting patchwork of housing that ensures that all generations of a family can live in the same neighborhood.

The Mt Laurel Apothecary will accommodate the resident's needs for an old fashioned pharmacy, accept all major prescription plans and feature home delivery. At the Mt Laurel Hardware Store, shoppers can buy a pound of nails, choose from a variety of do-it-yourself tools, get a cold drink from the antique Coca Cola drink box, or relax over a game of checkers, a genuine recreation of an old fashioned general store. When it's time to eat, residents can stroll down to The Standard Bistro. Alan Martin the Bistro's chef will offer lunch and dinner items ranging from roasted stuff quail, shrimp and grits, braised lamb and fresh sautéed flounder.

Add to this mix the Mt Laurel Organic Garden, offering members access to organically grown vegetables and fruits through the season and the Mt Laurel Farmers Market and Crafts Show, held in the Town Center through the spring and summer months, and it is easy to see why Mt Laurel was a runaway hit at the 2003 Spring Home Tour, posting two Gold awards and two Silver awards, including 'Best All Around Community' and 'Development of the Year.'

"Mt Laurel is an experience," states Elton B. Stephens, Jr. "We're not just building homes here. We're building an opportunity for community, for neighborhoods, for friendships, for a lifetime."

THOMPSON TRACTOR COMPANY

Mike Thompson was barely two years old when his father, Hall W. Thompson, moved the family from Nashville to Birmingham to assume ownership of the tractor company he had purchased here in 1957. Mike, who now serves as president of Thompson Tractor Company, notes that his earliest memories were of playing on and around tractors. His father's most vivid memory, however, is of the company's frightening first month in business.

"We made a single machine sale in the month of December, and lost $40,000 of our limited capital," Hall W. Thompson wrote on the 40th anniversary of the founding of the company.

Fortunately, that was the last red ink month the new company experienced. Over the ensuing four-and-a-half decades, Thompson Tractor Company grew through a series of carefully planned expansions of the line of products and equipment it carried and through its unwavering commitment to service after the sale to its customers.

From its origin as the Caterpillar dealer for the northern 39 counties in Alabama, Thompson Tractor Company has become the full line Caterpillar dealer for Alabama and northwest Florida and the Caterpillar forklift dealer for most of Georgia. The company, which specializes in the sale and service of Caterpillar earth moving, construction, and material handling equipment, is headquartered on Pinson Highway in Tarrant, and employs more than 1,100 people.

Diversification and responding to shifting market demands have been as important to the company's growth as was its representation of Caterpillar, a manufacturer with a worldwide reputation for quality design and construction. The Eisenhower Defense Act of 1956 led to a huge demand in heavy equipment for the construction of the interstate highway system that the Act authorized. Thompson Tractor was there to supply the bulldozers, scrapers, and graders needed for road building. The worldwide demand for coal in the early 1970's led to heady times in the strip mining industry which required tractors, loaders, and trucks. The boom in residential construction over the years and major construction projects such as the Tenn-Tombigbee Waterway and the Alaska Pipeline

also created additional demand for heavy machinery. In each instance, Thompson Tractor Company helped supply the equipment, parts, and service for the contractors doing the work.

"We'd like to be recognized as a business partner by our customers," Mike Thompson relates. "We provide our customers with one-stop shopping for equipment sales, parts, service, rentals, and leasing. We also offer options on used parts and used equipment as well. We want to be known for the value we offer."

Down time is costly in any business, but in the heavy construction industry it can be fatal. For that reason, Thompson Tractor provides customer support that includes field mechanics and technicians trained to keep equipment up and running, and a preventive maintenance program that helps customers extend the life of their equipment. Thompson' parts supply program makes overnight availability of parts to 98 percent of the company's service area.

Thompson provides a diverse array of services to customers in its region through four divisions: Thompson Tractor Company, Thompson Power Systems, Thompson Lift Truck Company, and Thompson Cat Rental Store.

Thompson Tractor Company provides sales and support of Caterpillar earth moving, general construction, forestry, and industrial equipment. In 1987, it became the sixth largest Caterpillar dealer in the U.S.

The Power Systems Division supplies Caterpillar diesel engines and power systems for any electric power generation applications as well as engines, parts, and service for trucks and marine propulsion applications. Thompson Lift Truck Company offers a complete line of material handling products and support from Caterpillar and other leading manufacturers.

The newest addition to the Thompson family of services, the Thompson Cat Rental Store, offers contractors the convenience of short-term rental equipment.

Following Hall Thompson's retirement in 1983, Mike, his sister, Judy, and his brother, George, each served as top officers in the company. Mike Thompson points to many of the company's key employees and their longevity with Thompson Tractor as a major reason for the success of the family business. He cites the contributions of Paul Chism, who was with the original company that Hall Thompson purchased in 1957 and who stayed on to eventually serve as chairman of the board of Thompson Tractor, as among the most important

"This company's greatest assets go home every night," says Mike Thompson, referring to the dedicated staff who have made Thompson Tractor Company what it is today and who will lead it into the 21st century.

Thompson Tractor Company is the full line Caterpillar dealer for Alabama and Northwest Florida and the forklift dealer for most of Georgia. The company is headquartered in Tarrant and employs more than 1,100 people. Mike Thompson, pictured above, is company president.

Terry Slaughter

The truth about design in the world of Terry Slaughter is that it makes a difference, a palatable difference in the lives of people. Founder and creative director of a Birmingham-based advertising agency, SlaughterHanson, that became nationally known for its creative work, Slaughter has seen his creativity move in many directions in recent years.

The overwhelming truth he has arrived at is a simple premise: Creativity can extend beyond self to reach out to serve others. Slaughter opened three separate galleries in English Village last year, galleries designed to give a structure, a home, to Slaughter's vision. The concept behind Terrence Denley, Gallery Geoffrin, and Chairity is based upon this notion of creativity for the common good—creativity that impacts the human condition. "Three galleries created to expose people to beautiful design, while at the same time extending beyond the aesthetic to enhance the lives of those in need.

Profits from the galleries will be used in various humanitarian efforts, including housing programs for the homeless in Mexico and programs that touch the lives of individuals in hospice care. When creativity serves, when design impacts the human condition, it is then that the beauty of design, of creativity, truly enlightens," according to Slaughter's web site designintruth.com.

The genesis of Terry Slaughter's commitment lies in his faith in God and in his experience leading his employees to Mexico to help build houses for the poor.

"Most of the time that I have given of my talent, it has been the talent of creativity. When I first started going down to Mexico, it was not about creativity. They just needed somebody to move some bricks around.

"When you're doing an advertising campaign, you know it's touching people but there's no connection to who it touches. It's all on an intellectual level. Well here, you're building this house, and in one week this family who was living in this box, who's right there on site with you, at the end of the week, they're living in a house. You know that because you were there, their life was changed. The life of the Sanchez family was changed that week because of what you did.

El Nidal is the organization founded to provide housing for Mexico's poor. Perenity is Terry Slaughter and his wife Jennifer's flower ministry. Jennifer creates about 100 flower arrangements every week, delivered by volunteers to hospice patients. The Perenity web site opens with a record-ing of a woman's voice: "We come into this world. We glow. We bring color to the lives of those around us and then we leave. Every flower has a story to tell."

Both of these efforts are funded in part by proceeds from the English Village art galleries: Terrence Denley, Chairity and Gallery Geoffrin. Terrence Denley is a retail gallery for Terrence Denley Garden Design, featuring items for the home and garden including sculpture, books, prints, urns-each piece chosen for its design qualities. Chairity displays one-of-a-kind chairs from the 19th and 20th centuries. Contemporary fine art in a museum quality setting is showcased at gallery geoffrin, named in honor of the 18th century arts patron Madame Marie Geoffrin who sold art to help the poor.

Spiritually and creatively Terry Slaughter is on a journey—a journey of discovery, a journey toward joy and peace, and a journey toward the finest in design.

"I think you know when it's good, you just have an intuitive sense and you just know what good design is. That doesn't mean it's the best design, but it's good. It shouldn't be the best—it's a journey. You never get to the destination, professionally or spiritually, but the journey should be evolving. It also should be rewarding to your psyche. I'm into psychic income right now more than anything."

Terry Slaughter moved to Birmingham after beginning his agency in his hometown of Dothan.

"I think that for a creative person, it comes down to, could you be the best you could be in a city like Birmingham? Yes, I can do that. I can do work that normal people in our industry could say, 'Oh, you could only do that if you lived in L.A. or San Francisco or New York. We've proven that living in this area that we can do great work, yet we have the quality of life that is so wonderful.

"I think just the livability of this area is extraordinary. There are so many things that make living here comfortable and enjoyable. But a lot of it comes down to the congeniality of people, and the willingness to give back. I go to different parts of the world a lot. And I know it's this way a lot of places, but very few places where I travel do I find a city that is willing to look at those less fortunate and want to try to do something about it. This is a city that I think embraces the idea that, 'I want to have a great place for my family to live, but I also want to make it better for other people.' And that's a wonderful thing. That's what I think runs through the veins, the fabric of this city."

Sonja Oliver

Sonja Oliver walks the spotless floors of the Mercedes plant in Vance waving and speaking to passing employees. She points at bright M-class bodies in various stages of assembly and explains what comes next.

The plant is a constant moving machine, car bodies are lifted and moved on conveyor belts, doors hang in single file moving steadily and employees attach parts, scoot by on lifts and ride three-wheeled cycles with baskets and bells.

"I don't ride those," Oliver says, laughing and pointing to the three-wheeled cycles.

This bright-faced energetic woman looks natural in her denim shirt, smiling and talking as if it is her energy that drives the moving parts.

"Mercedes was just opening when I came here (to Tuscaloosa from Hattiesburg, MS)," she says. "I was a marketing/human resources specialist in the banking industry. I am a quality management systems specialist here."

But her rise did not just happen.

"It wasn't like I just said 'I want to do that.' I started as a switchboard operator, then moved to the quality department first as switchboard operator, then as administrative assistant and then as a quality management systems specialist."

Oliver explains what a quality management systems specialist does: "We (Mercedes) have to abide by standards to ship cars to Europe. We have to make sure we have those standards in place here. I ensure that the company is ready for the audit. We do internal audits. We have to find things (that are being done wrong). I prepare an internal audit schedule and coordinate with internal auditors. I handle the documentation system for internal management. I train everyone. This morning it was the administrative staff and this afternoon it's group leaders and team leaders on the floor. At some point we train everybody in the company.

"A co-worker told me, 'Sonja, I don't know why everybody doesn't run from you.' And another one answered, 'It's because she smiles.' I'm going into my ninth year here. I love working here. I like the job and the people. We have a team concept. All our presidents and vice presidents are considered team members. It's not like the hierarchical chain of command."

Team is something she understands. Oliver's husband, Maurice, is a former professional football player.

"He played at Tampa Bay and New Orleans, the Canadian Football League and with the Birmingham Fire," she says. "He was an outside linebacker. (But) my teddy bear's not mean. I was only a (football) fan when he played. I used to watch him."

But both Olivers have learned something about team play in recent years. Their first child was born premature, after only 22 weeks, and died.

"We needed a neo-natal intensive care unit," she says. "When I got pregnant again we moved to Birmingham. Julius was 23 weeks and he weighed 1 lb., 3 ozs. Birmingham is important because it has everything from before birth, to after birth to now. Mo goes to the Epic School. We are working with him on learning different skills. This year he's playing baseball. We're trying to get him into activities that will help him develop.

"With the school's help and Children's Hospital's help, we're working to get him where he needs to be. It's a lot of work."

The Olivers' third child, 7-month-old India, was full term. So, is the family going to continue to grow?

"There are no plans for that. Mo (senior) says that's between me and my boyfriend," Oliver says, laughing.

So this working mother continues to drive 40-45 minutes to work.

"I hit the interstate and I go," she says.

What kind of vehicle does she drive?

"An M class," Oliver says, flashing that big smile.

Ann Miller

Ann Miller has a lot of family in Birmingham, a sister, cousins, "lots and lots of Robertses." And although she is a native of the city she was approaching 30 before she moved here and discovered her true calling.

Ms. Miller, the daughter of a naval officer, was born in Birmingham but soon moved on with her family. Her family traveled extensively and she attended a British boarding school in London and a French convent school in Paris. She earned a degree in Classical Greek from Swarthmore College in Pennsylvania where she planned to become an archaeologist. She studied Persian in anticipation of traveling to Iran to participate in a dig there. That fell through and she ended up in Mexico for a while before returning to New York City to work for three years as an assistant editor of children's books.

"That was the big city life, but I discovered I'm a nature girl," she says smiling, her strong hands laid flat on the table in front of her.

On this winter day atop Oak Mountain Ms. Miller is much more interested in the health of hawks, owls, squirrels, raccoons, assorted song birds and the coming "baby season" than she is Dr. Seuss or fossils.

This tall woman whose short, dark hair shows signs of graying, ended up in her native city not digging for artifacts, but caring for animals, first at the zoo, then in her back yard and finally at a beautiful facility in Oak Mountain State Park. Ms. Miller, executive director of the Alabama Wildlife Rehabilitation Center, used her retirement money saved from nine years of working at the zoo to devote more time to developing the center that cares for more than 2,000 injured and orphaned wild creatures.

She stresses that "this is not a zoo. It's for people to see how we take care of animals." The goal at the center is to nurse wild animals back to health and return them to their natural habitat. The Wildlife Rehabilitation Center occupies rent-free what was a restaurant in the state park. Of course, the center's relationship with the state park system is more of a partnership and goes far beyond just the building.

Ms. Miller says the Wildlife Center has a $300,000 annual budget, but counting work done by volunteers, probably operates at closer to $1 million a year.

"When dad retired from the Navy the family moved to Birmingham," she says. "I loved Alabama. Here were these beautiful hills. Spring unfolds for four glorious months. I began to get involved in conservation projects.

"Bob and Mary Burkes befriended me. They took me to Sipsey and taught me wild flowers, how to get around and how to live in the woods. That's when I became a zoo keeper. Later I used my pension fund to go full time (with the wildlife center) with the idea that I would raise funds, take care of the animals and organize the program. Each year the wildlife center has gotten stronger.

"I must admit my nose is to the grindstone," she says. "This requires every bit of concentration to keep it going. I'm very eager to expand the educational offerings to include schools and scouts. Now that we have this wonderful facility the idea is to have people interacting and understanding the wildlife we work with."

Ms. Miller is excited when she walks through the center, picking up handfuls of meal worms grown for birds and pointing to minnows that will feed another animal. She watches hawks in a beautiful bird facility. One flies straight up in the hopes of getting out. "Oh, don't do that," she says, explaining that a hawk can hurt itself. "When they start doing that they're ready to move out."

She points to examining rooms and explains that treating injured wild animals is much different than a veterinarian working with domesticated animals.

Ms. Miller, who describes herself as an animal rehabilitator, developed a way to reunite baby hawks and owls with their parents. When a baby falls from a nest and is brought to the center, she records its calls. Workers then make a nest using a clothes basket and sticks and twigs or return the baby to the original nest. They then begin to play the call and the parents come back.

"Once you're in the parenting mode, if it begs you feed it," she says.

COLONIAL PROPERTIES TRUST

"Where You Live, Work, and Shop"

A small ship's bell hangs in a corridor in the corporate headquarters of Colonial Properties Trust in downtown Birmingham. The company's staff members will sometimes ring that bell to announce a bit of breaking good news about Colonial Properties that they wish to share with their colleagues. Lately, that bell has been ringing quite a bit.

One of the largest diversified real estate investment trusts (REITs) in the United States, Colonial Properties Trust is among the largest developers, owners, and operators of multi-family, office, and retail properties in the Sunbelt region of the country. A self-administered and self-managed REIT,

the company is a fully integrated real estate company whose activities include development of new properties, acquisition of existing properties, build-to-suit development, and the provision of management, leasing, and brokerage services for its portfolio and properties owned by third parties. Colonial was founded in 1970, and completed its initial public offering in 1993.

Since its IPO, the company's total market capitalization has grown from $425 million to $2.8 billion. Headquartered in Birmingham, Colonial Properties Trust, through its subsidiaries, lists a portfolio of over 100 multi-family, office, and retail properties where people live, work, and shop. This translates into over 14,500 apartment units; 5.2 million square feet of office space, with about 80 percent

of that portfolio in office parks; and more than 15 million square feet of retail shopping space. The company's properties are concentrated in carefully targeted, high growth cities in Alabama, Florida, Georgia, Mississippi, North Carolina, South Carolina, Tennessee, Texas, and Virginia.

In a year characterized by a shaky economy and an uncertain stock market, Colonial Properties Trust in 2002 achieved 12.4 percent total annual return for its shareholders.

"One of the key reasons that our strategy has enabled us to achieve consistent long-term performance is our diversified property portfolio which provides the company with greater flexibility in operations, investments, and dispositions than many of our peers," states Thomas H. Lowder,

Colonial's president and CEO. "We believe that the market's interest in our company during 2002 reflects investor recognition of the many benefits that our diversification offers. That diversification also positions us with the financial flexibility to continue our growth."

The catalyst sparking Colonial's consistent long-term growth is the company's 'Colonial Star Strategy'. This highly disciplined initiative, designed to deliver steady financial results over a long term horizon, is based on a simple premise: to invest in a diversified portfolio of multi-family, office, and retail properties located in high potential Sunbelt cities. It also stresses managing those properties with an uncompromising focus on performance excellence.

Colonial's Multi-family division accounts for 25 percent of Colonial's net operating income. The 41 properties Colonial owns and manages in 18 cities located across the Sunbelt retain a healthy 92 to 96 percent occupancy rate. The Office division, which generates 25 percent of the company's net operating income, owns and operates 21 properties in six cities across the Sunbelt. The Retail division, which consists of 17 regional malls and 27 neighborhood shopping centers, is the largest segment in the company's diversified portfolio, generating 50 percent of the company's net operating income.

Colonial's steadfast adherence to its 'Star Strategy' has produced a stellar track record. The company has been recognized for projects ranging from a multi-family housing development in Sarasota and an expansion of an office park in Atlanta to a retail mall development in Huntsville and a neighborhood community center anchored by a Wal-Mart Supercenter in Birmingham.

The company's signature mixed-use community is Colonial TownPark Orlando in Florida. Encompassing the entire range of Colonial's property types, the 175-acre development features the 456-unit Colonial Grand Apartments, half million square feet of office buildings, and 200,000 square feet of retail shop space. Colonial TownPark Orlando epitomizes Colonial's commitment to provide a place where people actually live, work, and shop.

Closer to home, the jewel in the company's crown is its $50 million renovation of Brookwood Village. Embracing the philosophy that the 'shopping mall' concept of the 1970's has given way to 'lifestyle centers' featuring streetscape-style shopping, Colonial Properties Trust undertook a two-year transformation of Brookwood Village which not only provided a facelift, but also changed the inherent design structure of the facility. Anchored by Rich's and Parisian, the new 600,000 square foot Colonial Brookwood Village is home to over 40 unique specialty stores plus seven eating establishments ranging from fine dining restaurants to coffee and dessert shops. Many of the stores have dual indoor/outdoor entrances furthering the convenience and novelty of village shopping.

"The buzzword there is 'lifestyle centers' - shopping centers with a street scheme," says Reynolds Thompson, Colonial's chief operating officer. "I think we have the best combination of these by virtue of having not only the street shopping experience, but we also have the mall to complement it, along with convenient parking, which is a real plus for Brookwood."

In addition to the new access to the stores, Colonial Brookwood Village also features upscale interior design, better shopper access, and natural lighting. Part of the challenge that Colonial faced was in keeping Brookwood Village in operation during the renovation. The dramatic results indicate the company's desire to go the extra mile for its clients.

Other well-known malls that carry the Colonial Properties imprint include the 1.4 million square foot Colonial Mall in Macon Georgia; the Colonial Mall Bel Air in Mobile; and malls in Gadsden, Decatur, and Huntsville. The list of Colonial's corporate clients is a page from the national Who's Who in business: AT & T, Bank of America, Fiserv, BellSouth, IBM, MetLife, and Charles Schwab to name a few.

In the Birmingham area, Colonial Grand at Liberty Park stands out as one of Colonial Properties Trust's best known multi-family developments, one of the first in the local Class A+ housing market. Other familiar landmarks owned and managed by Colonial include Colonial Grand at Mountain Brook, Colonial Village at Cahaba Heights, The Colonnade, International Park, and Colonial Plaza. The corporate headquarters for Energen is another Colonial development, and the company received a Toby Award from the Building Owners and Management Association for its renovation of its own headquarters building. The state-of-the-art telecommunications and technology built into every building that bears the Colonial Properties signature has earned the company a reputation as a developer of 'high performance workplaces.'

Colonial's eye-catching performance has also been spotlighted on the national stage. When Standard & Poor's recognized the REIT industry, now a $150 billion national force, Colonial Properties Trust was one of six REITs added to the S&P indices, and is now included in the S&P SmallCap 600. The REITs must meet the same stringent guidelines covering liquidity, financial viability, market capitalization, ownership, and industry and sector representation that are used for other companies considered for the indices.

The company's strong support of civic activities begins with its leadership. Drawing on the lessons learned from his father, CEO Lowder is a big proponent of giving something back to the community that he feels has been such a strong supporter of Colonial Properties Trust. The company has been an active supporter of the American Heart Association, the Junior League, Alabama Shakespeare Festival, the American Red Cross, Children's Hospital, King's Ranch, and dozens of other organizations and causes. Lowder himself has served as the chairman for United Way of Central Alabama, and many company employees regularly participate in community fund raising events.

"After all," Thomas Lowder notes, "we live, work, and shop here too."

Left: Colonial Brookwood Village exterior and interior.
Below: Colonial Grand at Liberty Park.

JOHNSTON BARTON PROCTOR & POWELL LLP

Throughout its 75-year history, the law firm of Johnston Barton Proctor & Powell LLP has maintained a reputation within the legal community, and in the community at large, for its commitment to the very highest quality of work on behalf of its clients.

Founded in 1926, the firm originally became known for its representation of the earliest automobile dealers in Birmingham. Those clients led to the representation of a national commercial credit company that was formed to enable people to buy automobiles during the Depression. As Birmingham grew and changed, becoming more diversified, so did the firm. By the 1950s, the firm had expanded its focus to offer a full range of legal services to healthcare clients and Alabama newspapers, among others.

needs of its largest clients, it is small enough to develop a personal relationship with all of its clients, large and small. The firm recruits new lawyers from the top law schools throughout the United States. As young lawyers join the firm, they are instructed by example and exhortation that the personal attention the firm gives to each client lies at the core of the firm's tradition and is a matter of significant professional pride.

Johnston Barton's labor and employment lawyers advise clients on all types of issues in the changing workplace.

Johnston Barton's trial lawyers represent clients in state and federal courts throughout the United States.

Today, Johnston Barton Proctor & Powell LLP has expanded its practice throughout the United States and internationally to provide a wide range of services to clients, which range from major public corporations to closely held businesses and individuals. The firm has grown primarily in the practice areas of labor and employment (representing employers) and health care (representing hospitals, nursing homes, managed care organizations, and healthcare practitioners). True to its tradition, the firm has not grown larger simply for the sake of size, but it has expanded as necessary in order to continue to provide the quality and kinds of services its growing clientele has come to expect.

Although Johnston Barton Proctor & Powell LLP is large enough to meet the

The areas of legal services performed by Johnston Baron Proctor & Powell LLP, include antitrust, banking and finance, civil litigation, communications and media, construction, corporate and securities, health care, insurance, intellectual property, international, labor and employment, medical malpractice defense, products liability, real estate, taxation, trusts and estates, and white collar criminal defense. The firm is particularly recognized within the state and region for its extensive practice in labor and employment, health care, and media law.

The labor and employment law section at Johnston Barton Proctor & Powell LLP provides a full spectrum of workplace representation designed to assist national, regional, and local clients in both resolving and avoiding litigation. Attorneys in the firm's labor and employment practice group represent public and private management in all areas of labor and employment law, including litigation throughout the United States in state and federal courts as well as before arbitrators, the National Labor Relations Board, the Department of Labor, and the Equal Employment Opportunity Commission, among others. The firm's labor and employment law practice is headed by a former Chair of the Labor and

Employment Law Section of the American Bar Association. The firm holds an annual seminar for clients, which focuses on current developments in labor and employment law.

The firm's health care practice is one of the largest in the state. Johnston Barton Proctor & Powell LLP serves as general counsel for Alabama's largest hospital system and for several of Alabama's largest nursing home chains. The firm also represents managed care organizations, preferred provider organizations, and physician groups and individual physicians. Attorneys within the firm represent clients in all facets of healthcare law, including the defense of physicians, hospitals, and nursing homes in medical malpractice cases.

With more than 60 years of experience in media law work, Johnston Barton Proctor & Powell LLP has represented local and national newspapers, television and radio stations, magazines, advertising agencies, bookstore chains, television networks and production companies, media holding companies, authors, film makers, entertainers, and others. The firm's work for these clients includes defense of defamation and privacy actions, litigation for access to public meetings and records, and contract, labor relations, copyright, and trademark matters. The firm also serves as general counsel for the largest circulation newspaper in the state of Alabama and represents three of the four major television network affiliates in Birmingham.

The firm draws from its corporate and tax, real estate and other practice groups to provide full-range legal services to new and expanding industries and to investors and organizers of technology-based ventures. In September, 2001, the firm, together with veteran economic developers, formed World Business Advisors, LLC, which provides industries with site selection and industrial market analysis and assists localities with economic assessment and development.

Johnston Barton's health care lawyers represent hospitals, nursing homes, physicians, and management organizations.

Although the firm works on both a national and international scale, its attorneys remain committed to the Birmingham community. The diligence and insistence upon high quality work that are the hallmark of Johnston Barton Proctor & Powell LLP within the legal profession and the business community also make the firm a leader in its hometown. Members of the firm have served as president and members of the executive committee of the Birmingham Bar Association, president of the Birmingham Library Board, chairman of the Board of Governors of Indian Springs School, president of the Girl's Club of Birmingham, chair of the Birmingham Chapter of the American Red Cross, president of the Altamont School Board of Trustees, president of the Alabama Nursing Home Association, president of the Board of Directors of Big Brothers/Big Sisters, and Chancellor of the Episcopal Church in the Diocese of Alabama. The firm's attorneys are leaders of the bar and active participants in the charitable and community organizations, churches, and public institutions and agencies of Birmingham.

Johnston Barton's media lawyers are committed to knowing their clients' needs and meeting their deadlines.

Bruce Ayers

Bruce Ayers loves a good party.

He was the social chairman of his fraternity at Missouri Valley College, and except for a brief stint selling insurance to farmers in south Alabama, he has been throwing parties in Birmingham for almost 30 years.

Sure this owner of The Comedy Club is an extremely successful businessman. On this stormy Friday afternoon Ayers is wearing a neatly pressed white shirt. He sits behind a desk in his stylish dark office, surrounded by computer screens. His salt-and-pepper hair looks like it belongs on the head of an attorney strolling the courthouse halls downtown.

But even here, in the office of his business, Ayers' demeanor is not what it should be. He's just too boyish, too excited, too interested in telling stories and talking golf. And too interested in remembering great parties at Ski Lodge apartments and disco music and mechanical bulls and the ever-changing world of Birmingham entertainment.

Ayers is one of those lucky people who does what he loves. Even so, he really is a businessman. He graduated with a business degree. Then he learned his trade from the ground up before bringing the first comedy club to Birmingham in 1983.

"Selling insurance taught me a lot about the people of Alabama," he says. "I worked with a friend Don Lipscomb who opened The Cobblestone on Morris Avenue. Then in 1978 Brentwoods opened. At that time disco was hot. I was assistant manager. The more I was there the more I liked it. It was the coolest club.

"That started fading. Thank God for John Travolta and 'Urban Cowboy.' On opening night we booked a little band and we couldn't give tickets away. That band was Alabama. The next year they were selling out the BJCC. We had a mechanical bull in the back, the first one in town. We were Cassidy's for a year and then that started fading and we had to change again. We made it Singles, a dance club. That started fading after about a year and a half."

By 1983 Ayers had come to know Birmingham and the entertainment business. And he made a leap that has since put the city on the entertainment map.

"We were going to change to live entertainment. We went to Atlanta and—I don't know why, really—we went into a (comedy) club called The Punchline," he says. "So we came back and started doing live comedy two nights a week."

But there were lessons to be learned there, too.

"Dennis Miller was there the second night and it was his first job outside Pennsylvania. It didn't work that well with the audience.

"We opened The Comedy Club on Highway 31 and nobody knew what it was and nobody's ever heard of these comedians. It was hard. In November of that year I went to the airport to pick up an act. He was this big black guy. That night Andy Versiglio, one of the owners of the Piggly Wiggly, was in the club for his birthday. I asked the comedian to say something for Andy on his birthday.

"Sinbad went up on stage and did 30 minutes on the Piggly Wiggly. He became our first star. Ours was the first place he ever headlined. Every night he would just pick something. He got us on the map. It was a slow, slow, slow process of finding the right acts.

"Entertainment has always been my forte. Making people feel special, showing them a good time. I think I've figured out what Birmingham wants."

The Comedy Club moved to Greensprings Highway in Homewood and things were going great guns when in 1993, during the biggest snow storm in the city's history, the club burned to the ground. Carrot Top was headlining at the club then and his props burned with Ayers' business. But even that precipitated a change for the better.

"Carrot Top was scheduled to be on the Tonight show that Tuesday, but he couldn't because he lost all his props," Ayers says, taking a sip from a bottle of water. "Leno made some comment about the club. And then all the comedians who had been there started calling Jay and telling him what a great club that was. Jay called me and offered to do commercials for the club."

It was then that The Comedy Club moved to the Stardome in Hoover and gave Birmingham one of the truly great comedy venues in the country.

So does Ayers, the connoisseur of great parties, ever desire the spotlight?

"I want to pick the acts and decide on the commercials. We know what the people like. Comedy is more universal, but you target different segments of the market. This week we have an act geared to the 20-27-year-olds. James Gregory is for 30-35 and up. Nobody does it like we do.

"I don't want to be on stage. I want to be Ed Sullivan, orchestrating all the details. I'm the producer."

Shelley Stewart

This in a nutshell is the philosophy of Shelley Stewart, honed through six decades on this earth. He wrote it down in his best-selling memoir, *The Road South*, published to great national acclaim in 2002.

"Beyond being a description of a whirlwind life, I hope my story will do nothing if not inspire. If I can overcome the hurdles of poverty, abuse, and racism, then so can anyone. If life throws you a lemon, turn it into lemonade; accentuate that which is positive and life affirming. A person who maintains a faith in God and focuses on noble principles and fruitful goals can accomplish much…

"Now is the time to follow your inner voices over the din of a world bombarded with the sounds of discouragement and pessimism. In our nation we spend foolish amounts of time trying to separate under the guise of skin color or race. But if you look at the last four letters in the designations African American, Puerto Rican American, Mexican American, or white American, you will notice the words, I can.

"The individual can place this phrase into an assertive context; I can overcome the most formidable barriers to achieve success, whether it is within the maze of human relations or the obstacle course of the business world. Optimism and idealism are beleaguered but not dead. Hope and understanding may often be dormant, but they are not disemboweled. The individual is essential to a wider humanity, and lives nurtured in faith and determination can prove indomitable against astronomical odds. As I always say, Life is hard by the yard, but a cinch by the inch."

These are the words of a man who was fed fried rats by his stepmother, who saw his father kill his mother with an ax when he was five years old. He lived on a cold porch, caring for siblings at the tenderest of ages, and earned his keep by working in a stable. He experienced some kindness at the hands of a white family in the segregated South of the 1940s. He rescued his brothers from virtual slavery in rural Mississippi in the '40s. He struggled to nurture a natural love of learning in an environment that discouraged the schooling of young black men. And he overcame it all to become a pioneering black disc jockey, radio station owner and head of a large Birmingham advertising agency.

The odyssey of Shelley Stewart is a remarkable story of human desire and endurance, tempered by personality and the drama of the civil rights era.

Shelley The Playboy was the moniker in the Birmingham of the 1950s and 1960s. Radio was the medium.

From broadcasting black music and veiled instructions to civil rights marchers to later hosting a talk show that kept a beat on the pulse of the city, Shelley is a great communicator.

In a professional business career that has spanned everything from spinning records at wild dances to negotiating and selling radio advertising packages and campaigns to managing O2 Ideas, a complex modern advertising, marketing and branding agency, Shelley Stewart has come to understand the nuances of life and business lived on the leading edge.

Through the good and the evil, Birmingham has always been home.

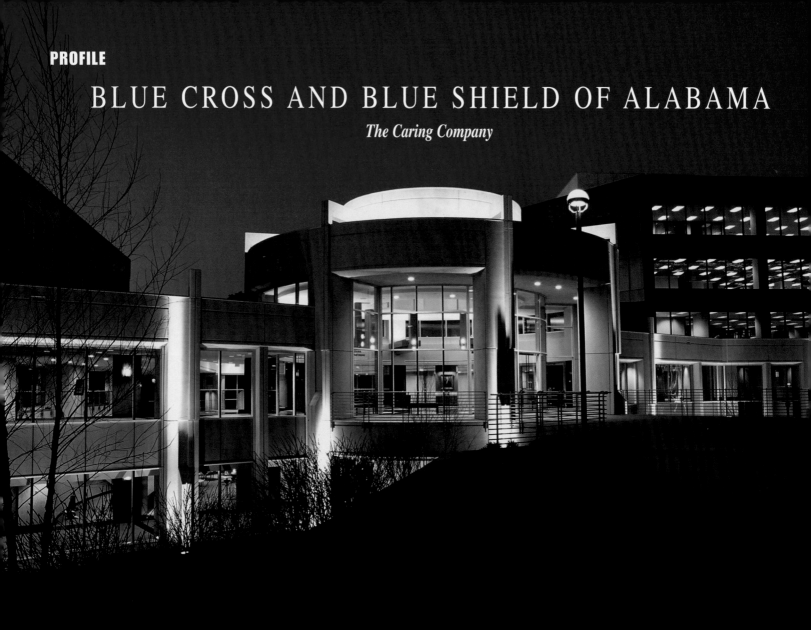

BLUE CROSS AND BLUE SHIELD OF ALABAMA

The Caring Company

lue Cross and Blue Shield of Alabama is the largest provider of health care coverage in the state and one of the largest in the country. As a recognized national leader in benefit administration, Blue Cross provides health and dental coverage through group or individual plans for more than 27,000 businesses in the state representing over three million members. Major companies with thousands of employees to the smallest cottage industry with as few as two workers have turned to Blue Cross and Blue Shield of Alabama to provide the best value at the most reasonable price.

Founded in 1936 as the Hospital Service Corporation, the company has grown to become the eighth largest member of the Blue Cross and Blue Shield Association.

"For more than 66 years, we've looked outward to our customers to determine how we can best serve them, and then we've acted accordingly," states Phillip Pope, the president of Blue Cross and Blue Shield of Alabama. "'Customer First' is more than a tradition with us. It is our daily commitment."

Pope and the leadership at Blue Cross have used this outward look, along with a careful inward analysis of the company's operation in charting the company's successful course. Blue Cross leads the market by making cost effective decisions, continuously evaluating and re-negotiating provider contracts, and keeping administrative costs low. In fact, more than 94 percent of each dollar

received goes directly to paying benefit costs. The company is also known for its efficient and timely processing of claims, 75 percent of which are filed electronically by its participating hospitals, physicians, and dentists. Probably the most compelling statement regarding Blue Cross' commitment to "Customer First" is the fact that the company has retained more than 98 percent of its customers during the past ten years.

In addition to the firm's corporate headquarters on Riverchase Parkway in Hoover, the familiar Blue Cross and Blue Shield of Alabama logo is over service centers in Montgomery, Huntsville, Mobile, and downtown Birmingham. Satellite offices also canvass the state from Foley on the Gulf of Mexico to Florence in north Alabama.

From these offices, thousands of specially trained associates process more than one million transactions every working day. As the Medicare Part A and B carrier for Alabama and the Medicare Part B carrier for Georgia and Mississippi, Blue Cross pays billions of dollars in benefits every year. In addition, the company serves as the Medicare intermediary claims processor for Puerto Rico and the administrator for Part A benefits in Iowa and South Dakota.

To address the needs of its customers effectively in this cyber age, Blue Cross professionals are continuously seeking and implementing the latest in leading edge technology. For example, the company developed InfoSolutions, a secure electronic medical information network designed to help physicians and hospital facilities enhance patient care. InfoSolutions serves as a centralized database for health care providers to access and share information such as patient medical history and medication sensitivities - information physicians need to make informed decisions accurately and more quickly.

Since most of us do not carry complete copies of our medical information with us at all times, InfoSolutions can be more than just a convenient service - it can be a lifesaver in an emergency. The secure online medical information network can provide authorized health care providers with instant access to med-

ication histories, lab results, allergies, chronic illnesses, and immunization status. Participation costs nothing, but delays and lack of information in a critical situation could cost dearly.

Other trails that Blue Cross has blazed include introducing the state's first Preferred Provider Organization (PPO), the Preferred Medical Doctor (PMD) network, in 1984. The company's Preferred Care program, with over 9,000 providers, is the largest provider network in the state. Blue Cross has also achieved 100 percent participation among Alabama's hospitals and over 90 percent of the state's outpatient facilities.

Blue Cross' Personal Choice physician program allows patients to select their own primary care doctor, who then oversees and coordinates the patient's health care and treatment. In addition, the Blue Cross Participating Prescription Drug Program, accepted at over 99 percent of the state's pharmacies and all the major pharmacy chains, offers prescription drugs to members at reduced prices.

A great source of pride to the dedicated employees of Blue Cross and Blue Shield of Alabama is the community service activities in which the company is involved, especially those initiatives that promote the health, safety, and wellness of the state's children. Blue Cross teams are constantly appearing at community fund raising events such as the Cancer Society's Relay for Life, the annual AIDS walk, and America's Walk for Diabetes. They also support the Birmingham area YWCA's day care for homeless children, the March of Dimes, the Alabama Kidney Foundation, and breast cancer and leukemia research. Blue Cross associates constantly rank at the top of the highest per capita contributors to the United Way.

The centerpiece of the company's commitment to good corporate citizenship is the Alabama Child Caring Foundation. Blue Cross and Blue Shield of Alabama established the non-profit Foundation in 1987 as the funding mechanism for its Alabama Caring Program for Children, which provides health care coverage for children whose parents cannot afford coverage on their own, but don't qualify for government assisted care.

Thousands of children in Alabama do not have access to adequate health care because their parents cannot afford medical coverage. The Caring Program for Children provides primary and preventive health care services designed to meet the typical needs of children. Blue Cross provides all administrative support for the Foundation so that every dollar contributed goes directly to providing health care coverage for the children. Blue Cross also matches every contribution dollar for dollar. Since the first child was enrolled in the program in 1998, over 40,000 children have received help through the Foundation.

Blue Cross is proud to sponsor the Body Trek trailer. Body Trek is a traveling exhibition that moves from school to school with exhibits and demonstrations touting accident prevention, health, and nutrition.

The company also sponsors Alabama's Poison Control Centers with operators on duty 24 hours a day, seven days a week giving adults a place to call if a child accidentally ingests a toxin. The Centers received over 100,000 calls last year.

At Blue Cross and Blue Shield of Alabama, "The Caring Company" is more than just a slogan. It is the cornerstone for the company's goal of providing the best health care coverage while responding to its customers with a sense of urgency and compassion.

The company's work has not gone unnoticed. Its strict adherence to "Customer First" and the other core values on which the company operates led Blue Cross and Blue Shield of Alabama to be recognized by the national Blue Cross and Blue Shield Association. Every year since 1995, the Birmingham-based organization has received the Brand Excellence Award for the highest degree of customer loyalty in the Blue Cross family of companies across the United States. In 1997, Child Times magazine named Blue Cross "Birmingham's Best Company for Working Parents" in the large company category. The company's PMD program has also been named in Consumer Reports as the number one Preferred Provider Organization in the United States.

As a recognized national leader in benefit administration, Blue Cross provides health and dental coverage through group or individual plans for more than 27,000 businesses in the state representing over three million members. Major companies with thousands of employees to the smallest cottage industry with as few as two workers have turned to Blue Cross and Blue Shield of Alabama to provide the best value at the most reasonable price.

Dr. Amrik Walia

The body and the mind. Together. Apart. In the world of medicine, in the realm of health, the interconnections of the mind and the body mean endless fascination to Dr. Amrik Walia.

He sits in the office in the building he built to house his Institute of Mind Body Medicine and Spa Moksha in Inverness. Dr. Walia has spent his life in pursuit of the connections between the physical and the mental.

Born in India, Walia came to the United States when he was a young man. He came to study and learn and build a life in his adopted country. Born in 1947 at a tumultuous time in the history of the subcontinent, Walia began his studies in his native country, earning a B.S. and M.S. in chemistry.

Still more than half of Walia's life, he has spent in the United States. In 1975, he finished his Phd in medical chemistry at Loyola University in New Orleans.

That same year he joined the department of surgery at UAB.

"I got very interested in immunology at UAB, which was regarded as one of the best in the nation," Walia recalls.

Walia immersed himself in research work at UAB, where he applied for an individual fellowship from the National Cancer Institute in immunotherapy, finishing his training in 1981.

Working on the faculty at UAB and as chief of government research at VA Hospital, Walia helped UAB start the Office for the Advancement of Developing Industries (OADI), a high technology incubator.

Fascinated by the study of the interaction of mind and body and the immune response, Walia studied mind-body medicine at Harvard Medical School in 1997 and 1998.

Studying with masters of mind-body medicine, working with luminaries such as Deepak Chopra and Dr. Herbert Benson, Walia has shared the awareness that people can create health within themselves. Mind-Body Medicine is a complementary mix of modern medicine and alternative health therapies—substantive therapies and programs with exercises, nutrition or cognitive thought restructuring (positive thinking).

"It is not mysterious. We are chemical molecules. How you work with chemical reactions in your body depends on you," says Walia, who is 55 years old and in excellent health.

"All of these reactions are taking place in the body at all times. It is hard to believe how much is involved in a single drop of blood. There are 50 to 60 million cells in a drop of blood."

Walia's work brings a vision of wholeness to a world that often seems irrevocably split. "People are going to die, but if you're going to live longer, living a healthful lifestyle is essential."

RAST CONSTRUCTION, INC.

Building for the Future

My dad always said 'Do a job once and do it right,' says Danny Rast, the second of three generations of a family celebrating a half century of providing quality construction services to commercial, industrial, and government clients. "We pride ourselves in our quality work and our reputation for integrity. Both are critical for success in this business."

And both have figured prominently in the success of Rast Construction, Inc., the heavy construction company to which Danny Rast alludes and which he and his brother, Bob, lead. The company was founded in 1952 by their father, Holt Rast, who made his entrance into the construction industry by building houses. He quickly found, however, that the home building boom underway at that time meant that the burgeoning municipalities in Jefferson County were in need of water and sewer lines. Rast shifted career gears, purchased a single backhoe, and began filling this need on the part of municipal and county governments for improved infrastructure.

For the past half century, Rast Construction, Inc. has been constructing water, gas, and sewer pipelines; water and sewage treatment plants; and pumping and transfer stations for a variety of clients. From the tiniest half-inch lines to 120-inch giants, Rast

Construction, Inc. has successfully completed jobs for Jefferson and Shelby Counties, Alagasco, Alabama Power, and a host of municipalities throughout Alabama and the Southeastern states.

"My goal has been to continue to operate the business on the principles on which it was founded by my father," says Bob Rast, the company's president. "We are happy to have been a participant over the years in the growth and development of the heavy construction industry in this area, and feel that we have had an impact in making the industry more responsive to the needs of the customer."

Contractors today must adhere to and be in compliance with a complex maze of state and federal guidelines in utility construction. The professionals at Rast Construction, Inc. take great care to complete their projects with minimal impact on the environment.

"We employ the latest technology and state-of-the-art equipment to focus on rehabilitating existing facilities where possible to bring them up to

standard," states Roy Weaver, Rast's vice-president of operations.

"Technology has come a long way since the 'pick and shovel' days when a problem in a pipeline caused serious construction concerns," adds Clay Bailey, the vice-president and general manager of rehabilitation operations. "In those days, contractors had to dig up much of the line to locate and correct a problem. We now employ a television camera that we can insert into a pipeline, videotape the interior, and exactly pinpoint a problem spot. We were one of the first building contractors in Jefferson County qualified to do this type of rehabilitative work. These minimally invasive procedures are much less damaging to the environment than the old 'dig up and replace' policy of only a few years ago. It's part of our commitment to quality work and to sustainable development."

The start-up construction company with a single backhoe has grown into a multi-million dollar operation employing approximately 140 people. The company is headquartered on a 10-acre site on Shannon Road in the Oxmoor Industrial Park. Construction equipment ranging from the smallest trenching machines to 16-foot tunnel boring behemoths regularly leave the equipment storage lot bound for projects throughout the Southeast. Projects on which Rast Construction, Inc. has

put its signature range from a $12 million sanitary sewer pumping station on Minor Parkway and a water treatment plant in Bessemer to five miles of 54-inch pre-stressed concrete water pipelines in Greenville, South Carolina and chilled water lines for UAB.

The dedication of Rast's employees has been a major factor in the development of the enviable reputation the firm has earned in the industry. "Probably a third of our employees have been here for 20 years or more," says Donna Jones, the firm's office manager and bookkeeper who has almost two decades of service to the company. "That's extremely rare in this business where company engineers and other technicians move frequently to accept other job offers. It's a statement on the family atmosphere that exists here."

Roy Weaver, vice president of operations, is joined by several other members of the Rast family in leading the company into the 21st century and building on the professional relationships that have come to identify Rast Construction, Inc. as an industry leader.

"We pledge to continue doing our best to satisfy a client's needs in terms of price, quality, and on-time delivery of construction services while providing stable employment for our employees and being a responsible corporate citizen," Bob Rast adds.

Right: Bessemer Water Filtration Facility located near Hueytown, Alabama for the City of Bessemer, Alabama. This facilty was designed for water filtration with a capacity of 12 MGPD (million gallons per day).

Above: Back Row—John Wanhatalo, Estimating; Roy Weaver, Vice President; Bob Rast, Chariman and President. Front Row— Daniel Rast, Vice President; Michael vonEschenbach, Accounting; Donna Jones, Accounting; Camelia Giambrone, Accounting; Bruce Jones, Estimating.

BRASFIELD & GORRIE

Their Work Is Everywhere

A visitor to London once inquired about the works of 17th century architect Sir Christopher Wren and received the response, "Look around you. They are everywhere."

The same might be said of the buildings and construction projects completed by Brasfield & Gorrie, a nationally ranked general contractor with headquarters in Birmingham. The company has in its portfolio of work some of the most recognized office, institutional, retail, healthcare, condominium, and industrial buildings and facilities from Virginia to Arizona and from Michigan to Florida.

The company began in 1964 when Miller Gorrie purchased the assets of the Thomas C. Brasfield Company, which began work in Birmingham in 1921. Three years later he changed the name to Brasfield & Gorrie. Over the next thirty five years, Gorrie directed the company's growth, an expansion that included offices in Orlando, Atlanta, Nashville, and Raleigh.

The company is organized as 14 operating divisions, each functioning as independent profit centers. More than 2,000 professionals give the company the ability to customize construction services to fit the unique needs of individual clients. From early planning stages through construction, the company uses a team approach to ensure that the client's needs and expectations shape the project design, schedule, and delivery. The company is recognized for its expertise in structural steel and concrete frame construction.

Although Brasfield & Gorrie has clients in 20 states and will go wherever clients need construction services, it has concentrated on providing design-build, construction management, and general contracting services in the Southeast. The company has been guided by a consistent vision to be recognized as an industry leader that provides exceptional services and exceeds every client's expectations.

As the churches and buildings designed by Christopher Wren have influenced London, so have the buildings constructed by Brasfield & Gorrie shaped the landscape in Birmingham The AmSouth/Harbert Plaza, the Birmingham Public Library, the Hugo L. Black Federal Courthouse, One Federal Place, Park Place Tower, Energen Place, the Financial Center, the Y.M.C.A., and the Criminal Justice Center were all built by Brasfield & Gorrie.

Religious facility construction has included, among many others, Briarwood Presbyterian Church and Hunter Street Baptist Church, and renovations at Church of the Advent and Temple Emanu-El.

Other significant Birmingham projects are the Colonnade development, the Meadow Brook Corporate Park, and Parisian and Saks at the Summit off Highway 280.

Brasfield & Gorrie is nationally recognized for its healthcare construction. In Birmingham, the company built most of the campus of Medical Center East and St. Vincent's Hospital and many buildings on the UAB and Baptist Medical Center campuses. In 2003, the company is serving as the construction manager on UAB's $350 million replacement hospital construction program.

Brasfield & Gorrie is listed as one of the Top 50 contractors in the nation. The success of Brasfield & Gorrie is reflected in the number of repeat clients, which amounts to 80 percent of its projects.

Left: McWane Center

Below: The Kirklin Clinic

EDS

Ordinary People, Extraordinary Achievement

In the Spring of 1962, Texas businessman Ross Perot was scribbling on a pledge envelope during a service at Highland Park Presbyterian Church in Dallas. Perot was mulling over potential names for a business he would incorporate for $1,000 in June of that year. Electronic Data Systems (EDS), the name he settled on, was launched with the vision of helping customers realize the maximum benefits from their computers.

EDS began processing its customers' data by purchasing unused time on other companies' computers, which often sat idle late at night. In the early days of the company, employees loaded reels of magnetic mainframe tapes in the trunk of a 1962 Chevrolet Bel Air, and drove to different locations to process work in the middle of the night. It would be three years after its incorporation before EDS first bought its own computer.

The birth of EDS in the 1960's came at a time when federal health insurance programs for the poor and the elderly were going into effect.

Health insurance organizations were deluged with a flood of claims to process under the new Medicare and Medicaid programs created by the Social Security Act of 1965. EDS offered solutions through one of the company's founding premises: companies need business and technology partners, not just computers and functionaries to run them.

Forty years after its inauspicious birth, EDS has become the information technology partner for more than 35,000 business and government clients in 60 countries around the world. The company is a global leader in information and technology designed to help its clients flourish in the digital economy. Almost 140,000 employees in more than 800 offices and service facilities assist clients in better serving their customers, competing in all aspects of e-business, and improving bottom line performance. The company supports more than 3.3 million desktops worldwide, managing about 50,000 servers and providing Web hosting for some 900 clients around the globe.

EDS now offers over 100 client services ranging from accounting

transaction management to government and industry consulting to workforce development systems.

When EDS went public in 1968, the company had fewer than 400 employees. Its first stock offering was $16.50 a share, and the company recorded revenue that year of $7.7 million. A year later, EDS' stock price hit $160 a share. In 2001, the company listed $21.5 billion in revenue, almost 40 percent of which came from outside the U.S. In the first quarter of 2002, the company had $5.34 billion in revenue, and established its 12th consecutive quarter of double digit growth.

The company's portfolio of scalable solutions draws on the expertise of EDS' professionals in four primary areas:

● Management Consulting. A.T. Kearney, the high-value management consulting subsidiary of EDS, focuses on CEO concerns and helps clients gain and sustain competitive advantage through a full spectrum of management consulting services, including strategy, operations, and information technology.

● Solutions Consulting. Solutions Consulting combines EDS' fast growing E.Solutions implementation consulting capability with its substantial applications services business.

● Operations Solutions. EDS' Operations Solutions integrates the company's traditional mainstay IT outsourcing operations—centralized and distributed systems and communications management—with its business process outsourcing capability.

● Product Lifecycle Management. PLM Solutions offers the most comprehensive digital product lifecycle management software products and services for companies seeking to integrate their customer and supplier strategies with product development, manufacturing, and service strategies. EDS' services are backed up by vast experience in supporting clients globally in every major industry, including communications, energy, financial services, government, healthcare, manufacturing and retail, and travel and transportation.

Over the course of the past four

decades, the company has pioneered a number of firsts and broken new ground in almost every market it now serves. EDS built the world's largest voice and data network, and conceived, built, and operated the world's most sophisticated network control facility located in its headquarters in Plano, Texas. The company became a leading services provider to the life insurance industry by introducing comprehensive solutions to handle every life insurance administration function.

EDS' work with government includes providing all the information technology services for the State of South Australia, as well as similar services for Inland Revenue, Great Britain's taxing agency. Major commercial clients include Chevron, General Motors Corporation, Commonwealth Bank of Australia, BellSouth, and a host of others. The company enables more than 13 billion business, consumer, and government transactions every day, including 2.5 million ATM transactions daily, making it the world's fourth largest ATM/EFT processor. EDS is also the largest mortgage processing out-sourcer in the world, handling approximately 2.3 million mortgages a year.

"The people who accomplished EDS' milestones were just regular folks," said vice-chairman Jeff Heller at his retirement last February after 34 years of service at EDS. "EDS has always been just ordinary people who came here and achieved more than they ever thought possible because of the opportunity and support they found."

Those ordinary people pioneered concepts and practices that are now centerpieces of the IT services industry, including systems management, systems integration, centralized transaction processing, and others. The company's innovation lies in its people's capacity for inventive implementation and creative methods.

Many of those people have had a profound effect on government and business right here in Alabama. EDS now employs more than 1,500 people in the state in offices in Birmingham, Athens, Cottondale, Mobile, Scottsboro, Gadsden, Montgomery, and Tuscaloosa. Alabama-based businesses that draw on EDS' expertise include Bruno's, BellSouth, Ruby Tuesday, Birmingham Steel, Alabama Title IX Medicaid, and the Veterans' Administration Hospital.

The company's employees are also active in their communities. EDS staffers in Birmingham helped improve the appearance of Parker High School as part of the company's Sixth Annual Global Volunteer Day. Through EDS' 'Partners in Education' efforts, the company partnered with Curry Elementary School to develop a computer lab and mentoring program for its students. EDS also sponsored a Thanksgiving food drive for the United Way, and allowed its employees to make financial contributions to the agency through a payroll deduction plan.

EDS has fulfilled its founding mission of helping manage the business and technology complexities in today's digital economy. The company's leadership is firmly committed to continued decisive action that builds trust among its customers, shareholders, and employees.

Far right to left:
Monitoring Customer Systems;
Facilities Planning; System Integration;
March of Dimes 2003 Walk-A-Thon

PROTECTIVE LIFE CORPORATION

"Doing the right thing is smart business."®

In 2002, when John D. Johns became the sixth CEO of Protective Life Corporation, he brought with him many of the qualities that Protective's previous leaders had demonstrated over the company's storied 95-year history. Those leadership qualities, combined with a continued reliance on the company's core values and management philosophy, have helped Protective become one of the fastest growing companies in the life insurance industry.

Protective's values-oriented management philosophy can be traced back to its founder, William Dorsey Jelks, who started Protective Life Insurance Company in 1907 with "a right, high purpose in mind." Today, that right, high purpose is expressed in Protective's unyielding devotion to its core values: quality, serving people, and growth. A former Chief Executive of Alabama, Jelks had been known as "Alabama's Business Governor" during his two terms of office in Montgomery. He advocated the same steady, conservative growth for Protective that he had promulgated for Alabama during his watch at the state's helm. Believing that serving people begins with being worthy of their trust, Jelks' commitment to Protective's customers, shareholders, and employees remains today the focus of the company's leadership.

Prudent financial discipline has been a hallmark of Protective since its inception. The company's success over the years was due in part to its ability to withstand the tough economic times that have periodically fallen upon the nation. Only a decade after its founding, the company was paying claims for young Americans who died liberating Europe in World War I. The nationwide flu epidemic after the War, part of the global epidemic that killed hundreds of thousands worldwide, also took a heavy toll on company resources.

Protective weathered those storms and, beginning in the 1920s, embarked on an expansion policy that by the end of the decade brought the amount of insurance in force to almost $6 million, a substantial sum in 1928.

Protective continued to grow, even through the dark economic times of the 1930s. Colonel William J. Rushton assumed the top leadership position at the company in 1937, and for the next three decades guided it with the same sound leadership that had come to characterize the company. Colonel Rushton also helped reinforce the company's reputation for integrity and fairness.

When William J. Rushton, III assumed the helm of the company in 1969, Protective had been operating primarily as a regional provider, serving customers throughout the South. The second Rushton to sit in Protective's CEO chair, William, or Billy as he insisted everyone call him, built upon his father's success, and drove substantial growth by introducing the company's family of products to all 50 states.

Whereas Billy expanded product distribution across the United States, Drayton Nabers, Jr., who succeeded Billy as CEO in 1992, grew the company by increasing its distribution across a variety of channels. He achieved this through both internal growth and acquisitions. The most significant of those acquisitions include:

• West Coast Life Insurance Company, the oldest life insurance company headquartered in San Francisco. Further solidifying Protective's position on the west coast, West Coast Life markets individual life insurance products through a strong network of brokerage general agents located throughout the U.S.

• The Lyndon Companies in St. Louis, Missouri, which doubled the size of Protective's Asset Protection Division.

• Matrix Direct, an innovative direct marketer of term life insurance products, located in San Diego, California.

As the life insurance industry has experienced significant consolidation over the last decade, closed blocks of insurance policies and annuities frequently became available for purchase. Since 1990, Protective's Acquisition Division has successfully invested approximately $700 million of capital in closed block-of-business acquisitions.

"This company has always been characterized by its optimism and positive attitude," states CEO John D. Johns. "These attributes are reflected in our core values and beliefs. We have been a key player in the growth and development of Birmingham over the years, and look forward to a future of continued service to the community."

Johns and the management team at Protective Life have outlined a growth strategy that is built upon the corporate philosophy to which the company's thousands of associates around the country ascribe: *"Doing the right thing is smart business."*®

"This has become more than a slogan at Protective Life," Johns points out. "It has come to symbolize a reflection of our core values, and it reiterates the intrinsic relationship between the company's basic business philosophy and its success."

That relationship has flourished over the years. The small company, founded by Alabama's 32nd governor, that paid its first $1,000 death benefit to a policyholder in 1909, now lists total Corporate assets of over $20 billion. In July of 2002, Protective Life Corporation reported second quarter pre-tax operating income of $68.6 million, a 20.4 percent increase over the same period of last year.

The company boasts an advanced technology platform that continues to improve. Protective's IT team has invested heavily in the company's core administrative systems, and believes they are as efficient as any in the industry.

Through its subsidiaries, Protective Life Corporation now markets a diverse array of insurance products and services. The company operates several divisions whose strategic focuses can be grouped into three general categories: life insurance, specialty insurance products, and retirement savings and investment products. Each division is generally distinguished by products and/or channels of distribution.

Protective's Life Insurance line of business consists of three divisions. The Individual Life Division markets term life, universal life, and variable universal life insurance through a network of independent insurance agents, financial planners, insurance brokers,

stock brokers, and direct response organizations. Within the Division, Empire General Life Assurance Corporation, based in Overland Park, Kansas, provides individual life insurance through Brokerage General Agents. The West Coast division sells universal life and level premium term-like insurance products in the life insurance brokerage market and in the bank-owned life insurance market. The Acquisitions Division acquires blocks of life insurance policies originally sold through other companies.

The Specialty Insurance Products business is made up of the Asset Protection Division, which special-

Protective's values-oriented management philosophy can be traced back to its founder, William Dorsey Jelks, who started Protective Life Insurance Company in 1907 with "a right, high purpose in mind."
"This company has always been characterized by its optimism and positive attitude," states CEO John D. Johns. "These attributes are reflected in our core values and beliefs."

izes in marketing vehicle and marine service contracts, credit life and disability insurance through dealer networks, banks, and consumer finance companies.

Protective's Retirement Savings and Investment Products businesses operate under the Stable Value

Products and Investment Products Divisions. The former markets guaranteed investment contracts, funding agreements and long-term annuity contracts to money market funds, government entities and qualified retirement savings plans such as 401 (k)s. The Investment Products

Division manufactures, sells, and supports fixed and variable annuities.

Building upon the strengths of the past with a keen, smart eye toward the future, Protective Life Corporation will soon mark its centennial year of service to the Birmingham community and to its

customers around the country. "We have an outstanding management team and employee group," Johns states. "Our people are smart, hard working, and productive. They have a passion for the business and are enthusiastic about our future."

Daniel Wolfe

Laura Wolfe remembers what it was like that hot August back in 1998. Her almost seven-year-old son, Daniel, had low-grade fevers and pain in his feet and legs. A routine doctor's visit showed her middle child didn't have mononucleosis or strep throat. But when three weeks came and went and still Daniel didn't get any better, her mother's intuition told Laura Wolfe something was very wrong. She insisted his blood be drawn.

It was leukemia. That diagnosis and the subsequent treatment began two and a half years of an intense medical voyage for Daniel.

Laura Wolfe thinks back on the worst of the nightmare. Beyond the bone-chilling knowledge that her son was sick, she and her husband Ed were by Daniel's side when he had spinal taps and bone marrow aspirations that started when he was six years old.

As nerve-wracking as the experience was and as scary as the treatments were, there were positive aspects, too.

"Daniel would practically run into Children's Hospital to see Meredith," Laura Wolfe recalls fondly of Meredith Weintraub, a pediatric nurse practitioner at Children's.

Weintraub saw Daniel through 19 spinal taps and five bone marrow aspirations. Those procedures weren't the only trials, but Daniel managed to maintain a stiff upper lip through them all.

"The first time I didn't know what was going on," Daniel recalls. "I had never had one before. They still hurt, but I got used to them." Weintraub started putting a cream on his skin to lessen the pain and then giving him a numbing shot. The stoic youngster eventually turned down the shot, facing the pain head-on. His mother says, "Most kids have general anesthesia. Daniel just had prayer and topical deadening cream."

"People always say I'm a trooper," Daniel says, "and I don't know what to say."

During the long and arduous treatment, Daniel's mom gave him an intramuscular shot once a week for two years. The Wolfe family was surrounded by support. Wendy Allison, the wife of the family's pastor, would hold the boy's hand and pray during each one. The Bible study group at Altadena Valley Presbyterian Church would pray for them every Tuesday.

Even though these were daunting times, Daniel kept doing what boys do. Instead of focusing on the medicine and the cancer and the concern, Daniel chose to focus on sports.

One day Daniel remembers he played soccer and scored goals in the morning, and then found he had pneumonia that afternoon. "People were surprised that I was out playing even though I had cancer. I just love sports so much it really didn't stop me."

If he wasn't playing on a team, he was playing soccer with his sister. "Emily likes soccer and basketball." Sometimes he can even talk younger brother Bryan into playing.

Sports are not the only thing important to Daniel. When asked what the past three years has taught Daniel, he says: "My relationship with God has gotten closer and closer. I really had to trust in him."

After thirty months of pretty intense treatments, it's over except for blood work and full exam every four weeks. Rightly proud, Daniel says, "I only take medicine for headaches and colds now. —Lynda Cardwell

JONES LANG LASALLE

The history of Jones Lang LaSalle is a blend of the best of dynamic American entrepreneurship with a 200-year old tradition of proven success in Europe. The company was born in 1999 through the merger of Chicago-based LaSalle Partners, Inc. and Jones Lang Wootton headquartered in London, England. The result was the creation of Jones Lang LaSalle, the industry's largest global real estate services and investment management firm.

With a global reach spanning more than 100 major markets, Jones Lang LaSalle is a leader in real estate services and investment management, employing more than 7,000 people worldwide. The firm has helped reshape the real estate landscape not only in its Americas headquarters in Chicago, but throughout the United States and around the world.

Since its inception, Jones Lang LaSalle has focused on forging strategic long-term relationships with its corporate, property owner and investor clients. The firm's reputation for delivering best-in-class real estate products and services has redefined the real estate industry.

"No other single company can match us in all four sectors of our business," said Christopher Peacock, president and CEO of Jones Lang LaSalle. "A number of other real estate services companies offer similar services that our Corporate Solutions and Investor Services units provide. Our Capital Markets group often goes head to head with investment banks, and our investment management business competes with other global and regional fund management businesses. We believe no other firm has the broad spread and depth of capacity to serve client real estate needs in all these areas, nor do they enjoy some of our synergies."

The firm's American component was founded in 1967 as IDC Real Estate by a group of real estate entrepreneurs in El Paso, Texas. They pinned their success on their ability to outperform competitors by taking a long-term, relationship-based approach to real estate as opposed to providing simple one-time transactions. This strategy was key to the company's early success, and led to its expansion and relocation in 1972 to Chicago. Five years later, it was renamed LaSalle Partners, Ltd. after its business address on LaSalle Street in downtown Chicago. Over the course of the next 25 years, the company developed into a publicly traded, fully integrated, global real estate firm.

Jones Lang Wootton, LaSalle's merger partner, was established in 1783 as an auction house in London. It was later combined with an estate agency business, and grew to prominence over the next century. After World War II, the firm was active in assisting in the reconstruction efforts of post-war London, which had been devastated by bombing. Jones Lang Wootton gained responsibility for a number of speculative development and leasing projects in the city, and solidified its position in the market.

Closer to home, Jones Lang LaSalle's clients include Compass Bank and BellSouth.

In the late 1950s, the firm expanded into Australian markets, opening offices in Sydney and Melbourne. It later branched out into Scotland, Ireland and continental Europe. Recognizing the potential opportunities provided by the political changes sweeping central and eastern Europe, the company opened new offices in Budapest, Prague and Warsaw. Expansion into North America led to the opening of an office in New York, where the company began meeting the needs of many foreign investors coming to terms with different market practices, valuation techniques and professional standards.

Meanwhile, LaSalle Partners was experiencing rapid growth in America. The company had been successful in expanding its real estate business by identifying a client's need, tackling it more professionally than the competition, and then expanding an initial assignment into an ongoing business relationship. The creation of its investment banking specialty, for example, was a response to market needs for more sophisticated financial expertise than was being offered by real estate firms and investment banks of the day. This resulted in LaSalle expanding its talent pool to include real estate investment bankers that represented buyers and sellers in some of the most significant real estate transactions of the 1970s and 1980s.

The merger of LaSalle Partners and Jones Lang Wootton in 1999 was a natural evolution of two firms with a common culture, strong client service foundations, synergistic operating philosophies and rich real estate service successes. The resulting Jones Lang LaSalle was thereby uniquely positioned to provide new opportunities for their clients, withstand and adapt to change, and continue to grow. In addition, the common service approach of the two companies, combined with their growth platforms and experience, enabled them to deliver cross-border real estate services and investment management expertise to multinational companies, property owners, and investors worldwide.

A leading real estate service concept pioneered by the firm and popular with many companies in the industry today is the tenant representation relationship. Rather than seeking

small individual transactions, Jones Lang LaSalle focuses on national relationships with major users of office facilities. This ensures long-term viability by providing long-term occupancy solutions for several of the nation's largest accounting firms, as well as clients in insurance, banking and financial services. The firm also serves corporate and investment clients as fee manager of major public development projects, such as the renovations of New York's Grand Central Terminal and the Symphony Center in Chicago.

The American headquarters of

Jones Lang LaSalle in Chicago perhaps best illustrates the full scope of the firm's broad range of expertise and services. The company's offices are located in the Windy City's towering Aon Center, a property the firm leased, occupied, sold and subleased to Aon Corporation.

Closer to home, Jones Lang LaSalle's clients include Compass Bank and BellSouth. Jones Lang LaSalle has a team of highly qualified and talented professionals providing on-site facility management services for 374 Compass Bank locations in seven states. The facilities under man-

agement total over 3 million square feet of space and include Compass' corporate offices, operation centers and banking offices. In addition, the company provides strategic real estate consulting and leasing services.

Jones Lang LaSalle partnered with BellSouth in 1996, and has continued to provide first class facility and project management services, as well as tenant representation. Jones Lang LaSalle manages 12 BellSouth facilities, encompassing 3.3 million square feet of corporate office and operation space located in Alabama, Kentucky and Tennessee.

ALABAMA CENTRAL CREDIT UNION

Making Dreams Come True

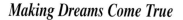

The U.S. economy was still foundering in the depths of the Great Depression in 1938 when the Alabama Central Credit Union opened its doors to its first customers. Since then, the organization has weathered good and bad economic times and not only survived, but expanded to provide quality financial benefits to the employees of over 800 companies around the state. With nine branches scattered throughout Alabama, the Credit Union employs 75 people dedicated to improving the quality of life for its members.

"At most banks, you are a number," states Ron C. Haas, CCUE, the president of Alabama Central. "As a member of a credit union, you are a stockholder in the company. That makes a tremendous difference. When a company joins a credit union, its employees become members of the organization. That means they can offer input and have a voice in the operation of the credit union. As owners of the organization, they are encouraged to participate in its operation."

Haas points to another major difference between Alabama Central and traditional banks. Alabama Central is governed by a Board of Directors made up of members of the credit union from around the state. Their service on the Board is voluntary. They are there solely because they believe in what Alabama Central does and in the products the institution offers.

In recent years, that list of products and services has grown to over 80 different features. In addition to standard checking and saving accounts, Alabama Central offers its members a variety of loan packages, certificates of deposit, money market funds, debit cards, IRA's, safe deposit boxes, credit cards, home banking with bill payment, and complete financial planning services.

Deposits in a credit union are insured by the federal government to $100,000 just as in a bank. Over 30,000 members throughout Alabama have now placed their trust in Alabama Central and its more than $155 million in total assets.

Alabama Central has acted as a safety net for thousands who would have lost their access to financial services when the companies they worked for closed or relocated. In 2001 alone, five plant closings from Florence in north Alabama to Creola just outside Mobile left members without credit union services. Alabama Central merged the failed companies' credit unions and their members into the Alabama Central family.

"We have merged over 50 credit unions into Alabama Central over the years," Haas states. "We are glad to be able to assist fellow Alabamians by providing our products and services to an ever-growing membership."

'Helping' has been the cornerstone philosophy at Alabama Central since its inception. Being good corporate citizens has also been high on the list of the institution's leaders and associates. Periodic promotional functions and themed events help perpetuate the camaraderie among the employees and the feeling of 'family' that characterizes each Alabama Central office.

The institution has also kept in step with the technological advances that are constantly impacting the financial industry. Alabama Central now offers the benefits and convenience of home banking via the Internet. Members can access Alabama Central's website and the institution's new 'eBranch' services where they can transfer money between accounts, request a withdrawal, make loan payments, and more.

"The continuous challenge is to provide the old fashioned service and personal attention that our members deserve in a progressive, high tech environment," said David W. Metcalf, the Chairman of the Board of Alabama Central in his annual report last year. "We care about what happens in the lives of our members. As an organization, we are financially strong, healthy, and secure. As a company, we are staffed by dedicated employees who take pride in the credit union. Alabama Central is here to help our members/owners build better lives as we travel through the 21st century."

Left: Ten convenient branches throughout Alabama...and growing.
Below: "Making Dreams Come True" for our members and their families.

SOURCE MEDICAL

Leading Outpatient Information Solutions

With over 20 years of experience in outpatient healthcare, P. Daryl Brown possesses the vision and expertise required to foresee unique opportunities in the marketplace. That vision and expertise—coupled with a burning desire to create his own corporate legacy—inspired Mr. Brown to found Source Medical Solutions, Inc. in November 2000.

Two years later, Birmingham-based Source Medical is the world's leading provider of outpatient information solutions, with products installed in over 3,500 facilities throughout the United States, Canada, Mexico, and Guam.

Mr. Brown's original vision culmi-nated from the recognition of two key trends—a migration toward outpatient care as a result of increasing health-care costs, and recent advancements in information technologies, including the maturation of wireless computing. Combined, these trends presented an amazing opportunity.

"Our solutions empower healthcare providers to spend more time doing what they were trained to do—care for their patients," said Brown. "Our products help healthcare professionals quickly and easily collect information about their patients using the latest computer technologies, dramatically reducing paperwork and errors associ-ated with more traditional methods of medical documentation."

In fact, Source Medical's solutions assist throughout every step of the patient care process, from scheduling appointments to treatment to billing. This unique 'end-to-end' approach is proven to reduce costs, improve infor-mation accuracy, and increase clinical efficiency.

Today, Source Medical offers lead-ing solutions for a wide variety of healthcare providers, including ambu-latory surgery centers, surgical hospi-tals, rehabilitation therapy clinics, radi-ology facilities, and physician practices.

Prior to founding Source Medical, Mr. Brown served on HealthSouth Corporation's Board of Directors and was President and Chief Operating Officer of HealthSouth's entire Eastern Division. Mr. Brown holds a Master's Degree in Business Administration from Samford University, completed the Kellogg Graduate School of Management's Executive Development Institute at Northwestern University, and completed his under-graduate work in economics at the University of Alabama at Birmingham. Mr. Brown also serves on the Board of Directors of the American Sports Medicine Institute, and is active in numerous other charitable and civic

organizations.

Under P. Daryl Brown's continued leadership as President and Chief Executive Officer, over 400 employees currently support Source Medical's unique vision for the future of health-care, and more than 20,000 healthcare professionals use the Company's prod-ucts to document over 80,000 patient visits per day.

"And we're just getting started," said Brown.

Top from left: Tom Hui, CTO; H. Sonny Crumpler, CFO; P. Daryl Brown, President & CEO; Michael A. Plaia, COO; Richard L. Chambers, Senior Vice President, Administration.

Left: Source Medical's solutions reduce healthcare costs, improve information accuracy and increase clinical efficiency.

AmMARK GLOBAL MARKETING

Any business owner who has ever experimented with direct mail as a means of reaching potential customers knows that this marketing method has the potential for being a highly successful venture. It can also be a very expensive failure. The difference is in selecting a specialist in direct marketing that can provide a comprehensive strategy aimed at getting your company's information into the hands of qualified prospects.

AmMark Global Marketing has compiled a successful track record in doing just that. The company, headquartered on Commerce Circle in Irondale with a satellite office in Atlanta, is a full service direct marketing firm that specializes in total turnkey solutions for their clients.

In today's fast paced competitive business environment, companies tend to have fewer employees shouldering more responsibilities. AmMark partners with its clients to become an extension of their marketing, advertising, corporate relations, and production departments. The company serves as a one-stop shopping source for projects by eliminating the need to deal with multiple vendors. AmMark offers a single source for expertise in the areas of concept, design, printing, list acquisition, list management, fulfillment, direct mail, and postal regulations.

"It is extremely important to have a complete understanding of the entire project and how variations in any of these components can drastically affect the overall quality, price, deliverability, and success of the campaign," says Jack E. Hartley, the chairman of AmMark. "This proactive approach to total business management, partnering with our clients to understand their needs, goals, and objectives, allows us to outline marketing strategies and more efficient methods to meet those objectives."

The company, originally founded in 1991 as a direct mail operation, was acquired by Hartley in 1997. The Birmingham native had 40 years experience in the printing side of the business, but was searching for a motivated professional with a marketing background to join him in turning the business around and getting it back on track. A few months after he took over the reins of the business, Hartley found the person he was looking for.

Jeffrey W. Cooke, now the president of AmMark, had a background in marketing, having launched several successful marketing campaigns for a variety of national retailers. Together, he and Hartley grew AmMark from first year earnings of around $200,000 to a company that topped $7 million in revenue last year.

"The key is in building relationships," Cooke explains. "You must also have a thorough knowledge of this business where a one to three percent response rate is considered a huge success. Thirdly, you've got to offer the highest level of customer service. We have been able to think outside the lines of traditional business when necessary to do whatever it takes to deliver quality and service to our clients on a timely basis. And we deal in total honesty. We've actually turned down potential business when we felt that the product or service was not right for a direct marketing campaign."

Hartley and Cooke now head a team of 42 professionals imbued with enthusiasm and a wealth of expertise in total marketing and distribution programs. They have designed and implemented complete nationwide marketing campaigns for companies ranging from Fortune 500 headliners such as Reebok, Champs Sports, the National Football League, the National Basketball Association, and BellSouth to the smallest local mortgage company sending out solicitations for home mortgages.

It's a long way from being a small company that was gasping for breath five years ago when Hartley and Cooke assumed the helm to second place on the *Birmingham Business Journal's* 'Fast Track 25' list of the Magic City's fastest growing companies. Presiding over that impressive turnaround and the 2,400 percent growth it recorded earned Cooke the *Birmingham Business Journal's* 'Rising Star' award in 2001. It will certainly not be the last time that AmMark and its management team will be cited for excellence as the company continues its tradition of service to its clients.

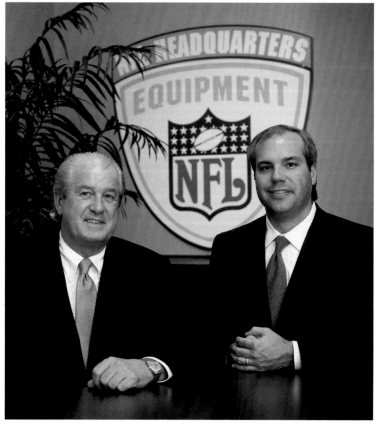

(L to R) Jack E. Hartley, Chairman and Jeffrey W. Cooke, President and Chief Executive Officer.

ENERGEN RESOURCES CORPORATION

Energen Resources Corporation, a subsidiary of Birmingham-based Energen Corporation, acquires, develops and explores for oil and natural gas in North America. Energen Resources is among the top 20 independent oil and gas production companies in the United States.

The company's roots trace back to 1971 when it was named Alagasco Energy Company and its focus was the exploration of gas and oil in northwest Alabama. In 1986, the company changed its name to Taurus Exploration Corporation and again in 1988 to Energen Resources Corporation as it is known today.

Energen Resources employs more than 250 people. In addition to its corporate headquarters in Birmingham, Energen Resources has a business office in Houston, Texas and field offices in Oak Grove, Ala; Vance, Ala; Farmington, N.M. and Arcadia, La.

Energen Resources employees are active participants in a variety of volunteer organizations. From serving as United Way campaign volunteers to coaching Little League athletic teams, employees are involved in the communities they serve.

In its early years, Energen Resources was involved in coalbed methane drilling in the Black Warrior Basin in Tuscaloosa and Jefferson counties. Coalbed methane is natural gas found in coal seams. The coalbed methane industry in Alabama has invested almost $2 billion in the state and created jobs, directly or indirectly, for 13,000 people at the peak of drilling activities. Energen Resources is still the largest coalbed methane operator in the Black Warrior Basin.

Energen Resources' growth strategy depends on acquiring proved reserves and pursuing exploitation rather than exploration. In the 1990s, the company switched its direction to pursue a more diversified supply portfolio by investing $850 million in acquisitions and related development. Building on its acquisition success, Energen Resources is poised to spend more than $900 million on property acquisitions and further exploitation of existing properties by 2006.

The company adheres to its strict investment criteria when evaluating possible property acquisitions. Natural gas properties are preferred over oil, although the company does not rule out oil properties that otherwise meet the acquisition criteria. Because of the control that comes with being the operator, Energen Resources' clear choice is to acquire operated properties.

For Energen Resources, the target property must have these three characteristics: located onshore North America, substantial exploitation potential and a long-lived reserve base. This less-risky approach offers the immediate benefit of existing, proven production and the potential for higher return.

Major acquisitions for Energen Resources include San Juan Basin properties in New Mexico from Burlington Resources; coalbed methane properties in Alabama from Amoco and Burlington; TOTAL Minatome Corporation and Permian Basin oil reserves.

Past success has earned Energen Resources a positive reputation in the acquisition marketplace. The company is respected for its evaluation speed and ability to close a deal. This status helps ensure that Energen Resources is invited to review and assess property packages as they become available.

The company is now active in six reserve areas: San Juan Basin (New Mexico), Black Warrior Basin (Alabama), Permian Basin (New Mexico and Texas), North Louisiana/East Texas, Gulf Coast Onshore (Texas and Louisiana) and the Rocky Mountains (North Dakota, South Dakota and Wyoming). In the areas in which the company operates, Energen Resources is consistently one of the most active companies in terms of exploitation and operational enhancements.

Energen Resources operates nearly 6,800 wells and produces approximately 6.3 billion cubic feet equivalent (Bcfe) of gas monthly. Since 1995, proved oil and gas reserves have risen from less than 100 Bcfe to more than 1 trillion cubic feet equivalent (Tcfe). In the same period, annual production has grown from less than 10 Bcfe to more than 75 Bcfe.

Energen Resources and its sister subsidiary, Alagasco, contribute to Energen Corporation's strength. Energen depends on Energen Resources to be the source of its earnings growth. Energen Resources' portion of Energen's consolidated net income rose from 18 percent in 1995 to 63 percent in 2001. To continue growth at that pace, the company will adhere to its low-risk business strategy. If the past is any indication of the future, Energen Resources is looking ahead to continued acquisition and exploitation success.

Inset: Energen Resources' growth strategy depends on acquiring proved reserves, such as this site in the San Juan Basin of New Mexico, and pursuing exploitation rather than exploration.

Below: The success of this development well is evident from the flare of natural gas. Energen Resources operates nearly 6,800 wells and produces approximately 6.3 billion cubic feet equivalent of gas monthly.

Photos by Billy Brown

Dr. Michael Saag

Michael Saag is a big, excitable dreamer. A sandal-wearing, tieless man who could be mistaken for a history professor ...or a Deadhead. But Dr. Saag isn't a Deadhead. He's not even a history professor.

He is a world-renowned HIV/AIDS researcher at UAB, the author of at least 24 articles or book chapters on HIV/AIDS and the head of the 1917 AIDS Outpatient Clinic where the world turns for answers in its battle with the worst plague in history.

Sitting at a round table—the only clear space in a cluttered institutional-style office in the UAB Community Care Building—Dr. Saag explains the decision to work in a field that is not exactly glamorous.

"Most physicians will say they went into medicine to make a difference and I can say I've made a difference," he said. "I remember growing up and reading history and wondering 'What's going to happen in my lifetime?' It seemed everything had been done. Then I stumble into this epidemic that is without question the largest plague in the history of mankind. I'm able to make a difference.

"There is a political aspect of this. I get to go and represent disenfranchised people."

Dr. Saag talks about his children, his wife, his life. He gets excited, talking fast. He is sincere and humble, describing himself as a jack of all trades with ideas for plays in his mind and a library of music videos that he has made. And that excitement and sincerity spill over into his career choice.

"I cannot fully comprehend the power of this epidemic," he said. "What happens if people 20-to-50 years old virtually die out? How does a society function if you have five-year-old orphans wandering the street? What is culture for these people without homes? Where are the rules, laws. Concept of religion? I can't comprehend what that means globally.

"Here we are just at the end of the beginning. We haven't begun to see the worst ravages. It's silent and it's exploding among young people What about the U.S.? Your kids, my kids? You can preach abstinence until you are blue in the face and it means nothing."

Dr. Saag came to UAB to go into cardiology and "got bored with asking questions about chest pain. Midway through the first year I got interested in infectious diseases."

He began working with HIV and in 1986 he "got lucky and stumbled onto a finding that HIV existed as a swarm of viruses, each genetically distinct. By 1987 I had to define who I was going to be. There was a tremendous opportunity at UAB to establish a clinic."

About 1988 he solidified his idea for a clinic that would handle patient care, social service, research, education of health providers and community outreach. "There was an incredible environment here at UAB," Dr. Saag said. "I've been to most major universities in the U.S. and there is nothing compared to what we have here—general academic freedom, visionary leadership. This is almost a university without walls. We work with different departments seamlessly."

Of course, there is a downside to working with a deadly disease.

"If I'm a good clinician I care about the patients who come to see me," Dr. Saag said, placing his hands flat on the table. "I need to know these people. That relationship is what being a physician is all about. When I see someone who is very sick and I'm able to help them, there's no better reward. But there are times when nature and the disease win.

"(Our patients) have been infected 10-12 years before they ever show up at our doorstep. No matter what we do, they die in four years. That's a tremendous loss. It's losing a friend and the closeness of a relationship."

Then, sounding somewhat un-doctor-like, he says, "You find beauty in the fact that all of us are different. ...The judgmental folks are forgetting what our historical religious leaders used to do. Who was the one who helped lepers and had genuine concern for the sick?"

Priscilla Hancock-Cooper

Priscilla Hancock-Cooper, hands folded in front of her on the table, looked out the window of the Civil Rights Institute board room to the 16th Street Baptist Church across the street. She was dressed like a young girl at summer camp—baseball cap, pedal pushers, a tee-shirt and a jacket—but she had a serious, distant expression on her face.

"When I came through—black writers in particular—you were indoctrinated into the idea that you had a responsibility to your community. It isn't just about you. What you are saying, why you are saying it. What's it doing to your community? We had to answer those questions. That discussion was out there and on the table."

Clearly Hancock-Cooper is a talented writer with the soul of a poet and the social conscience that goes along with it. But she has another talent that serves her and the art well: She is, in a sense, an actress, performing her work as well as the work of other poets.

"We call our performances poetic concerts. It's not hip-hop, but it's adding drama to poetry. It's music and acting; oral interpretation. It's really theater, putting the poetry on stage."

"I started performing because it is a way to get people interested in literature. It's an effective way to introduce people to that body of work."

It's also an effective way to make needed change.

"It allows you to tell the story of the history and to introduce culture that's not as threatening to people. You can cover the horror of slavery. It allows people to be relaxed enough to explore topics that may be difficult."

Hancock-Cooper tours with three shows of her work, and one of them, "Ebony Legacy: The Oral Tradition of African-American Literature," is often seen on Alabama Public Television. She also is the founder and director of Nia Institute, Inc., a day camp where children, parents and teachers can learn about African-American history and culture. Hancock-Cooper also wrote the copy for the permanent exhibit at the Civil Rights Institute.

And she works with girls ages 12-18 at the Girls Facility at Chalkville, teaching them to write.

"Being African American I'm more sensitive to the realities of the criminal justice system. I don't think it makes me automatically more (sympathetic toward troubled teens). It's a function of who I am, period. I love working with young people. I respect them probably because there were adults who respected me.

"I marvel at their honesty and am amazed by their resilience. They retain a zest for living. I'm probably not as judgmental. I know that life's circumstances can put you in places."

Her life's circumstances certainly put Hancock-Cooper in an interesting place.

"My mother was my first great influence. I knew my mother used to direct a group that did choral readings. That instilled in me a love of literature in ways I didn't understand.

"I heard the writer Haki Madhubuti when I was in high school. He did the oral performance thing. I was inspired during his readings."

Hancock-Cooper is loud, boisterous, fun at times and pensive at others. Her big smile can give way in a moment to a thoughtful, near-pained expression. Discussing race relations in the shadow of the 16th Street Baptist Church invariably leads to serious, low tones.

"Birmingham in 1963 spoke to courage. It's one thing to watch it on television and entirely different to have lived it. Birmingham's sacrifices benefited the whole country.

"With all the talk about reconciliation you hear little talk about repentance. There are a lot of black victims, but few white people who are taking the blame.

"To raise children in a world where they don't interact with people of different colors and culture is a disservice. The workforce isn't like that. That's reality."

Her gaze leaves the church and turns back into the board room.

"I have a strong belief in the importance of teaching our history and culture. I believe in children and believe in the power of arts to transform and change lives."

ST. VINCENT'S HOSPITAL

A Legacy of Caring

In a city with a world-wide reputation for medical research and quality healthcare facilities, one name stands out as having served the people of Birmingham longer than any other hospital. In fact, the Magic City itself was still a rowdy boomtown less than 30 years old in 1898 when three passengers destined to leave a legacy of caring descended from a train in Birmingham's Union Station. Sisters Benedicta and Magdeline, two members of the Daughters of Charity of St. Vincent de Paul, and Father R.A. Lennon were met by Father Patrick O'Reilly of St. Paul's Catholic Church, and were whisked away from the station on Morris Avenue to begin working on the realization of Father O'Reilly's dream of a hospital for the bustling new community.

to sustain and improve the health of not only individuals but also of the community.

"Being Birmingham's first healthcare facility is a statement of the commitment of St. Vincent's Hospital more than a century ago to provide quality healthcare services to the community," states Curtis James, FACHE, the hospital's president and CEO. "We are very proud of the reputation we've built for ministering to the whole person - body, mind, and spirit. Our goal is to work hard to continue that commitment into the future."

The nerve center of St. Vincent's medical complex is the main hospital building, an acute-care facility located at University Boulevard and St. Vincent's Drive. In addition to the 338-bed, all-private hospital rooms, the building also provides medical care in more than 50 specialties ranging from allergy/immunology to vascular surgery. More than 300 physi-

Center. St. Vincent's caregivers designed its birth suites with a home-like atmosphere that includes a rocking chair, TV/VCR, and pull-out loveseat for family members who wish to spend the night. More than 100 pediatricians and pediatric sub-specialties address patients' individual needs, from labor/delivery/postpartum care to lactation support. The Neonatal Intensive Care Unit provides the highest level of care available to newborns. The hospital, through its Good Health School, offers a variety of perinatal classes to meet the healthcare needs of the mother and her baby. All this has led to St. Vincent's growth in its obstetrical services.

Three professional buildings are also on the main campus. In addition to physicians' offices, St. Vincent's professional buildings house the Lee J. and Nancy M. Bruno Rehabilitation Center. The $4.3 million gift from the Bruno family for the Center, which

highlighted by the Linn-Henley Auditorium and include the tiered Mary Bruno Lecture Hall, a computer education center, and several classrooms with satellite downlink, cable phone, and data connections.

The spiritual center of the St. Vincent's complex is the Chapel. Serving as the heart of the hospital, it has provided a haven for those who seek the solace of prayer and meditation. The new chapel features seven carefully crafted panes of stained glass. When viewed from the outside, the exquisite panels overlooking the Red Mountain Expressway serve as a beacon on the hill in a building that has long been a distinctive Birmingham landmark.

But St. Vincent's commitment to the Magic City is not limited to its resources at its main campus. Its goal to take wellness beyond the walls of its hospital led to St. Vincent's reaching out to the community to make its

President and CEO Curtis James promotes the use of the latest healthcare technology available to enhance the quality of patient care at St. Vincent's.

Sculpted in bronze, "Sisters' Vigil" greets patients and visitors at St. Vincent's main entrance, in recognition of the four Daughters of Charity credited with founding the hospital in 1898.

Sister Magdeline and Father Lennon soon left, but Sister Benedicta stayed and was joined by other members of her order. They took up residence in the DeBardeleben house on Southside where they first began administering medical care to the city's residents.

From that inauspicious birth a little more than a century ago, St. Vincent's Hospital has grown to become a world-class healthcare facility. St. Vincent's has built a reputation as a healthcare ministry dedicated to spiritually centered, holistic care designed

cians, 83 percent of whom are board certified, lead a staff of nurses, support personnel, and volunteers in providing everything from the latest medical technology to a simple prayer at a patient's bedside.

The hospital is also home to the Joseph S. and Theresa R. Bruno Cancer Center. The facility, made possible through a $1.5 million donation by the Bruno family, is known for the comprehensive cancer care and support services it offers.

Attached to the main building is St. Vincent's Women's and Children's

opened in 1992, was not only the largest donation ever made to St. Vincent's, but it was also the largest ever given to a private hospital in Alabama. A cardiopulmonary rehabilitation facility, a mammography center, diagnostic center, and pharmacy are located in the professional buildings.

The main campus is also home to the Bruno Conference Center. The multi-purpose Center is part of the hospital's ongoing effort to unite the corporate world with the healthcare industry. The Center's resources are

services conveniently available to residents throughout Birmingham and central Alabama.

St. Vincent's offers an Occupational Health Clinic on its campus and on Lakeshore Drive in Homewood. The Clinics handle cases involving workers' compensation, offer occupational medicine, treatment of job-related injuries, work-related exams, drug screening, and physical and occupational therapy. Last year, these Clinics served more than 27,000 patients.

The addition of St. Vincent's Centennial Lodge in December 2000 provides comfortable, homelike accommodations for those who want to be near a loved one in the hospital. Funded by St. Vincent's Foundation, the Centennial Lodge offers several amenities to support families who may be coping with a loved one's illness.

In April 2000, St. Vincent's teamed with Rich's Department Store at Riverchase Galleria to make mammography, breast care, self-exam instruction, and additional services available through St. Vincent's Women's Center at Rich's.

The hospital's Wellness Van canvasses many underserved areas of Jefferson County as well as corporate sites. It has provided thousands of mammograms to women at their places of employment in addition to screenings for blood pressure, cholesterol, and glucose. The hospital's Good Health School reaches more than 30,000 people each year through

care, St. Vincent's began laying the foundation for a completely digital hospital as early as 1992. Ten years later, St. Vincent's cardiovascular intensive care unit (CVICU) is slated to become the hospital's first totally digital unit. Named one of the "100 Most Wired Hospitals" in the country, St. Vincent's partners with numerous organizations to develop and implement technology.

"We are committed to employing technology in a way that enables our caregivers to provide better care," states Curtis James, president and CEO of the hospital. "Making more data and patient information available electronically through handheld computers at the patient's bedside helps our staff streamline patient care and eliminate potential miscommunication. We have filmless x-rays, completely electronic medical records, bar codes on patient wrist bands, and other innovations in our

Ascension Health. The faith-based organization is dedicated to the shared healing mission of the four provinces of the Daughters of Charity and the Sisters of St. Joseph.

As a member of Ascension Health, St. Vincent's is part of an $8.9 billion healthcare leader, the nation's largest not-for-profit health system. Ascension now has more than 83,000 associates working in hundreds of health facilities in 15 states and the District of Columbia.

One measure of Ascension Health's commitment to improving access and delivering quality care, particularly for those who are poor and vulnerable, is the $352 million that the health system annually provides for community benefit services and care of the poor. Locally, St. Vincent's demonstrates a measure of that commitment through the provision of hospital services to the uninsured and Medicaid/Medicare

Birmingham, regardless of their ability to pay. In keeping with the tenets of ministering to the poor, on which the Daughters of Charity of St. Vincent de Paul was founded in the 17th century, St. Vincent's hospital today remains focused on providing the best possible healthcare to all the people of this area, regardless of their economic status.

St. Vincent's mission of service and its commitment to operating under the highest standards of medical ethics are best exemplified by one of its own staff members. Sister Virginia Delaney, the vice-president of mission services at the hospital, recently was honored with the Pellegrino Medal for Ethics awarded by the Health Ethics and Law Institute of Samford University. The award honors individuals recognized nationally as leaders in the contribution to healthcare ethics.

"Our mission can best be summed

Homelike Birth Suites in St. Vincent's Women's & Children's Center surround new moms and their babies in comfort, and each suite provides a sofa bed for dad or a family member or friend to spend the night.

Sr. Virginia Delaney has been recognized with the prestigious Pellegrino Medal of Ethics, a national award presented to those who exhibit leadership in healthcare ethics.

corporate and community wellness programming.

In May 2000, St. Vincent's was named one of the nation's top 100 hospitals for heart care by HCIA-Sachs in its Cardiovascular Benchmarks for Success study. The Bruno Memorial Heart Care Center provides the technology and treatment of all types of cardiac problems. It also offers community-wide education programs promoting healthier individual lifestyles.

Embracing the latest technology to streamline and improve patient

efforts to become totally wireless. Vital signs are recorded by computer, and a new digital system in the Pharmacy Services Department saves time and increases accuracy by scanning prescription orders. All these efforts result in our caregivers being able to spend more bedside time with their patients."

In 1999, St. Vincent's marked another milestone in its history. The Daughters of Charity National Health System, under which St. Vincent's operated, and the Sisters of St. Joseph Health System merged to become

enrollees. Another example is seen in the multitude of community benefit programs sponsored by St. Vincent's which serve not only the indigent, but also certain segments of the population, such as youth and the elderly, who have special needs.

Despite its phenomenal physical and technological growth over the past century, St. Vincent's has never lost sight of the original mission that Father O'Reilly and the two Sisters had when they arrived in Birmingham more than a century ago—to provide quality healthcare to the people of

up in a quote from St. Vincent de Paul," Sister Virginia relates. "In 1657, he said, 'Come now, let us engage ourselves with renewed love to serve the sick and poor, let us even seek out the poorest and most abandoned of all. They look on us as people sent by God to help them.' This statement is as timely today as it was when St. Vincent de Paul made it 350 years ago."

MERCEDES-BENZ U.S. INTERNATIONAL

New Products, New Jobs, Even Greater Economic Impact.

 decade after Daimler-Benz AG (now DaimlerChrysler AG) surprised the world and selected Alabama as the home for its first passenger vehicle plant outside of Germany, Mercedes-Benz U.S. International (MBUSI) is getting ready for the next chapter of its life. New products, more jobs, and an even greater economic impact are what the Birmingham community will soon see coming out of the Mercedes plant.

The story all began in September, 1993 when, after a five month intensive site selection process, the company selected a location about 35 miles west of Birmingham in Tuscaloosa County to build a new plant, to produce a new vehicle, with "team members" who had never before built an automobile.

Today, more than 80,000 M-Class sport utility vehicles are built annually in the $400 million, 1.2 million square foot facility. Some 350 vehicles come off the line each day and are sold in more than 135 countries around the world.

In forming the new organization in Alabama, Mercedes-Benz U.S. International, Inc. (MBUSI) created a "melting pot" of cultures and experiences. Individuals with experience from Mercedes-Benz were joined with colleagues from both the U.S. and Japanese automakers to bring together the "best of the best" in terms of ideas and ways to produce an automobile and work with suppliers.

The worldwide success of the M-Class, and the Alabama-based company that builds it, paved the way for the $600 million expansion which is underway to double capacity at the plant to 160,000 vehicles annually. To support this expansion, some 2,000 new "team members" will be hired, bringing the total workforce to 4,000.

The expansion will also double the plant's size to three million square feet. The new facility, which will include two assembly shops, two paint shops, and an expanded body shop, will build the next generation M-Class, as well as an entirely new vehicle—the Mercedes-Benz GST (Grand Sports Tourer). The GST will combine vehicle concepts from a sports sedan, station wagon, mini-van, and sport utility vehicle. Both the future M-Class and the GST will hit the market as 2005 vehicles.

"The worldwide demand for the M-Class has exceeded all expectations and shows that Mercedes-Benz made the

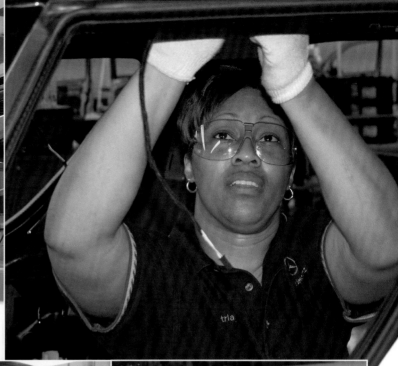

right decision when it came to Alabama to build it," said MBUSI president and CEO Bill Taylor. "Our success would not have been possible without the great partnerships we have formed within the state and our local communities, and without the strong workforce that we have found here. Alabama has become an important home for Mercedes-Benz."

Becoming a part of that workforce proved to be high on the list of many job seekers in Alabama. More than 46,000 applications were received for the first 1,500 jobs at Mercedes. Some 25,000 applications were received for the 2,000 additional jobs associated with the plant expansion. The majority of the workforce comes from a 75-mile radius of the plant, spanning the Birmingham and Tuscaloosa corridor, but it's not uncommon for "team members" to come from as far away as Anniston, Huntsville, and Montgomery.

Economic impact of the Mercedes plant has been felt statewide. Even before the expansion, the Mercedes plant is said to represent a $1.3 billion economic impact annually. On top of that, MBUSI is the state's largest exporter, with more than $1 billion in finished vehicles and parts leaving the state every year. Another $1 billion in purchases are made within Alabama each year, thanks to the Mercedes plant. More than 10,000 jobs, both direct and indirect, are attributed to MBUSI. All this before the company's $600 million expansion is complete.

ONE TEAM CULTURE

The feeling of being a part of a winning team is underscored in many ways. Probably the most noticeable is the atmosphere of "one team" that permeates the facility. To begin with, all production shops, along with the administrative offices, are under one roof to foster good communication flow. In addition, there are no private offices in the facility; rather, wall-less workstations fill the environment. Even the company's president and CEO sits in an open office, readily accessible to team members. Absent also are executive parking and executive-only dining areas.

In addition, "team members," whether in the plant or in the office, wear "team wear"—uniform clothing that displays an individual's first name and the Mercedes logo, further illustrating the "team" concept.

FAMILY AND COMMUNITY: IMPORTANT VALUES AT MBUSI

MBUSI believes that family and community are just as important as building a top quality product. In May, 2002, MBUSI opened a state-of-the-art Childcare and Wellness center on its property. Team members' children can take advantage of the exceptional learning and development activities, while their parents work right next door. The wellness center, which includes a gym, weight room, aerobics classes, and organized team sports, is open practically round-the-clock to accommodate day and evening shifts at the plant.

The M-Class is the official vehicle of the Kid One Transport System, a non-profit organization that provides transportation for children and expectant mothers who need medical care, yet don't have access to transportation. MBUSI has donated M-Class vehicles to Kid One since the organization was formed in 1997.

MBUSI is also the proud sponsor of the Mercedes Marathon, an annual event held in Birmingham which brings thousands of visitors into our city, while raising money for local charities.

These and dozens of other outreach initiatives impacting the environment, the arts, health and social welfare, and education form the key components of the company's community outreach.

SOUTHTRUST CORPORATION

Trust is a critical commodity in the business world, and nowhere is it more important than in the selection of a financial services provider. For more than a century, SouthTrust has built its business on establishing trust by consistently meeting and exceeding the needs of its customers.

Founded in Birmingham in 1887, SouthTrust has grown into one of the 20 largest bank holding companies in America. The company is listed on the Nasdaq stock exchange, is a Fortune 500 and a Forbes Platinum 400 company, and is a member of the S&P 500 and the Keefe, Bruyette, and Woods, BKX indices. The company's focus on providing comprehensive products and services combined with unmatched customer service has established SouthTrust as a financial leader in 19 of the South's largest cities in nine states from Virginia to Texas.

"SouthTrust is the largest Alabama-based bank holding company, and is the cornerstone of Birmingham's nationally recognized financial services industry," says Glenn Eubanks, SouthTrust's president and chief banking officer.

SouthTrust's success has revolved around focusing on high growth markets, establishing a presence in those markets, and growing internally. Three primary lines of business drive the company's growth and service to customers ñ Retail Banking, Commercial Banking, and Capital Management.

RETAIL BANKING

SouthTrust's employees focus every day on ways to make it easy to do business with the company. SouthTrust has a network of more than 700 banking and loan offices and 850 ATMs, as well as full-service online banking.

This extensive infrastructure helps deliver traditional banking products and services to customers. SouthTrust has checking and savings accounts to fit any need and a full menu of CDs and money market accounts to help customers put their money to work for them. And SouthTrust offers a complete line of mortgages, consumer loans, and business loans.

COMMERCIAL BANKING

What makes SouthTrust's Commercial Banking group different from other banks? SouthTrust has built a team of highly experienced banking professionals to provide a unique, customized service to clients. The commercial banking group consists of real estate lenders, corporate bankers, middle market and business bankers who focus on companies with revenues of $10 million to $250 million.

Each relationship is treated as an important opportunity to add value to a client's business. With that relationship comes a strong and competitive lineup of loans, corporate real estate services, cash management products, and international banking services.

SouthTrust's professionals have significant experience working with private and public companies, advising them on a variety of corporate finance and treasury needs. SouthTrust works to offer flexible, aggressive structures that align the client's interests with those of the bank.

CAPITAL MANAGEMENT

SouthTrust's Capital Management Group delivers a combination of brokerage, institutional sales, trust, trading, investment banking, private banking, and insurance products and services. These services are designed to maximize the financial well-being of SouthTrust's customers.

Through SouthTrust Securities, individual investors benefit from SouthTrust's extensive lineup of competitive investment funds and full-service brokerage products. Tax-exempt organizations and corporations have access to a variety of investment banking and institutional brokerage options through the SouthTrust Securities Capital Markets Group.

SouthTrust also has an experienced trust team that offers a comprehensive group of trust and estate planning services, and the SouthTrust Insurance Agency provides life, disability, auto, homeowners, business, and many other insurance products.

SouthTrust Bank, founded in 1887

A COMMITMENT TO BIRMINGHAM

SouthTrust is among the Birmingham metro area's largest employers. The company's 4,000-person local workforce exemplifies the company's commitment to the communities where it does business. Employees, such as Ollie Sandlin, regularly donate their time to programs and initiatives that benefit civic and chari-

Ollie Sandlin
SouthTrust employee since 1953

The Wildwood Campus, off of Lakeshore Drive in Homewood,
was completed in June 2002

SouthTrust employees donating their time to local organizations.

table organizations. Ollie started at SouthTrust nearly 50 years ago, and through the years has been a strong community leader in local organizations, such as the Birmingham Area Chamber of Commerce. He has single-handedly raised over half a million dollars for the Chamber, and has been their top producer for six consecutive years. Other organizations that SouthTrust actively supports are: United Cerebral Palsy, the Children's Hospital, the YMCA, and dozens of organizations that rely on the company's Fair Share contributions to the United Way.

In addition to its headquarters location in the SouthTrust Tower in the heart of Birmingham's financial district, SouthTrust maintains a strong presence throughout the metro area. Along with its 40 conveniently located branch offices, the company completed in June of 2002 the newest of three building on its Wildwood Campus off Lakeshore Drive in Homewood.

The new four-story building provides 124,000 square feet of office space for about 1,000 additional SouthTrust employees. Together with the Wildwood I and II buildings, the new facility will house portions of the bank's mortgage, human resources, data processing, and other administration operations.

SOUTHTRUST'S SECRET TO SUCCESS

SouthTrust's 13,000 total employees are the real story behind the company's success. Those dedicated professionals, almost half of whom are shareholders, have a personal stake in the success of the company. That's why the customer always comes first.

"At SouthTrust, we feel that the personalized, friendly service we provide is one of the main reasons we've been able to sustain and grow our company," Eubanks says. "We've been doing business that way for more than 100 years. We take very seriously our slogan that at SouthTrust, you're not just another customer and we're not just another bank."

AMERICA'S FIRST FEDERAL CREDIT UNION

Focusing on Service

The same iron and steel furnaces which forged the sinews of Birmingham's economy in the 19th and part of the 20th centuries were also the birthplace for one of Alabama's largest credit unions. America's First Federal Credit Union was founded in 1936 as a credit union offering financial services to workers at U.S. Steel's Ensley

1,300 select employee groups representing over 80,000 members.

Functioning as a not-for-profit cooperative, America's First offers a variety of benefits to its members. A steadfast emphasis over the years on service rather than on profits allows the credit union to offer a variety of high quality products and services without the accompanying high fees charged at a bank. America's First's commitment to serving the underserved translates very simply

tors. These unpaid volunteers represent company sponsors and members of America's First, and chart the direction of the credit union in ways most beneficial to the membership.

This includes featuring a complete range of traditional services offered by a financial institution—savings and checking accounts, money market funds, certificates of deposit, and IRA's. Accounts are federally insured for up to $100,000 by the National Credit Union Association, and qualifying accounts are insured for up to an additional $250,000 by American Share Insurance. The credit union also offers a full compliment of consumer loans, including mortgages and credit cards, as well as financial planning, insurance, and investment services.

Striving to make its services convenient to all its members, America's First operates 12 full service locations

throughout the Birmingham metropolitan area with additional branches in Mobile, Cullman, Anniston, and Talladega.

The institution's emphasis on convenience is also evident in the ease with which members can shop for and purchase a car. Members can research a purchase or trade-in, become pre-approved for an auto loan, browse from a variety of terms and rates designed to fit individual needs, and close the deal at one of the credit union's 80 Wheel Power Dealerships. Monthly payments can even be deducted from the member's America's First account. The same ease of shopping extends to members looking for a new home equity line of credit.

"Providing the ultimate in service to our members is what we're all about," says David Adcock, president and CEO of the institution. "We were founded on this principle, and look to the future with an eye focused on continuing to respond to the needs of the people we serve."

Standing Strong for over 65 years...

America's First Federal Credit Union is one of the strongest credit unions in the nation with over $400 million in assets.

plant. Struggling to cope with the loss of jobs and homes and the numerous bank closings that marked the Great Depression, these workers were in need of a financial institution that would help them re-build their lives. The Iron and Steel Workers Credit Union, the predecessor of America's First, opened its door to these underserved individuals, and have kept those doors open for over 65 years.

Today, America's First Federal Credit Union is one of the strongest credit unions in the nation. Listing over $400 million in assets, America's First extends service to more than

into people helping people.

"We constantly strive to be a one-stop, full service financial institution that always puts our members first," says R. Gary Goff, the chairman of the institution's board of directors. "Our main objective is to find innovative products and services that will meet the changing needs of our members."

Every member of America's First owns a share of the credit union, and has a voice in the operation of the institution. They make that voice heard in their election of the members of the credit union's board of direc-

VESTA INSURANCE GROUP

Vesta's focus and commitment are to the personal lines insurance business. The Birmingham-based insurance holding company offers a wide range of personal insurance products through its member companies. Vesta's family of protection includes standard residential property and automobile insurance, traditional life insurance, health insurance, and non-standard automobile agency and insurance operations in selected markets.

Strategic acquisitions, some allowing the company to enter new markets while others designed for geographic expansion, have been key to Vesta's growth. Those acquisitions have enabled the New York Stock Exchange company to leverage its infrastructure and capital to offer complimentary products.

The company has achieved growth while providing an outstanding work environment for its more than 1,600 employees, 350 of whom work at Vesta's national headquarters in Birmingham.

Through the 2001 acquisition of Florida Select, Vesta acquired a proven residential property team that can build a profitable business in catastrophe exposed states. The Vesta management team uses quantitative risk models to build the optimal portfolio of business while protecting the company's balance sheet with solid reinsurance catastrophe protection.

Vesta entered the life insurance market in June of 2000 through the acquisition of American Founders' Financial Corporation, an Arizona-based firm that offers traditional and universal life products as well as annuities and pension contracts. Vesta is now positioned to offer a wide range of life insurance and savings oriented, tax advantaged annuities, and related products.

Vesta's leaders also see great potential for growth in the non-standard automobile market. To gain entry into this market, Vesta made a series of acquisitions for a number of non-standard auto insurance agencies, allowing Vesta to control the premium at the source. These acquisitions provided Vesta an opportunity to grow its business through a distribution channel backed up by a full service call center to field customer inquiries, facilitate policy applications, and administer the process of issuing new policies.

The company has achieved growth while providing an outstanding work environment for its more than 1,600 employees, 350 of whom work at Vesta's national headquarters in Birmingham.

Ronnie Bruno

It's the same quick paced walk, the same intent gaze, the same no-nonsense conversation. Much is the same with Ronnie Bruno, but much is different. The suit and tie have been replaced by an open collar short-sleeved shirt and a gold chain. The phone rings and instead of a problem with a store in Tennessee, he's talking with his father-in-law about an Alabama football game.

Now there is time to coach soccer or attend his son Gregory's basketball game or take a quick trip to the coast with his wife Lee Ann. And now there is time to give back to the community that has been his lifelong home.

Bruno knows what he was given.

"The community was extremely good to our business and we feel we need to give back," he said. "I was given a gift, a tremendous company to run. The obligation to give back never ends."

Bruno was 43 when he sold the family business that had grown from one grocery story to a $2.9 billion southeastern grocery retailer.

"I was in the business 25 years," he said. "I grew up in it. It took several years to kind of unwind. It was more than a job. You never get it out of your mind. You live it. It took me a while to get out of that mode. I used to be concerned about a lot of different things every day.

"I miss the daily contact and the vendor relationships. I miss the people in the supermarket business; the people I worked with on a day-in, day-out basis. The company had some wonderful people. But I'm happy the company is doing well. The family name is still in the business and it has great leadership. It took me quite a while. I'm happy now."

Bruno serves on the boards of the Russell Corporation, SouthTrust Bank and Books A Million. He also is deeply involved in community activity, serving as a board member of The Metropolitan Development Board, United Way, The Club and St. Vincent's Hospital Foundation of Alabama.

And, of course, there is the Bruno's Memorial Classic, the senior PGA tour event he founded in 1991. Bruno serves as chairman of the foundation's board of directors,

overseeing one of the premier senior PGA events and one that has given more than $6 million to local charities.

Bruno is known nationally in the sport of golf because of the tournament and the Bruno Event Team—a sports marketing company with 30 employees—that he and Gene Hallman founded in 1995. So, what's his handicap?

"Eighteen. I've been playing a long time. Sometimes I play a round and I think it'll be the last," he said, smiling.

Really, even though the 80-hour weeks he worked as chairman and CEO of Bruno's, Inc. are behind him, Bruno stays too busy to get in much golf. In addition to his obligations on boards and to the Bruno Event Team, he is president of the Bruno Capital Management Corporation, a family investment company.

"I stay busy enough," he said. "I don't do just one thing a day. I shift gears a lot. I'm usually here a little after 7 a.m."

But to Bruno, life is much more than running a business, staying busy. He points out that he has a family tradition of community service. His mother runs the Ann and Angelo Bruno Foundation, and unlike many charitable organizations founded by the wealthy, the Brunos spend their money not on the arts or cultural activities for the advantaged, but on programs for the less fortunate.

There is a reason for that. Ten years ago, not long after the death of his father, Bruno said in an interview that his faith helped him overcome adversity and run Bruno's, Inc. in a way that was fair to stockholders and employees.

Now, behind a different desk, in a different time, he explains his motivation: "Religion is the foundation of what we're all about. It's the guidance behind you. I know what I am. You try to make your decisions and you hope to be guided."

ALABAMA POWER COMPANY

Most of us who flip the switches on and off at home and at work are aware that Alabama Power is the utility company that brings light to our world. But what many people do not realize is the extent to which Alabama Power is involved in improving the quality of life for all of us in Alabama.

"The people at Alabama Power are committed to our customers and committed to making Alabama an even better place to live, work, and do business," said Charles McCrary, the company's president and CEO.

Alabama Power is the second largest subsidiary of Southern Company, one of the nation's largest generators of electricity. An investor-owned, tax-paying utility, Alabama Power provides electricity to more than 1.3 million homes, businesses and industries in the southern two-thirds of Alabama, and does so at a cost well below the national average.

In addition to supplying electricity, Alabama Power serves Alabama communities in myriad ways. From providing flood control and recreation to protecting the environment, from encouraging economic growth to supporting worthy causes through its charitable foundation, Alabama Power is working to preserve and improve on what makes Alabama great.

In 1924, Alabama Power created its Economic Development department, the first utility in the nation to take such a step. Since then, the department has assisted thousands of companies in their search for the right location to build a plant or expand an existing operation. Among the names that have looked to the company's Economic Development specialists are Mercedes-Benz, Honda America, Hyundai Motor Company, General Electric, Michelin Tire Company, Briggs and Stratton Motors and a host of others. In addition, the department partners with local communities throughout the state, offering a variety of services ranging from strategic planning and leadership development to assistance with downtown revitalization projects.

Since the company was founded almost a century ago, Alabama Power's employees have never wavered in their commitment to provide electric power at a reasonable price and to be responsible stewards of the environment. To these ends, the company has pursued a balanced approach to fuel diversity to ensure affordable, reliable and increasingly clean energy production. In addition to coal, the company looks to hydropower, nuclear power and state-of-the-art natural gas-fired cogeneration and combined-cycle units to meet its customers' future energy needs.

Hydropower has long been a mainstay of our country's national electrical power system and is one of the cleanest and most environmentally safe and affordable sources of energy. The cost to operate and maintain hydroelectric facilities is approximately one-third that of fossil or nuclear generation plants. Alabama Power operates 14 hydroelectric plants on three river systems, providing a dependable, stable source of power.

But Alabama Power's hydroelectric generating plants do more than supply customers clean, reliable electric energy. The lakes created by Alabama Power hydro facilities on the Tallapoosa, Coosa and Black Warrior Rivers offer more than 4,000 miles of shoreline, beaches, boat ramps, picnic areas, trails and camping sites for the public's enjoyment. The lakes are also an integral part of the state's flood control efforts and provide water for drinking, for agriculture, for industry, and to protect critical habitat for fish and wildlife.

Alabama Power now employs more than 6,700 people in dozens of different job descriptions, but all work toward the same goals: keeping reliability high and rates low. In 2002, the company exceeded its previous service-reliability record while continuing to boast some of the lowest utility rates in the nation. In fact, Alabama

Far left: Alabama Power volunteers help clean up the Coosa River, part of the Renew Our Rivers campaign spearheaded by Alabama Power; Inset facing page: Alabama power corporate headquarters in Birmingham at dusk.

Background image this page: Jordan Dam at sunset; Top inset:: Children frolic at Mitchell Lake; Lower inset: Special-needs children fishing at the Exceptional Anglers event at Oak Mountain State Park. Alabama Power is a key sponsor of the event; Far right: An Alabama Power employee monitors environmental equipment. Every day, Alabama Power employees are working on environmental solutions to help protect the state's air, land and water.

Power's average retail price for electricity is roughly the same it was ten years ago.

The company has also posted an impressive record in its efforts to safeguard our environment. Since the 1970s, Alabama Power has invested more than $1.3 billion in environmental protection equipment, research and development. The company ranks in the top 10 of all investor-owned utilities in the country for its investment in equipment and technology to improve the environment.

The investment is paying off. Since 1990, Alabama Power has reduced emission rates of sulfur dioxide (SO_2) and nitrogen oxide (NO_x) by 47 percent, while at the same time increasing electricity production to meet the growing energy needs of the state. Those emission rates will drop even further as new equipment comes on line. The company has consistently met or done better than the standards set by the federal government for air emissions designed to protect human health and the environment. Emissions

of SO_2 from Alabama Power plants are at half the levels allowable under state standards, which are so stringent that many power plants around the country could not operate in Alabama. In Birmingham, ambient air quality is 85 percent below the SO_2 standard set to protect public health.

But that's just the beginning. From now through 2010, Alabama Power expects to spend $1.5 billion on environmental upgrades to meet future air standards. Those upgrades include a $500 million initiative, already underway, to install Selective Catalytic Reduction (SCR) and other NO_x-reduction technology at Alabama Power plants. NO_x is a component of ground-level ozone.

But environmental technology and research are only part of Alabama Power's commitment to protecting the state's valuable natural resources. Believing that environmental stewardship begins with education, Alabama Power teamed up with the Alabama chapter of the Nature Conservancy to create a Web site, nowandforeveral-

abama.org that offers a wealth of information for teachers, students and parents about some of Alabama's most unique wild places. Alabama Power also partners with other environmental groups, schools, civic organizations, homeowners and boat owners in clean-up efforts on several of the state's lakes and river systems. Alabama Power's "Renew the Coosa" campaign has been recognized as one of the largest river clean-up initiatives in the Southern United States. In 2002, Alabama Power received a national award from Keep America Beautiful for its role in Renew the Coosa, which will now be known as "Renew Our Rivers" because of its broad impact, in the state and beyond. The company also sponsors and supports environmental groups such as the Nature Conservancy, Keep Alabama Beautiful, the Alabama Wildlife Federation and Legacy-Partners in Environmental Education.

Further recognition of the company's environmental stewardship efforts includes receiving the National

Hydropower Association's Outstanding Stewardship for American Rivers Award for its efforts on the Yates and Thurlow dams. The company and its employees have also been recognized recently by the Alabama Wildlife Federation, the Electric Power Research Institute and the Southeastern Electric Exchange for its environmental initiatives.

The greatest recognition, however, comes from the customers of Alabama Power, who consistently rank the company near the top in customer satisfaction.

As the company prepares for its 100th birthday in 2006, Alabama Power is focused on fulfilling its responsibility to provide affordable, reliable electric power and superior customer service while continuing to reduce its impact on the environment. During its second century, Alabama Power will remain committed to satisfying the state's growing demand for energy while working to help preserve, protect and improve Alabama for future generations.

Ona Watson

Ona Watson stood outside the music room that bears his name and pointed to a plaque bolted to the brick beside the door. The neon sign glowed and Watson, clad in cool leather pants and a brimless felt hat rolled up in the front, smiled.

"This is my motto," he says.

The plaque reads: "To all that enter this door. Bring an open mind and heart along with peace and love."

Earlier, in the cluttered office of Ona's Music Room amid boxes of potato chips and pork rinds and a bottle of Louisiana hot sauce that the proprieter says causes him dire gastric difficulties, Watson says: "We have ministers that come in here. Recently for Valentine's Day we gave a church free admission for one weekend and they used it in a raffle.

"We do music and it's good, clean music. No adjectives involved. You can come here and enjoy yourself regardless of what religion you are or what color you are. I had a lady celebrating her 85th birthday and she was on the dance floor swinging."

Watson, who fidgets during an interview, opening drawers, looking at mail, squirming in his seat, talks in smooth, understated tones and drops interesting phrases into conversation.

• "I want one of those things. That thing is called a Grammy."

• "I lived in New York for a while and in LA for a minute."

• "If I didn't own this place I'd be coming here anyway because it's a nice place."

• "I still say a b flat is a b flat and if you can play, you can play."

He also takes an interesting view of music, refusing to classify himself as a jazz singer.

"Jazz and hymns are the same, only the lyrics change. I'm more or less an entertainer. We do jazz and blues and big band and even country. It's not just jazz; that's why I call it a music room.

"I like ballads. I like songs about being in love because that's what I'm about. I like the lyrics. One of the things that bugs me about TV is sometimes we dwell on war too much. Not that we don't need to protect our country, but I think singing and doing music about love is refreshing.

"I like cowboys and westerns. Looking at the old black and white pictures you don't hear any curse words. Even if they fire a gun it's still OK."

Perhaps Watson's humble beginnings have affected his view.

"I've been singing since I was 12," he says. "I was in the choir at the Groveland Baptist Church in Woodlawn where my dad was the minister. I used to listen to Frank Sinatra, James Brown, Ella Fitzgerald. I used to listen to a lot of that stuff. My dad used to play those big records, those old fashioned ones, 78s. He said, 'If you want to do good in this business you gotta learn some of these songs.'

"My Dad said, 'Get a real job,' but then he decided that if this is what I want to do I should learn the basics."

Was his father a singer? "He could hold a note."

Watson has three brothers and a sister and all of them can sing. Two of his brothers are in a gospel group and his sister, a special education teacher in Washington, DC, "is the best singer of all of us. I'm more of an entertainer.

"If I died this very second, let it be on stage. I like performing live because you get an instant response. I've recorded and not gotten a response from that record for years to come."

So this singer and leader of a band called Champagne has found a good way to stay in front of an audience.

"I've always wanted to own a club," Watson says. "I had no idea of all the things you had to do, from mopping the floors to doing inventory. Why would I settle in Birmingham? I got tired of seeing people leave. I wanted to make a difference, that's why I stayed here.

"I get e-mails and calls from all over the world from people asking to come and play in my club."

Will Pearson

Imagine a dorm room at Duke University. A bunch of kids sitting around. Smart already, or they wouldn't be at Duke. Smart but wondering why they know some things and not others. Wondering what they really should know. Wondering most of all, "Who really cares?"

Will Pearson is a Duke graduate, as are the other founders of an unlikely magazine publishing phenomenon, *Mental Floss*, that also includes plans for books and additional products. The publisher has a regular segment on CNN's Headline News.

"We lived in the same freshman dorm. There was a group of people who would get together in the evenings and just talk about whatever was on our minds. And one evening we started talking about education, and the purpose behind education. Because we're all taught that we should know the plays of Shakespeare. We're all taught we should understand the periodic chart in chemistry. But we never really ask ourselves, why are we learning these things? Or we do from time to time, but we never really come up with an answer.

"And even that evening when we were talking about it, we didn't really know why we had to learn all of these things; but we agreed on one thing, and that was the fact that people like to feel smart. People like to feel well educated. They love to watch an episode of Jeopardy and be able to answer every single question. Why there's this yearning for this knowledge, we don't know, but we decided it would be nice if you could receive a magazine that was almost your education in monthly installments. So we decided, there's not a magazine that's quick, quirky and fun that teaches all of these things, so let's try and start one."

Start a magazine? That's a notion many an entrepreneur has tried to pursue, but few with the initial success of Will Pearson and company. Their prototype issues, sold nationally through chains such as Barnes and Noble and Books A Million, had a sell-through percentage on the newsstand of 65 percent, twice the national average.

"From the very beginning of launching this, we put up a website and would ask for reader feedback. That was a huge motivational factor in continuing this, because we would get so many e-mails from people saying, 'This is exactly what I was looking for, because you're right—I've always wanted to feel smart. I've always wanted to learn these things, but I don't want to read the textbook. I want somebody to tell me what the Dead Sea Scrolls are in one page, or what black holes are in a couple of pages, and break it down into terms I can understand.' So it was really the reader feedback initially that was a factor in helping us continue this," Pearson says.

With the magazine up and running, Pearson moved the company back to his hometown of Birmingham. (He was born and raised in Hoover). Now he and 10 staffers are working on future issues of *Mental Floss* from offices here.

"We're looking into a few other product line extensions. We begin work on a book series called *Condensed Knowledge* with Harper Collins next month. We're brainstorming on a couple of other ideas. There's a company that's interested in maybe trying to turn this concept into a board game within the next couple of years," Pearson says.

"I see *Mental Floss* the magazine being the backbone of a company that's doing a number of different things. But, long run, when people hear the name Mental Floss, we want them to understand that it's a company that tries to blur the lines between a great education and great entertainment—whether it be in reading the magazine or reading one of our books or playing a board game. In whatever way they decide to approach us, they'll know that if they want to understand certain topics, they can pick up *Mental Floss*."

MASONRYARTS

September 11, 2001: MasonryArts' Physical Security Division, a Bessemer, Alabama-based company, was 5 days from completing the installation of the blast resistant window and curtain wall system in Wedge I of the Pentagon when hijacked Flight 77 hit. 125 Pentagon workers and 64 airline passengers and crew were killed as the plane struck Wedge 1 and part of Wedge 2, which was awaiting renovation. Had the plane hit directly at any other non-renovated wedge, the resulting loss of life would have been even more devastating.

MasonryArts was again selected by the U.S. Department of Defense after 9/11 to participate in what would be known as the PenRen Phoenix Project, named after the ancient mythical phoenix rising from the ashes. In an ironic twist of history, the original construction of the Pentagon was begun 9/11/41, and as such, it is a National Historic landmark. MasonryArts was set to the task

of recreating the original Indiana limestone façade, employing cutting techniques from 60 years before, as well as historically replicating the original windows with a blast resistant curtain wall and window system.

The blast resistant windows needed to match exactly the exterior look of the originals. MasonryArts was able to accomplish this feat, down to the little little tabs in the corners used to hold screens before the air conditioning system was installed. Steel beams reinforce the walls around the specially constructed blast-resistant units, and geo-technical material covering the wall between the steel beams are designed to "catch" debris in the event of an explosion, preventing debris from causing injury to the occupants in the room. The entire Phoenix Project was completed in nine months' time, which was three months ahead of the scheduled September 11, 2002 completion date. Everyone involved with the project attributed the project's speed to the workers' personal motivation and dedication.

John Swindal, having been in the masonry business for over 50

Top: Workers unfurl an American flag at the Pentagon. Left: The Kirklin Clinic on the campus of UAB.

years, founded his first business on the cornerstones of Quality Workmanship, Absolute Integrity, On-time Project Completion and brought this tradition of excellence with him when he and his son, Roy, created MasonryArts in 1979. MasonryArts is a single-source cladding contractor possessing unique abilities, services and skills, designing, fabricating and erecting high-rise glass curtain wall, stone cladding systems, and installs commercial and industrial masonry and pre-cast concrete. MasonryArts operates its own 60,000 sq. ft. custom curtain wall and window production facility and has top secret facility clearance from the Department of Defense.

MasonryArts offers renovation, restoration, and demolition services for exterior building skins as well as providing forensic investigation services, budget and systems analysis, and emergency stabilization/dry-in measures for damaged, unstable, or leaking building exteriors. Although Bessemer-based, the company has offices in Washington, D.C., Miami, Pensacola and Orlando. Downtown Birmingham houses a stone showroom, part of the company's stone division specializing in the importation and fabrication of natural stone for commercial and custom residential projects. Physical Security by MasonryArts is a separate entity within MasonryArts devoted exclusively to designing, fabricating and installing blast resistant, ballistic and forced entry resistant security products and systems.

In addition to the Pentagon, MasonryArts' more well-known projects have included the Sears Tower; the U.S. Embassy, Moscow; the Federal Buiding, Oklahoma; and the FEMA Headquarters, D.C. Birmingham and Atlanta's urban landscape is dotted with numerous MasonryArts' stone, brick, glass and metal projects and are a testament to the company's tradition of excellence. MasonryArts has put its signature on hundreds of projects in this country and abroad.

Integral to the company's

Above: The U.S. Embassy in Moscow.

immense success has been John Swindal's unique leadership style and a talented, dedicated field, manufacturing, and administrative staff. Roy Swindal, President of MasonryArts, Inc. and John Swindal's only son, reminisces, "My father always taught me to never get so caught up in my own success that I forget that it's the people who work for the company who are responsible for that success."

MasonryArts is proud to have been selected by the Department of Defense to manufacture the custom blast resistant wall and window systems for Wedges 2, 3, 4, & 5 of the Pentagon and presently was awarded the contract by the U.S. General Services Administration to manufacture and install specially designed blast resistant windows, replicating historical profiles of the Old War Office Building, also in Washington, D.C.

Scottie McCallum

In the office of the mayor of Vestavia the constantly ringing telephones sound like a hand bell choir at practice. Late on this December day there is muffled talk of finding sites for business and heavy, hurried footsteps.

This is the perfect place for Dr. Charles "Scottie" McCallum, retired president of the University of Alabama at Birmingham and now mayor of the city of Vestavia. Mayor McCallum is that rare mix of energy and intellect. He's the guy who is always "getting talked into" projects and ends up changing the face of a city.

Explaining how he came to be mayor after a long career as a doctor and university president, he said, "I had helped with United Way and was active in the chamber, the Metropolitan Development Board and the symphony, doing those things you need to do. As a person in the university you have a responsibility to the community.

"I'd always felt responsible as a part of the faculty, yet I had never been involved in the city where my family grew up. I had never given a lot to this specific community where I had lived for so many years. Some people wanted me to get involved in running for public office. I wasn't particularly interested, but a group of young people wanted me to run for mayor. I viewed it as a way to pay back for all the things that I have received."

It's dark outside and the secretary has left. It is the end of a day that began more than 12 hours ago at 5:30 a.m. with a two-mile walk.

"I'm usually here by 6:45 or 7 in the morning," the mayor said, shifting in the comfortable chair in his large office. "My day ends about 7:30 p.m. I have a lot of functions at night; regional planning organizations, the whole issue of transportation, meeting with other government leaders."

But that's not all.

"I still cover clinics. I have students and residents in outpatient clinics and I volunteer to go down and work with them as a teacher while they see patients. There are a lot of things at the university that I still participate in. I spend at least 40 hours a week being mayor of Vestavia.

"I'm pretty busy from early in the morning until late at night. My wife might not enjoy it if I were home all the time."

Mayor McCallum is humble, excitable and he talks fast. He has a grasp of the larger issues facing the Birmingham area:

"Most people who live here work in Birmingham. They know they need to make a contribution to the greater metro area. We realize the zoo, the symphony, the McWane Center and the Botanical Gardens are not just Birmingham's responsibility.

"Birmingham is so much better than it gets credit for being. It's about time we take credit for our accomplishments. Look at the enrollment of African Americans at UAB and it's fantastic. We need to take some pride. I love for people to come from other countries to come and visit with us. People who have come here have made this a very cosmopolitan community. People from Vietnam, Thailand, Iraq, Germany, Norway, Italy and Pakistan. These people contribute so much to our community and make it richer.

"I look at this as a team effort. I hope the city is going to continue to move forward. As long as you can get people to help and give input, you're making progress."

Progress to Mayor McCallum is more than just big time politics. On this night he also has sidewalks, a public park and a Christmas parade on his mind.

"The (Vestavia) Christmas parade was great. The children were great. We had a big turnout It's wonderful to see bands and the youth participate in the parade."

Then:

"We just closed on 35 acres on Little Shades Creek. We're going to have walking trails, ballparks and gazebos. And we need sidewalks."

KPMG

A Hallmark of Personalized Service.

PMG LLP, one of the recognized 'Big Four' in the world of accounting, has had a presence in Birmingham since 1958. Located in the heart of the city's financial district, the firm is part of the 103,000 KPMG professionals in 152 countries around the world that collaborate across industry, service, and national boundaries to deliver the highest quality accounting services to its clients.

Companies face a host of new challenges in today's economy. The global marketplace is distinguished by remarkable growth and consolidation. KPMG focuses on helping clients successfully respond to changing opportunities by providing professional services whenever and wherever they are needed.

KPMG has tailored those services, including tax, assurance, litigation support, and risk advisory services, to address the complex business challenges faced by its clients. Through the firm's international network of industry professionals, among the best people, products, and technologies are combined to enhance services with industry insights and best practices.

Under the leadership of Steven H. Richards, Birmingham's managing partner, the Birmingham office has nearly 100 professionals with diverse backgrounds, capable of delivering a sophisticated and broad range of services related to assurance, tax, and litigation support. The firm's client base is a mix of industry leaders, many of whom are international and publicly held companies in the financial services, manufacturing, retail, distribution, and healthcare sectors. Each receives the attention to detail and personalized service that have become the hallmark of KPMG.

"As complicated as the business world has become today, companies are realizing that they need the professional services of an accounting firm that is proficient in all aspects of business," says Richards. "Our people work with attorneys, investment bankers, underwriters, and others on tax issues, mergers, compliance, acquisitions, estate planning, and other financial services. We're part of a total financial team for our clients. We work with a variety of companies ranging from small start-ups to the state's largest banks and insurance companies."

KPMG has become one of the leading accounting firms in the region and the state by adhering to the same standards of excellence for which the firm has become known around the world. Its professionals in 750 cities apply common business processes and global account management through a globally integrated infrastructure.

The professionals at KPMG in Birmingham actively support our local civic, community, and educational institutions. KPMG partners and employees contribute to local colleges and universities, and devote many hours of service to a number of Birmingham area organizations such as Junior Achievement, the United Way, the American Heart Association, and the American Cancer Society. These activities have also included leadership positions in the Chamber of Commerce, various area churches, the Birmingham International Festival, and the McWane Center. KPMG's partners and employees are committed to their clients and community.

Above: KPMG partners (from left) — Woody York, David Lasater, Sam McGarr, Steve Richards, Wally Dunn, Matt Lusco and David Turner.

Left: KPMG professionals (from left) — Robert Pittman, Karria Myers, Amy Kendrick (seated), Donald Howell, Denise Hill and Paula Berry.

HRH METALS

Ever wondered what happens to those giant roller-mounted bins at construction and demolition projects when they become filled with the scrap metal collected at those sites? Many of those bins are trucked to HRH Metals in Moody where their contents are sorted, processed, and shipped to manufacturing centers to be recycled into new products. This collection and transformation of scrap metal is having a tremendous impact on our environment and, thus, on the lives of the more than five billion of us that call this planet our home.

The business was born among the pipe shops and steel fabricating plants of North Birmingham in 1942 when Ed Robinson and Roy Hoffman joined forces to open a small scrap metal yard. The original operation employed five people and served the manufacturing and industrial operations in the Birmingham region.

Six decades later, HRH Metals serves as a major broker buying scrap metal and selling it to foundries, steel mills, and manufacturing operations across the country. The company's headquarters and storage yard are on a 10-acre site in Moody just off Interstate 20 in St. Clair County.

HRH concentrates on scrap metal collection from military bases, manufacturers, utilities, demolition companies, and building contractors. In addition, any business that manufactures metal products, from airplanes to nuts and bolts, has scrap associated with that manufacturing. Collecting, processing, and recycling that scrap back into other finished products keeps thousands of tons of scrap metal from finding its way into our already overloaded landfills.

"Most people know about us only from our brokerage side," explains Ed Robinson, whose grandfather and father co-

founded the business. "We collect, however, all types of scrap metal, including aluminum, stainless steel, alloys, and ferrous and non-ferrous metals. Here at the yard, it is sorted, cut, cleaned, and packaged to meet the specific needs of our customers. We now ship to customers around the country and to overseas markets as well. Our expansion into global markets will increase as the emphasis on recycling and protecting the environment becomes more widespread."

Robinson had graduated from Auburn in 1970, and was about to accept a position with a company in south Alabama when his father asked him if he would lend a hand at the family business for just six months during his grandfather's illness. The younger Robinson found that he was perfectly suited for the brokering and marketing end of the business, and has remained there ever since. The third key player, Marlin Hinds, later joined Hoffman and Robinson and became the other "H" in HRH Metals. Together, they grew the business from a small neighborhood operation to a major player in the metals processing and recycling business. They are joined now by Steve Crawford and a staff of 25 people, some of whom have over 25 years of service to the company.

In addition to the tons of scrap metal they collect and process, the company takes very seriously its stewardship role in environmental protection. As a member of the Cahaba River Society and other organizations, HRH promotes efforts aimed at recycling as much of what we use on a daily basis as possible.

"In the future, I'd like to see us expand more into foreign markets," Robinson notes. "Our continued growth will probably lead us to look at additional plants and storage sites. The need to recycle scrap metal globally will become increasingly important in the future as we attempt to balance continued growth with a clean environment."

Serving the scrap industry for over 60 years, HRH Metals eagerly awaits the opportunity to help with all of your metal recycling needs.

PROASSURANCE CORPORATION

A Promise of Protection

The medical liability industry today faces unprecedented financial and legal challenges that can only be met by a company with a commitment to customer service and the financial stability to keep that commitment. The merger of Medical Assurance and ProNational Insurance Company in June of 2001 combined two companies with those strengths to create an even stronger company, which is today the nation's third largest provider of professional liability insurance for physicians, dentists, hospitals, clinics, and other individuals in the healthcare industry.

Birmingham-based ProAssurance Corporation continues the tradition of ten policyholder founded companies that were acquired by, or sold books of business to, Medical Assurance and/or ProNational over the past 12 years. True to those roots, ProAssurance is dedicated to delivering high-quality medical liability

insurance to its insureds.

"The mission of ProAssurance Corporation is to be the recognized leader in providing insurance solutions for the professionals we serve," states A. Derrill Crowe, M.D., the chairman and CEO of ProAssurance Corporation. "We will offer our insureds an aggressive defense for non-meritorious claims, an unmatched level of customer service, and innovative risk management support, all provided by motivated employees who treat our customers with professionalism and support."

Two start-up specialty property and casualty insurance groups founded by policyholders in the 1970's, Birmingham's Medical Assurance and Professionals Group, based in Michigan, grew in 25 years to become industry leaders. Their merger into ProAssurance Corporation further solidified the strong foundations of its predecessors and underscored their dedication to maximizing long term shareholder value.

With the merger, ProAssurance also became the majority owner of

Michigan Educational Employees Mutual Insurance Company (MEEMIC), a subsidiary of Professionals Group, and one of the nation's 100 largest writers of automobile insurance. MEEMIC, which presently operates only in Michigan, provides auto and homeowners coverages, primarily for educational employees and their families.

The medical malpractice crisis of the 1970's made it evident that the

medical professional liability market needed the specialized expertise, deep financial resources, and dedication of a company with seasoned professionals capable of vigorously defending all claims that are without merit and settling meritorious claims as expeditiously as possible. With an asset base of over $2 billion and over $400 million in equity, ProAssurance brings together the financial strength and long-term stability needed for the third largest writer of professional liability insurance in the nation. More than 30,000 policyholders rely on the company's wise counsel and strong service ethic.

ProAssurance is also known for its risk management expertise, specializing in providing ongoing support in implementing risk reduction strategies within healthcare organizations to provide protection in today's ever-changing liability and regulatory climate.

ProAssurance understands that healthcare professionals have earned their reputations for quality care and compassion through years of hard work and dedication. The company's 500 dedicated employees work hard to protect the reputations of their clients because their own reputations were built in the exact same manner.

Top: Victor T. Adamo, Esq. ProAssurance's President and COO (left) and A. Derrill Crowe, M.D., ProAssurance's Chairman and CEO (right) sign the merger documents that created ProAssurance in June, 2001.

Left: Almost 600 ProAssurance employees serve the needs of more than 32,000 policyholders in the Southeast and Midwest.

BAKER, DONELSON, BEARMAN, CALDWELL & BERKOWITZ

The unwavering focus on human rights, civic involvement, and pro-business advocacy that came to identify the law firm of Berkowitz, Lefkovits, Isom and Kushner spanned almost seven decades and stemmed from the vision of one man—Abe Berkowitz. That focus will be continued following the merger that created Baker, Donelson, Bearman, Caldwell & Berkowitz.

A prominent member of Birmingham's legal community since opening his own law practice in 1928, Berkowitz founded the firm six years later with a commitment to open-mindedness, fairness, and responsibility to the community. He put his philosophy into practice during the turbulent 1960's championing the causes of justice and social equality and playing a key role in the conversion of Birmingham's city government to a mayor-council format. The firm today maintains an ongoing commitment to social justice, corporate citizenship, and the betterment of society.

The firm's 320-plus lawyers, over 60 of whom are in the Birmingham office, focus on serving the legal needs of businesses, professionals, and a wide variety of commercial enterprises. They represent a broad range of businesses ranging from family-owned operations to large publicly held corporations. Through their commitment to teamwork and relationship building, the attorneys partner with their clients to provide highly informed, creative, and innovative solutions to their legal needs. This team approach assures prompt, cost-effective responsiveness and practical answers specifically suited for their clients' individual circumstances and objectives.

"We want to be known as the city's premier business law firm," states Denise Killebrew, the firm's managing partner. "We pursue that goal by combining our expertise with an understanding of the practical needs of our clients. Most recently, we have merged with one of the region's most respected multi-city law firms to add new areas of practice, depth and the ability to address multi-state issues. Our focus is on real-world issues as well as legal principles."

Baker, Donelson, Bearman, Caldwell & Berkowitz maintains its reputation for excellence by recruiting outstanding lawyers and law students who bring their specific skills and expertise in various aspects of law, such as business formations and acquisitions, equipment leasing, anti-trust, mediation, employment, construction, taxation, commercial litigation, and real estate, to the firm. In response to its clients' changing needs, the merger added offices in Tennessee, Washington, D.C., Mississippi, Georgia and Beijing, and expertise in white-collar crime litigation, health care, securities, and commercial lending

law. The firm's team approach involves individual attorneys concentrating their practices in specific areas of the law, while remaining closely involved in all aspects of their clients' legal representation.

As one of the first law firms in Birmingham to admit women as partners, Baker, Donelson, Bearman, Caldwell & Berkowitz continues to emphasize diversity in its recruiting and hiring practices. The firm views this not only as a method of providing equal opportunity, but also building a more complete and well balanced organization. During the years that he practiced law, Abe Berkowitz focused on people and practical issues, rather than vague legal principles. He surrounded himself with men and women from diverse backgrounds. All, however, were characterized by outstanding academic credentials, and each became imbued with the same compassion and vision held by the firm's founder. They remain dedicated to those principles today as they continue the founder's vision of providing the finest in legal services to their clients.

Standing: D. J. Simonetti, Anne W. Mitchell, Henry I. Frohsin, Nancy C. Hughes, Steven B. Corenblum.

Sitting: B. G. Minisman, Jr., Harold B. Kushner, Chervis Isom, Frank S. James, III.

Guillermo Castro

"It's all about passion," says Guillermo Castro. "In this industry you satisfy people...

A customer entering Sol y Luna waved to someone in the back of the restaurant and absent-mindedly kicked the welcome mat, turning up the corner.

Castro, still finishing the sentence in his even, heavily-accented voice, got up from the table at the front of the restaurant and fixed the mat.

"...and don't look at this like a job. When people decide to go out and spend money you are putting yourself on the line to provide satisfaction for the customer."

A few minutes later, and the restaurant is getting loud. This busy, artfully decorated space is alive with excited, rising voices and the smells of a working kitchen. It's simple and joyful like your mother's house on Thanksgiving.

"I wanted to share something that I believed and make people happy," says Castro, who has a bronze complexion and an open, thoughtful face. "In Mexico, eating was a celebration of life. I learned etiquette from my father and on Sunday after church we always went to a good restaurant. When I got to Birmingham 15 or 16 years ago there were no authentic Mexican restaurants. I thought, 'Why not offer something that is real.'"

So he worked in Atlanta and around Birmingham for a few years. Then he leased the space for Sol y Luna and spent a year remodeling.

"When the time came to open Sol y Luna ... basically God shows the way and you know it's time. At that time there were a lot of Mexican restaurants opening. I struggled for a year and had time to think about the inside operations.

"I'm Catholic. I have very strong beliefs. My approach with God is realizing that He puts things in along the way. God tells you that things are there for you. It's up to you to reach them. I'm not going to get involved in something I don't know. Sooner or later everybody finds their way and you do well. God is watching me."

Castro, who went to school in Mexico to learn architecture, found that his artistic nature could best be expressed in a restaurant.

"When I was going to architecture school I started working for an Italian restaurant and became assistant manager. I worked there through the school years. I met a regional manager for Victoria Station. He invited me to Houston to get more exposed to the restaurant industry. It was a learning experience.

"I graduated and worked three years as an architect. During my last two years as an architect my father invested in a restaurant. I remodeled it and worked there."

Then Castro visited Birmingham to see the woman he eventually married. He continued to work in the restaurant business, learning and getting ideas about the proper Mexican restaurant for this Southern city.

"I knew I had to work on the five senses—smell, tastes, sounds, textures and sights," he says. "They are all involved.

"I'm the executive chef. I have kitchen managers. Working in the kitchen is the fun part of my job. It's the passion. You try to mix things with your own niche."

But the restaurant business is about more than his work in the kitchen. Sol y Luna offers Castro a chance to share his culture with others.

"Next week I'm taking a group of local professional people to Mexico," he says. "We're going to Oaxaca, the culinary capital of Mexico. The idea is to work with a chef and stay in an old Mexican hacienda. I'm from Mexico and for me it's another way to share what my passion is. It's realizing that people are interested in the culture."

They also are interested in Castro's work at Sol y Luna and his newest restaurant, Los Angeles, which is next door. Los Angeles—opened two years ago—was mentioned in Southwest Airlines magazine as one of the top four new Mexican restaurants in the U.S. *The Miami Herald* featured Sol y Luna in its style section and *Outfitters* magazine named the marguerites at Sol y Luna the best in the country.

All this notoriety is not lost on Castro's 10-year-old son, Marcus.

"He asked me if he will be a great chef. Of course I tell him that he can do what he puts his mind to. He asked if my name would help him get into one of the cooking schools in New York. I had to smile. They don't know me."

BOOKER T. WASHINGTON INSURANCE COMPANY
SMITH AND GASTON FUNERAL DIRECTORS
A.G. GASTON CONSTRUCTION
CITIZENS FEDERAL SAVINGS BANK

Introduction

An entire family of companies emerged from the vision of Birmingham's noted entrepreneur and philanthropist Dr. A G. Gaston. Based upon his philosophy of identifying a need in the community and then offering a product or service to meet that need, Dr. Gaston not only achieved the American dream for himself but also offered the opportunity to thousands to achieve that same dream. Dr. Gaston's business acumen fostered an impressive portfolio of successful companies, four of which continue to play a significant role in Birmingham's economy.

BTW INSURANCE

In the early 1900s majority-owned insurance companies routinely regarded African Americans as "uninsurable." As a result, African Americans faced great difficulty obtaining life insurance and burial services. Observing this void, and acting upon his philosophy of needs identification and solutions, Dr. Gaston launched Booker T. Washington Insurance Company in 1923. The company has served the people of Alabama continuously for more than three quarters of a century, and it has grown steadily from modest beginnings to its current asset base of $58 million and $1.3 bil-lion of insurance in force.

"Our model of a multi-business corporation has served us well. It will help us meet today's challenges where diversification seems imperative to survive," notes Walter Howlett, Jr., the firm's chairman, president and CEO. "We remain committed to Dr. Gaston's legacy of finding a need and fulfilling it."

SMITH AND GASTON FUNERAL DIRECTORS

Dr. Gaston also founded Smith and Gaston Funeral Directors in 1923 to help provide decent burial services to the then-underserved black communi-ty. In doing so, he also greatly diminished the unsavory practice of dishonest neighborhood solicitations for funerals. Smith and Gaston became the servicing agent for burial policies of the Booker T. Washington Insurance Company, and the company is now in its seventh decade, providing families with funeral arrangements of quiet dignity and distinction.

"We're here to assist families in times of need," says Paul Gardner, the director of the company. "Dr. Gaston founded this business on a principle of service to the community, and we continue to operate it that way today."

A.G. GASTON CONSTRUCTION COMPANY

A.G. Gaston Construction Company is the newest enterprise in the Gaston corporate family. In 1984, Dr. Gaston endorsed U.S. Department of Housing and Urban Development Secretary Samuel Pierce's idea for a program that would combine renovation and maintenance work in Birmingham's public housing developments with job training and employment opportunities for the residents. The company was immediately successful, and in 1986 acquired another local general contracting company and expanded from working

Above: (from L-R) Paul G. Gardner, Mrs. Edna M. Gardner and Eric A. Gardner of Smith & Gaston Funeral Services, Inc.

Left: Seated, Walter Howlett, Jr., Chairman, President and CEO, Booker T. Washington Insurance Company and standing, Cleophus Thomas, Jr., CEO of A. G. Gaston Corporation.

116

Left: Gaston provided construction management services for a major renovation and addition to Minor Elementary School.

Below: Bunny Stokes, President of Citizens Trust, Birmingham.

exclusively on properties of the Housing Authority of the Birmingham District to competing on the open market. A. G. Gaston Construction has continued to grow and evolve, and is now a multi-million dollar professional firm providing construction/program management services to a wide range of public and private sector clients. The company typically serves governmental, commercial and industrial clients on major infrastructure or capital facilities projects.

Headquartered in Birmingham, A.G. Gaston Construction also maintains a branch office in Atlanta.

"We are well positioned for regional growth across the Southeast, even as we continue to serve our local client base," says Warren Jones, the firm's Senior Vice President. "We use

a full complement of internet-based project management tools, so we can deliver both staff and technical expertise and home-office oversight to any project, regardless of its location."

The executives that now direct these companies remain committed and true to their founder's vision of serving the communities in which they live and work. As a team, they continue to uphold Dr. Gaston's principles as they lead these businesses into the twenty-first century.

CITIZENS FEDERAL SAVINGS BANK

Citizens Federal Savings Bank is another company started by Dr. Gaston. The firm was originally founded in 1956 to provide home

mortgages to Birmingham's black community. With its motto "A part of all that you earn is yours to keep," Citizens Federal has been a financial beacon, promoting the virtues of fiscal responsibility to four generations of Alabamians. The institution remains a community-based and community-oriented bank, headquartered in downtown Birmingham since its inception. Citizens Federal's operations are driven by a commitment to safeguarding the depositors' interests, preserving and building capital, and providing home and consumer financing to our customers in Jefferson, Shelby and Greene counties. Beginning with initial assets of just over $300,000 in 1957, Citizens Federal now lists assets in excess of $100 million. Net earnings in 2001 increased by more than

18 percent over those of 2000.

"Our mission has not changed as we navigate through these turbulent economic times," said Bunny Stokes, Jr., the bank's chairman and chief executive officer. "We remain focused, and we intend to keep the bank safe, strong and profitable. To enhance customer service and increase the efficiency of our operations, we are implementing a significant upgrade in our technology. We also plan to establish an Internet presence to complement our new telephone banking system, which already provides 24-hour account accessibility to our customers."

Citizens Federal Savings Bank is now formally Citizens Trust, having merged with Citizens Trust of Atlanta as of February 28, 2003.

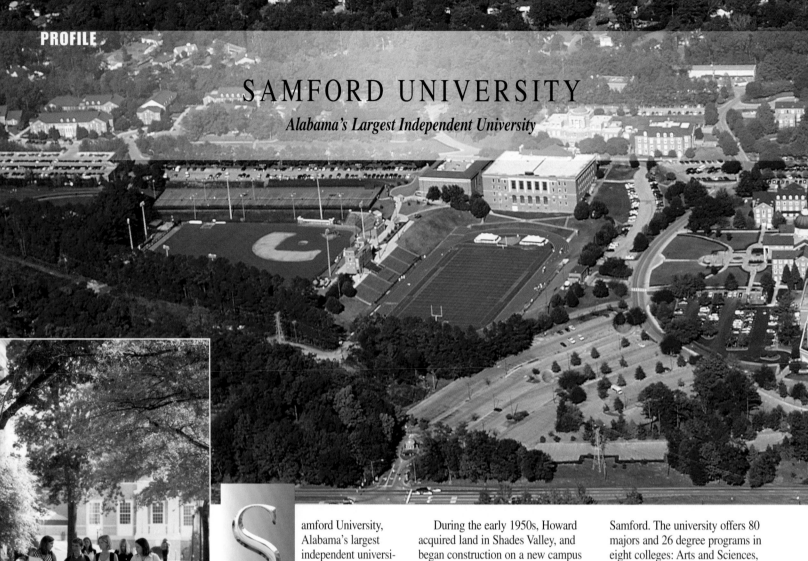

SAMFORD UNIVERSITY
Alabama's Largest Independent University

Above: Samford attracts students from 40 states and 22 nations to its Birmingham campus.

Aerial: Samford University's Georgian Colonial campus is one of the nation's most beautiful.

Far right: Samford's new $27 million Sciencenter houses a medicinal plants conservatory (foreground), a 100-seat planetarium, the Vulcan Materials Environmental Studies Center and facilities for the departments of biology, chemistry and physics.

Samford University, Alabama's largest independent university, has traveled a long road since its predecessor, Howard College, was sold at public auction in 1884 on the steps of the Perry County Courthouse. Founded in 1841 by a group of educational, economic, and religious leaders at Marion, Alabama, the college had been plagued by financial problems since the Civil War and Reconstruction. Fortunately, two Howard trustees put up their own funds to buy the school property and save the institution by deeding it back to Alabama Baptists.

Lured to Birmingham with the promise of support from the bustling new city that was fast becoming known as an iron and steel manufacturing center, the college moved to its new home in the East Lake section of the Magic City in 1887. Struggling in the beginning at its new site, the college grew stronger as the 20th century approached. By 1920, it had become a charter member of the Southern Association of Colleges and Schools. In 1927 it began a pharmacy program. By the mid-1940s, Howard had outgrown its East Lake campus.

During the early 1950s, Howard acquired land in Shades Valley, and began construction on a new campus in 1954. Three years later, the school moved to its present location on Lakeshore Drive, laying the groundwork for its growth and development into what it is today—Samford University.

The university's mission is to nurture students, offering learning experiences and relationships in a Christian community, so that each participant may develop personal empowerment, academic and career competency, social and civic responsibility, and ethical and spiritual strength. Key to achieving that mission is Samford's dedication to rigorous academic inquiry in a Christian setting. The university encourages students to think and act in ways that will positively impact not only their college years, but the rest of their lives.

"Our times call for a Christian university that rises to the academic challenge, but which makes no apology for seeking to influence the character of young people," Samford President Thomas E. Corts has said. "That is what the founders of this institution had in mind more than 160 years ago."

More than 4,300 students from 40 states and 22 nations are enrolled at

Samford. The university offers 80 majors and 26 degree programs in eight colleges: Arts and Sciences, Business, Divinity, Education and Professional Studies, Law, Nursing, Performing Arts, and Pharmacy. The university's more than 250 full-time faculty members have earned degrees in more than 160 colleges in the U.S. and around the world. They share experiences and knowledge with students in a well-rounded program which leads to a liberal education, a deep appreciation of cultural pursuits, and a sound background for graduate and professional study.

"Almost every state has a flagship private university complementing state institutions," says Dr. Corts. "Samford's location in Birmingham, the state's prime urban center, makes it extra important to Alabama. Samford's Cumberland School of Law is the only private law school in the state, and one of two accredited law schools. McWhorter School of Pharmacy at Samford is one of only two accredited schools of pharmacy and the only private, and, along with Ida V. Moffett School of Nursing, gives Samford special prominence in this medically oriented city. Beeson Divinity School is the only theological degree-granting entity in our state. And the Orlean Bullard Beeson School of Education

and Professional Studies received the U.S. Department of Education's first National Award for Effective Teacher Preparation."

Samford ranked fifth in the South among master's degree universities in *U.S. News & World Report's* 2003 selection of 'America's Best Colleges." The university is listed in the *Princeton Review "Guide to the Best 331 Colleges'* and rated as "Very Competitive" in *Barron's "Profiles of American Colleges."*

With an endowment fund of some $230 million, Samford ranks in the top five percent of the more than 3,600 colleges and universities in America. Alabama Baptists have supported Samford faithfully over the years, and the university continues to receive generous annual support from the Alabama Baptist State Convention.

Samford's Georgian Colonial campus of more than 60 buildings is considered one of the nation's most beautiful. The latest addition, a $27 million Sciencenter that opened in the fall of 2001, is also one of the most striking. The 90,000 square foot structure houses the departments of biology, chemistry and physics, and offers the latest in electronic, audio-visual and wet-lab learning opportunities. With 35 research labs, a botanical conservatory, and the largest

planetarium at a teaching institution in Alabama, the Sciencenter is unrivaled in the region. During the fall of 2002, as part of the Sciencenter, Samford unveiled the Vulcan Materials Center for Environmental Education to help encourage good stewardship of the earth's natural resources.

Samford University enriches the total individual by providing broad-based social, cultural and athletic activities and programs as well as a strong academic environment. The university is home to national sororities and fraternities, and lists more than 100 social, service, reli-gious, honorary and professional organizations on campus. As an NCAA Division I school, Samford offers 17 intercollegiate sports for men and women. In 2003, the university became a member of the Ohio Valley Conference.

Located just six miles from the heart of downtown Birmingham, Samford plays an important role in

weaving the cultural fabric of the Magic City. Samford's Leslie Stephen Wright Fine Arts Center serves as one of Birmingham's premier arts venues. The Benjamin F. Harrison Theatre, the Samford Recital Hall and Samford Gallery also showcase a wide range of cultural events. F. Page Seibert Stadium and F. Page Seibert Hall anchor the university's athletics facilities.

"A university of 4,400 has the benefit brought by professional schools, while affording close personal attention to individuals," Dr. Corts says. "Our emphasis with undergradu-ates is to facilitate a total experience. We want a great deal to happen in the life of each student intellectually, morally, spiritually, socially, physical-ly. It is no accident that surveys show Samford undergraduates are more engaged in their education than most. A university degree is not a drive-by happening; it is an experience!"

Dr. Corts assumed the office of president of Samford University in 1983. His leadership has been a major impetus behind the university's growth over the past 20 years. Under his watch, Samford has gained recogni-tion in national publications, attracted growing numbers of students from other states, established a London Study Centre as the keystone of an international program that touches five continents, completed major building projects, and nurtured an endowment that has grown by more than $200 million since his arrival.

In terms of facilities and intellectual scope and success, Samford University is far removed from the school that was auctioned over a century ago to pay its debts. The university now is a living, thriving monument to the generations who built the institution, and serves as a beacon to those who will lead it to continued success in the future.

SOUTHWIRE

ne man's desire to be able to offer his grandmother the opportunity to sit under an electric light in her own house led to the foundation of a company that has become one of the world's leading manufacturers of wire and cable.

Roy Richards, Sr. returned in 1945 to Carroll County in Georgia after serving in the U.S. Army during World War II. A 1935 graduate of Georgia Tech, Richards discovered that the War had virtually put on hold the activities of a company he had founded in 1937. Richards and Associates had strung over 3,500 miles of cable on utility poles the company had erected under contract with the Rural Electrification Administration (REA). The REA had been bringing the convenience of electricity to much of the rural South in the 1930's, and Richards' company had become the second largest REA contractor in the nation. He was eager to provide the infrastructure needed to light his native Carroll County, and he was especially committed to bringing the service to his grandmother's house.

"My grandmother is 85 years old, and she has never had the pleasure of sitting under an electric

light in her own house," he had told a wire manufacturer at that time. "She's seen it two times she's been to Atlanta, but she's never had it."

The War halted all REA construction. Post-war shortages in wire left the power poles his company had erected sitting wireless for months. He decided the only way to ensure a steady supply of wire was to make it himself.

Richards founded Southwire in March of 1950 with 12 employees. Frustrated by the time consuming, inefficient process of wire making at that time, Richards sought the services of an Italian industrialist who had developed a method for continuously casting and rolling rod by a wheel-and-belt method. Even though the process had never been used in creating electrical wire, Richards bought one of the man's machines and had a team of Southwire engineers adapt the procedure to produce aluminum and copper rod.

The technology immediately catapulted Southwire to a leadership position in the

industry. Within two years of launching the business, Richards' company had shipped five million pounds of wire, and doubled the size of its plant in Georgia. Southwire began selling its patented Southwire Continuous Rod (SCR) systems and wire and cable products around the world. By 1967, the company listed six manufacturing plants, an aluminum smelter, a copper refinery and operations in Carrollton, Georgia; Hawesville, Kentucky; and Flora, Illinois. Today, half the copper rod for electrical wire and cable is made using Richards' SCR method.

A second generation of the family continued to grow the business through the 1980's. Roy Richards, Jr., the founder's son, had worked at Southwire plants since he was ten years old, learning the

business from the ground up. Under his leadership, Southwire continued to focus on its core business of wire and cable manufacturing, but the company also expanded to keep pace with technology and meet the needs of its customers.

A machinery division was founded to produce SCR system components, wire making equipment, and other machinery. A technology center was created to provide a home for ongoing research and development in wire and cable design, metallurgy, and plastics compounding. Scientists and engineers utilize the center's cutting-edge facilities for product testing and improvement of manufacturing processes. The center has been the incubator for innovations that are revolutionizing the industry.

Southwire, in conjunction with the Oak Ridge National Laboratory, the U.S. Department of Energy, and several industrial partners, has developed the next generation of power cables. These superconductor cables suffer only a half percent of power loss through resistance compared to between five and eight percent loss for traditional power lines. They can also carry three to five times the load of traditional cables, providing more power to urban areas to serve a growing demand for electricity.

The company's customer service commitments have mirrored its technological advancements. A revamping of Southwire's logistics department created nine master services centers from a system of more than 50 warehouses. Additional plants have been opened in West Jordan, Utah, and Heflin, Alabama.

Southwire now supplies customers throughout the United States and Canada, including 135 of the nation's top power companies and dozens of utility companies abroad. More than a third of the homes in the U.S. contain wire from Southwire.

Stuart Thorn is the man now leading Southwire into the 21st century. The first non-family member tapped as chief executive officer of the company, Thorn brings a wealth of insight and experience gained while serving as a former top executive for several major companies. Impressive credentials on his resume include serving as the former president and chief operating officer of Beaulieu of America, a $2 billion carpet and rug manufacturer headquartered in Dalton, Georgia; vice-president of international finance with Campbell's Soup Company; and director of finance for North American consumer products for S.C. Johnson.

"For more than 50 years, Southwire has been a model of success and has revolutionized the wire and cable business by developing groundbreaking new products and technologies," Thorn said in an interview for the company's historical biography (from which this information was gleaned). "I am excited about helping continue that strong tradition as we discover and capitalize on the challenges of the next half century."

The world headquarters of Southwire remain today where the company was founded a half century ago in Carrollton, Georgia, about 40 miles west of Atlanta. Much of Carroll County has changed during those 50 years. Commercial, industrial, and residential development on an unprecedented scale has enabled Atlanta to mushroom into a major international city. Much of that development has spread into Carroll County. A major player in the phenomenal growth of the region has been the company founded by the man who dreamed of bringing electric lighting into the home of his grandmother.

Southwire is North America's largest building wire manufacturer and one of the world's leading wire and cable producers. The company's products include copper and aluminum rod, building wire and cable, utility cable products, industrial power cable and flexible power cord. Southwire is a pioneering researcher in the development of high-temperature superconducting power cables, which are nearly immune to resistance and which carry three to five times more electricity than traditional power cables.

Southwire conducts advanced research at the D.B, Cofer Technology Center. One of the world's leading centers for wire and cable technology, the Cofer center is home to Southwire's superconducting power cable program.

ALABAMA GAS CORPORATION

Alabama Gas Corporation (Alagasco) is the largest natural gas utility in Alabama and a subsidiary of Birmingham-based Energen Corporation. The company serves approximately 463,000 customers in nearly 200 cities and 27 counties in central and north Alabama.

The company got its start in 1852 as the Montgomery Gas Light Company. Today, Alagasco has more than 1,000 employees at work in seven operating divisions—Anniston, Birmingham, Gadsden, Montgomery, Opelika, Selma and Tuscaloosa—and in smaller district offices in the surrounding areas.

In the early 1980s, Alagasco purchased nearly all of its natural gas supply from one major interstate pipeline. Today, the company purchases its gas from more than 20 different suppliers. The gas is transported to Alagasco's distribution system through two major interstate and two smaller intrastate pipelines. The distribution system, which includes service lines for individual customers, encompasses nearly 20,000 miles of pipe.

A portion of Alagasco's gas supply comes from sources in Alabama, such as Mobile Bay, the gas fields of Tuscaloosa and the coal seams in Oak Grove and Vance. Additional supplies come from the Gulf of Mexico, Texas and Louisiana. A diversified gas supply portfolio allows the company to offer its customers the lowest possible price and be more flexible in its gas purchases.

Alagasco fosters a work environment that supports its employees' efforts to provide superior service to internal and external customers. The corporate culture encourages employees to have pride and take ownership of their work. Alagasco has twice been named to *Fortune* magazine's list of "The 100 Best Companies to Work For in America."

To supplement normal customer growth in its service area, Alagasco has purchased more than 20 municipally-owned gas systems in Alabama since 1985. With the initial count and subsequent growth, these acquisitions have added more than 46,000 customers to the company's service base. Alagasco evaluates the purchase of every system based on the benefits for the municipality and its customers as well as Alagasco's existing customers.

Alagasco has been a key player in attracting new businesses and industries to the state. Alagasco's new business development team is active in recruiting new industries that provide jobs for Alabamians and a larger tax base that benefits the communities in its service area. Company representatives have been instrumental in recent years helping shape the state as the new automotive center of the South.

Many of Alagasco's customers select natural gas for its convenience and reliability. As an added bonus, their fuel of choice also has environmental benefits. Natural gas is the cleanest fossil fuel available.

Along with developing new markets for natural gas in the home, the company promotes natural gas as a clean-burning fuel for vehicles. In addition to a portion of Alagasco's fleet, several of Birmingham's Metro Area Express (MAX) buses run on compressed natural gas. Gasoline and diesel-powered vehicles are to blame for more than 60 percent of all carbon monoxide pollution. These vehicles also produce large quantities of hydrocarbons and nitrogen oxides, the primary components of unhealthful ground-level ozone.

In the Birmingham metropolitan area, ground-level ozone has resulted in federally mandated sanctions that could threaten the region's economic development.

Recent investments in infrastructure improvements help guarantee reliable natural gas service to Alagasco's customers into the future. One such improvement is a new liquefier installed at the company's liquefied natural gas facility in Pinson. This new equipment ensures gas availability to customers during periods of peak demand.

Alagasco is involved in a long-term business and technology initiative that will help it become a more efficient and more competitive company. The initiative consists of a series of software projects involving finance, engineering, customer relationship management, human resources and e-commerce. These projects will give employees the tools they need to further improve service for customers.

Alagasco does more than just provide natural gas to its customers. The company also takes an active role in the communities it serves. Employees share their time and talents with organizations such as, American Red Cross and United Way. Throughout its service territory, Alagasco participates in the Adopt-a-School program, which gives employees the opportunity to positively influence the educational experience of local students.

Alagasco's community affairs department administers the company's volunteer efforts, including the Volunteer Investment Program. Through this program, grant money is awarded to qualifying non-profit organizations in which employees and retirees of Energen and its subsidiaries actively serve as volunteers. In addition, the company matches financial contributions its employees make to educational, charitable and cultural organizations. Employees also represent the company on the boards of directors of various organizations.

Alagasco is proud to be a co-sponsor of Project SHARE (Service to Help Alabamians with Relief on Energy). The program has helped thousands of eligible Alabamians by providing money to pay energy bills. Contributions from Alagasco customers help fund Project SHARE, which is administered by the American Red Cross. A person who qualifies can receive assistance one time during the winter and one additional time during the summer if severely high temperatures cause a health threat. Project SHARE helps people 62 or older on low, fixed incomes with no other source of funds and people, who for health reasons, cannot keep up a normal family income.

In addition, Alagasco offer services for its visually impaired customers. Customers can receive a large print or Braille bill to make it easier to read their monthly statement. Customers can also request modified knobs on their gas cooking equipment. These modifications include rivets, notches or Braille stickers to mark the various heat settings on existing range controls.

Alagasco offers its customers some options to make bill payment more convenient. More than 25,000 customers are enrolled in the Bank Draft Plan. The Bank Draft Plan lets customers pay their gas bill directly from a checking or savings account. In addition, more than 10,000 customers are taking advantage of Ebill. Ebill allows customers to view their bill at Alagasco's Web site and pay with a credit card or a bank debit transaction.

The Gatekeeper Program trains Alagasco customer contact employees, such as meter readers, to notice unattended and overlooked elderly people who may need help. When problems are identified through Gatekeeper,

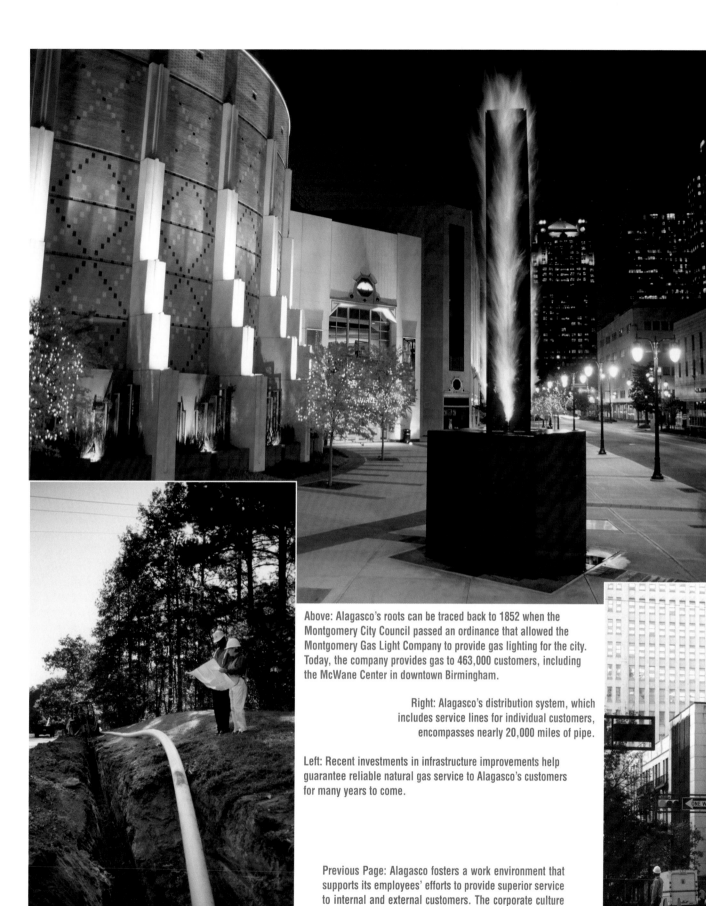

Above: Alagasco's roots can be traced back to 1852 when the Montgomery City Council passed an ordinance that allowed the Montgomery Gas Light Company to provide gas lighting for the city. Today, the company provides gas to 463,000 customers, including the McWane Center in downtown Birmingham.

Right: Alagasco's distribution system, which includes service lines for individual customers, encompasses nearly 20,000 miles of pipe.

Left: Recent investments in infrastructure improvements help guarantee reliable natural gas service to Alagasco's customers for many years to come.

Previous Page: Alagasco fosters a work environment that supports its employees' efforts to provide superior service to internal and external customers. The corporate culture encourages employees to have pride and take ownership of their work. Photos by Billy Brown

Alagasco contacts social service agencies that investigate and offer help to the customer in need.

Alagasco is active in several industry organizations, including the American Gas Association and the Southern Gas Association. The company has been recognized for its best practices by industry and business groups.

Alagasco and its sister subsidiary, Energen Resources, contribute to Energen Corporation's strength. Energen looks to Alagasco as the strong foundation for its growth strategy. With a history that spans 150 years, Alagasco is well-positioned to remain Alabama's leading natural gas service provider for many years to come.

Odessa Woolfolk

Some people are such forces of nature they change the very nature of the world they inhabit. Some are also as subtle as a gentle but earth-sculpting rainfall—you don't see the wind blowing or the trees bending—until one day you look up and the landscape has changed utterly. Odessa Woolfolk is like that.

Odessa Woolfolk grew up in Titusville and attended Birmingham's public schools.

She received a B.A. in history and political science from Talladega and an M.A. in urban studies from Occidental College in California She completed additional graduate studies in political science at the University of Chicago and was a National Urban Fellow at Yale University in urban and regional community development.

Woolfolk taught at Ullman High School in Birmingham and later in her career held senior administrative positions in D.C. with the Urban Reinvestment Task Force, the New York State Urban Development Corporation, YWCA of Utica, New York; and the Arbor Hill Community Center and Interracial Council in Albany, New York.

Here in Birmingham her career has always centered around the creation of opportunity and positive growth in the modern urban world. She was executive director of The Birmingham Opportunity Industrialization Center and associate executive director of the Jefferson County Committee for Economic Opportunity (JCCEO). For a decade she served as the director of the University of Alabama at Birmingham Center for Urban Affairs. She also served as assistant to the president for community relations at UAB.

Upon her retirement from UAB in November 1993, the university established the Odessa Woolfolk Presidential Community Service Award, which includes a cash prize presented annually to a UAB faculty member. The UAB National Alumni Society gave her its Honorary Alumni Award in 2000. She was inducted into the Gallery of Distinguished Citizens back in 1994, selected by the mayor and city council of Birmingham. In December 1998 she received the UAB President's Medal. In November 1999, the board of directors of the Birmingham Civil Rights Institute named a gallery in her honor.

Woolfolk's previous community involvement includes board memberships in a veritable who's who of community organizations: YWCA, Alabama Symphonic Association, United Way, Birmingham Regional Chamber of Commerce, the Housing Authority, Metropolitan Arts Council, Urban League, Metropolitan Development Board, Alabama School of Math and Science, Alabama Institute for the Deaf and Blind, Alabama Advisory Committee to the U.S. Commission on Civil Rights, Indian Springs School, National Conference for Community and Justice, Community Affairs Committee of Operation New Birmingham. She was the founding co-chair of the Martin Luther King, Jr. Unity Breakfast. And her work with the Civil Rights Institute will mold generations to come.

THE HACKNEY GROUP

T. Morris Hackney went on a shopping spree in the 1980's, and he hasn't stopped yet. The Birmingham native is the owner of The Hackney Group, a private equity group which specializes in the acquisition, operation, and development of low-tech manufacturing and fabricating companies. The firm, headquartered in SouthBridge Office Park, focuses primarily on middle market companies in the $10 to $15 million range in the Southeastern United States.

The founder and former chairman of the board of Citation Corporation, Hackney grew that company from a small single location to one of the nation's largest networks of cast metal production foundries. He brought the same sharply focused business acumen on which he relied to steer the growth of Citation to the acquisition and development of the 17 companies that The Hackney Group now operates.

The firm does not purchase any businesses to keep. Instead, it focuses on targeting companies that have demonstrated consistent earnings power. After acquiring them, Hackney's management team introduces proven business systems designed to allow the companies to achieve their full potential in the marketplace. Hackney will hold the company for anywhere from three to seven years, build the management team, add value to the company, then sell it. Whether it is a determination to take the business to the next level or to develop a tax advantageous exit strategy, The Hackney Group structures transactions to fit the individual needs of the business owner.

Hackney receives hundreds of acquisition proposals annually. His success in building a 17-company portfolio with annual revenues that top $200 million has been in selecting the right company to buy and knowing when to sell it.

"We locate qualified companies through a network of business brokers and referrals from associates," Hackney relates. "We're looking to receive a return on the business owner's equity by making the company grow and increase profitability. Our goal is to generate an annual return of 20 to 30 percent on our acquisitions. Normally, these aren't business turnarounds or distressed acquisitions. We buy good companies and make them better."

Hackney is a firm believer in the business principle of "You can't improve what you can't manage and you can't manage what you can't measure." Operating on that premise, his team focuses on respecting the importance of the existing company culture. After an acquisition, they never make changes merely for the sake of change. They offer only the management and organizational direction that experience has proven will lead to increased company strength and profitability.

Many times, the owners of companies that Hackney has acquired have not had the capital necessary to develop the business to its full potential. In other instances, the company is one that has grown from a small start-up to a size where the owner is ready to realize a short-term profit. In all cases, business owners sell to Hackney with the confidence that their company will be well cared for after they relinquish ownership. And business intermediaries know that Hackney's reputation in the marketplace ensures their own reputation will be enhanced.

Since its foundation in 1989, The Hackney Group has become known for its integrity and its financial strength. Whether it's a company that sells fire trucks or one that operates a heavy plate metal fabricating plant, T. Morris Hackney has carefully scrutinized every business proposal that has come through the door. After all, when you're on a shopping spree that lasts for over 20 years, you develop the discerning eye of a savvy shopper.

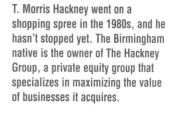

T. Morris Hackney went on a shopping spree in the 1980s, and he hasn't stopped yet. The Birmingham native is the owner of The Hackney Group, a private equity group that specializes in maximizing the value of businesses it acquires.

CHILDREN'S HEALTH SYSTEM

"Children are the Center of Our Lives"

children's Health System traces its roots to three men in 1911 who were touched by the plight of Birmingham's many sick and needy children. They spearheaded the efforts of a small group of Episcopalian men and women who founded the Holy Innocents Hospital as a "charity institution for children alone." The simple frame house they converted into a 12-bed hospital evolved over the next 90 years into a statewide network of primary and specialty pediatric healthcare centers.

Children remain the focus of Children's Health System today, and providing the finest pediatric health services to all children in an environment that fosters excellence in research and medical education remains the organization's mission.

"Throughout our entire 90 plus year history, Children's has worked to ensure that the best care and latest technology are available for all Alabama youngsters at a moment's notice," says Dr. Jim Dearth, the CEO of Children's Health System. "We believe there should only be one class of care for children—the best available care, and that is why we keep children at the center of our lives."

Children's Hospital, the nucleus of Children's Health System, is a 225-bed private, not-for-profit hospital. The facility is home to a diagnostic center, emergency department with a level I trauma center, kidney dialysis center, and one of the largest outpatient pediatric centers in the U.S. In addition, the Hospital is a leading pediatric hematology/oncology center, and operates the largest pediatric burn unit in the Southeast. Children's Hospital also serves as the primary teaching facility for the University of Alabama at Birmingham's (UAB) Department of Pediatrics, and boasts a renowned medical research facility.

The integrated approach to healthcare offered by Children's Health System incorporates the services of pediatricians, pediatric sub-specialists, family physicians, nurses, educators, and child advocates from across the state. This approach begins with an emphasis on overall wellness and prevention programs and extends to hospitalization, rehabilitation, and continuing care.

"Children's Hospital has been a lifeline for Alabama's children for over 90 years," states Margaret Porter, the 2002-2003 Board of Trustees Chair for Children's Health System. "We are a family that is committed to providing quality care and compassion for patients and their families. All of our efforts, from cutting edge research to hugs from our nurses, reinforce our belief that children are at the center of our lives."

Under the guidance of its Advocacy Department, Children's Health System works tirelessly as a leading advocate for children in Alabama. Through newsletters, a 24-hour regional poison control hotline, health fairs, parenting seminars, community events, and other strategic initiatives, Children's has helped to improve the quality of life for Alabama's youth. The Children's Health System's award-winning Website, www.chsys.org, also provides a wealth of information to the community on the organization's services, physicians, and a wide variety of health topics.

Children's Health System's leaders realize that the organization's strength lies in the skill, commitment, and compassion of its almost 2,900 employees, and the System continues to invest in those people in order to maintain its reputation as an employer of choice in Alabama. That commitment was recognized in 2001 when Children's Health System was chosen by Birmingham Family Times magazine as one of the premier companies in Birmingham for working families.

The compassion shown in 1911 by a group of concerned citizens for Birmingham's sick and needy children has never diminished over the past nine decades. Rather, it has grown over time to manifest itself into a world-class medical system meeting the needs of Alabama's children now and into the future.

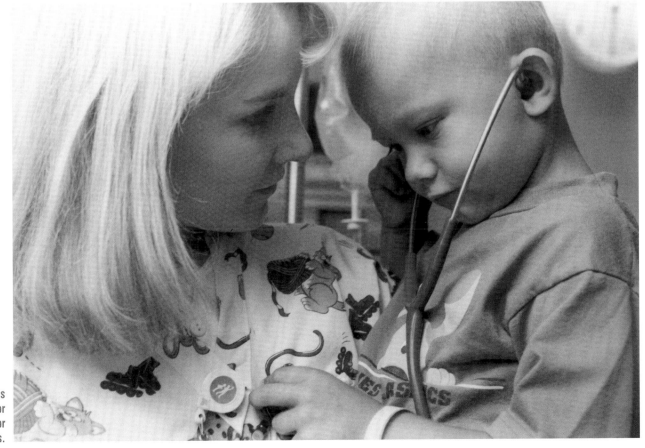

Children's Hospital has been a lifeline for Alabama's children for over 90 years.

SOUTHERN NATURAL GAS COMPANY

Southern Natural Gas Company was founded almost eight decades ago through the vision of a group of business leaders in the South seeking to deliver natural gas to the cities of Birmingham and Atlanta. Their pioneering efforts in building a pipeline across the Mississippi River brought natural gas from the oil and gas fields of Louisiana and the Gulf of Mexico to fuel the needs of residential and commercial

customers in Alabama and Georgia. Today, Southern Natural Gas Company is an integral part of the delivery system that brings clean burning natural gas to thousands of homes, businesses, and industries in eight Southeastern states.

From its Birmingham headquarters in the AmSouth Center, Southern Natural Gas has become a recognized leader in natural gas transmission. Southern Natural's pipeline system has steadily expanded to serve the burgeoning markets in the Southeast,

which are growing at a rate 60 percent higher than the rest of the nation. The company now owns and operates more than 14,000 miles of pipeline to bring natural gas to its customers. "Energy infrastructure is a vital component to attracting industries and maintaining a strong economy in Birmingham and throughout the region," said Jim Yardley, president of Southern Natural Gas. "We're proud to have our roots firmly planted here,

and will continue to serve the growing Southeast."

In 1999, Southern Natural Gas became part of El Paso Corporation, the leading provider of natural gas services and the largest pipeline company in North America. El Paso has leading positions in natural gas production, gathering and processing, and transmission, as well as liquefied natural gas transport and receiving, petroleum logistics, power generation, and merchant energy

From left to right: Bear Creek Storage facility, completed and put in service in 1981, was the second major underground storage facility owned by Southern Natural gas; Bell Mills, a Southern Natural Gas compressor station in eastern Alabama moves a high volume of gas throughout the region; a Southern Natural gas subsidiary on Elba Island, Georgia converts liquefied natural gas into regular natural gas for use in homes, businesses and industries throughout North America.

Southern Natural Gas Company, headquartered in Birmingham, Alabama, transports gas to much of the Southeast.

services. El Paso Corporation is fully integrated across the natural gas value chain, and is committed to developing new supplies and technologies to deliver energy to communities around the world.

As a member of the El Paso family, Southern Natural Gas shares in the Corporation's continuing commitment to the environment, health, and safety.

That commitment is rooted in a firm belief that the energy solutions the Corporation provides can help improve the environment. It also requires that its businesses be operated and its facilities maintained in a safe manner. Excellence in performance and personal responsibility are emphasized throughout the organization, from field personnel to executive management.

Putting those principles into prac-

tice, Southern Natural Gas and all the El Paso companies comply fully with all applicable laws and regulations, assess risks before initiating a new activity, and design and operate facilities worldwide utilizing the latest technology and practices necessary to protect human health and the environment. The company believes that outstanding business performance and outstanding environmental, health, and safety performance must go hand in hand.

Southern Natural also takes its civic responsibilities very seriously.

"We have a long history of being involved in the local community," said Yardley. "Through our corporate involvement, and through the many employees at Southern Natural Gas who volunteer on a variety of civic projects, we are committed to doing our part to make Birmingham a great place to work and live."

ELEMENTS, INC.

Sharply Focused on Public Relations Solutions and Strategy

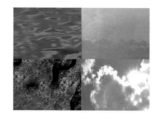

Elements, Inc. has been pioneering communications solutions for its clients for a half century. Founded in 1952 as Jesse J. Lewis & Associates, the firm broke new ground as the first African-American advertising agency of record in America. It has since grown to become an industry leader in innovation through its sharply focused marketing and public relations campaigns designed to produce solid results for its clients.

That quest for excellence was rooted in a number of carefully crafted and continuously honed principles and strategies. Christopher Bazuaye, the firm's president and CEO, is a firm believer that every successful marketing and public

relations campaign begins with a solid strategy, supported by a coordinated plan of action. He and his associates are quick to lay the groundwork for a plan custom designed for each individual client.

The firm emphasizes that the first step of the initiative is simply to listen. The company's communication and public relations specialists meet with the client to identify and understand exactly what goals and objectives the client has for the service or product to be promoted. They access a full range of the latest technological resources to research and track an issue, analyzing trends over time and differentiating audiences.

They are then ready to brainstorm the project and interact closely in the exchange of ideas and possible solutions. They weigh a number of options before arriving at a comprehensive program combining the right elements geared to achieving the stated goals.

The third phase of the process is to implement the solutions they have formulated. The firm understands that building an image or sustaining a company's position requires more than paid media can deliver. They are passionate about projecting the client's unique voice within the market with fresh, inspired approaches utilizing electronic and print media and hard-hitting public relations initiatives.

Finally, they partner with their clients to monitor the effectiveness of the campaign. The firm feels that the national recognition that many of their clients have received as a result of Elements' programs is the true measure of the company's success.

Many of these programs have been recognized with national and regional awards given by their peers and the industry. The North Alabama Communication Plan developed by Elements won the March of Dimes National Communication Award in 1996. The firm also won the Outstanding Community Service Award in 1992 for the Bryan Foods/Spirit of the South "African-American Promotion." The company has also been tapped as the Marketing Firm of the Year by the American Marketing Association.

More importantly in the PR professional's opinion is the fact that these and other of the company's award-winning campaigns have translated into bottom-line success for their clients. Their "Stars Fell on Alabama" campaign for the Alabama Bureau of Travel & Tourism resulted in an influx of $300 million in revenue, vaulting tourism to the number two spot in the list of the state's top

"We have a number of very talented people working here who could choose to be working in much larger markets. They come here because we all share a common professional passion. We focus on our customers, and we love utilizing our creativity to achieve positive results for each of them," says company president and CEO Christopher Bazuaye.

industries. It also saw an almost 16 percent increase in tourist expenditures, a state record. Another marketing program helped turn a local automobile dealership's $8 million deficit into $52 million in revenue. And it was accomplished with a per unit advertising cost that was 30 percent below the national average. The firm also worked for HBO on the phenomenally successful *4 Little Girls* produced by Spike Lee. They were responsible for the public relations work on the *Tuskegee Airmen* premiere sponsored by Alabama Power Company. Elements recently won an ADDY for this project.

There are many career high water marks that the company can point to, but one defining moment will always remain near the top of the list. "In 1998, we were handling a campaign in Choctaw County in south Alabama," Bazuaye recalls. "We had been asked to design an initiative aimed at persuading the county's voters to approve a referendum calling for a property tax increase for education. The campaign was successful and the referendum passed. On the drive home, I reflected on how rewarding it is to be able to do something for those young students, especially considering their circumstances. The school Board had been unsuccessful in passing a tax increase referendum on several attempts over the past 30 years. Our team and the client really worked hard and closely on that campaign. It reminded me that nothing is impossible if you pursue your dream with passion and direction from God."

Bazuaye's infectious enthusiasm for his work has spread to other associates who make up the firm's staff. "We are not a huge company like some of the larger marketing and public relations firms," notes an account executive at Elements. "We look at that, however, as an advantage. It allows us to focus quality time on our clients. We have a number of very talented and qualified people working here who could choose to be working in much larger markets. They come here because we all share a common work ethic. We focus on our customers and we love utilizing our creativity to achieve positive results for each client."

OGIHARA AMERICA CORPORATION

gihara Corporation, a world renowned Japanese tool and dye company, founded the American arm of its business in Michigan in 1987 to provide the stamping and sub-assembly of body panels for the automobile industry. A decade later, the company turned a 110-acre pasture in the Tarrant-Pinson Valley just outside Birmingham into an $85 million plant producing sidewalls, doors, hoods, fenders, and tailgates for the Mercedes M-class vehicles being produced just down the road from the Magic City in Vance, Alabama.

"The switch here is that Mr. Ogihara located the first operation in the Detroit area, the hub of the already established auto manufacturing industry, while the plant in Birmingham was built and the industry grew around us," notes Danny Collins, the associate relations manager for Ogihara America Corporation. "Just six years after the Mercedes plant went on-line, the state also attracted Honda to Lincoln, Alabama and Hyundai to Hope Hull just outside Montgomery. Nissan went into Canton, Mississippi, and a Saturn plant is now in operation in Springfield, Tennessee. That's five major automobile manufacturing and

assembly operations within about a 300 mile radius of Birmingham. Mr. Ogihara has a reputation as a man of vision, and, in this case, it was 20-20."

That vision led to the growth of Ogihara Corporation from a small dye shop in Japan in 1951 to the world's largest manufacturer of industrial stamping dyes. The company today operates 15 plants and offices around the world, and is a highly respected Tier 1 supplier of Class A and related body panels.

The Birmingham facility now employs over 300 people including engineers, production associates, technicians, tool and dye makers, quality control inspectors, and other skilled labor, mostly from Jefferson County. Since turning out its first body panels in 1997 for Mercedes, Ogihara has increased its capacity to that automaker from panels for 65,000 to 85,000 and then to 105,000 vehicles annually. In addition, the plant now provides hood and tailgate panels for the Saturn

plant in Tennessee, and stamps panels for the Nissan plant in Mississippi as well. Interestingly enough, all this was accomplished without increasing its floor space.

Collins cites technology and improved efficiency as the keys. The company relies on continuing improvements in automation and robotics to squeeze more technology into the same work space.

Ogihara's associates are keenly aware that the stamping industry in which they work is not one of huge inventories of finished products stored in warehouses waiting to be assembled. The door assemblies they manufacture in the morning for Mercedes will be part of an M-class vehicle the next day. For this reason, their goal of total customer satisfaction is achieved through a commitment to providing the best-in-class quality door panels and full service tool manufacturing and maintenance capabilities assuring continued production. Their modular production with just-in-time delivery makes them a leader in sub-assembly work.

Ogihara is also known for providing engineering, technical

assistance, and on-site expertise for new stamping plants. The company's cost reduction initiatives provide solutions through lean manufacturing techniques and total production maintenance.

Ogihara was faced with a number of challenges when they selected the Birmingham area as the site for their Southern production facility. The company had to recruit and train a labor force for an industry that was unknown here as recently as six years ago. The training team also had to school their new associates in sophisticated automated equipment that would be turning out body panels, the most visible features for the SUVs of Mercedes, an automaker with a name synonymous with quality. There could be no compromising on quality and on-time delivery.

Ogihara met those challenges by identifying and creating a successful process whereby the company would manufacture a high quality product and deliver it on-time to its customers. Since its inception, the company has continuously studied and refined that process to improve productivity. Ogihara America Corporation remains committed to even more refinement and improvement as the company expands the scope of its operations in the future to meet the growing demands of the automobile industry in the South.

Above: Ogihara's Birmingham facility has grown from 285,000 square feet in 1997 to 450,000 square feet in 2003.

Left: Ogihara has two tandem press lines with a 2,000 ton capacity on "A" Line and 2,300 tons on "B" Line.

LIBERTY NATIONAL LIFE INSURANCE

A Torchmark Corporation Company

A symbol of business success in Birmingham, Liberty National Life established a presence in Alabama back in 1900 when it was founded as The Heralds of Liberty, a fraternal organization established to sell life insurance. Today, Liberty National's up-stream holding company, Torchmark Corporation, also of Birmingham, owns a group of companies specializing in life and health insurance. Liberty National is one of the most prominent traditional insurance companies in the United States.

It was at the height of the Depression that Liberty National started its journey of growth and expansion in 1929 when it incorporated as a legal reserve stock life insurance company under the name Liberty National Life Insurance Company. The Company's first major expansion was in 1943 with the acquisition of Brown-Service Insurance Company, gaining a strong market share in Alabama selling burial insurance packages.

In the 1960's and 1970's, Liberty National branched out into health insurance, primarily supplemental cancer insurance. By the late 1970's, Liberty National was ready to expand beyond its traditional southeastern marketplace, and in 1979 acquired Globe Life And Accident Insurance Company of Oklahoma City. Also in 1980, Liberty National Insurance Holding Company was formed as the parent company of Liberty National and Globe Life, setting the stage for future acquisitions.

During the two years following the holding company's formation, it acquired Waddell & Reed, a mutual fund management company, and United Investors Life Insurance Company, both of Kansas City, as well as United American Insurance Company, Dallas, and other insurers. Liberty National Insurance Holding Company became Torchmark Corporation in 1982. In 1994, Torchmark made its most recent major acquisition, American Income Life Insurance Company of Waco, Texas.

Torchmark Corporation, a New York Stock Exchange traded company and a member of the S&P 500, has had only three chairmen since incorporation: Frank P. Samford, Jr., the son of Liberty founding-father Frank P. Samford; R. K. Richey, who became Chairman in 1986; and C. B. Hudson, Chairman since 1998. Under the leadership of these three highly respected insurance industry executives, by year-end 2001, Torchmark had grown to $12 billion of assets and had annualized life and health insurance premiums in force of $2 billion.

Torchmark is known as one of the most cost-efficient providers in the life and health insurance industry. While Torchmark has gained those efficiencies in part by integrating the administrative functions of its subsidiaries, it chooses to market its products under the name of each subsidiary, rather than the Torchmark name, in order to take advantage of the market recognition that each has earned in its market niche. Clearly, the name and reputation of Liberty National, its 109 offices and over 2,000 agent representatives carry a long legacy of community good citizenship, not just in Birmingham, but throughout the Southeast. Liberty National is an outstanding example of the many successful Birmingham companies that have retained the best of their long heritages and modernized them for success in today's business world.

Steve Yoder

Steve Yoder sat on a concrete bench outside the Birmingham Museum of Art and looked at Vulcan's huge head, repaired and freshly painted and on loan for a time awaiting work that will return the statue to the top of its pedestal on Red Mountain.

A breeze hummed through tree branches as Yoder, chairman of the Vulcan Park Foundation, said "...It was touching, to see this frail woman bending over and rubbing the name of her grandfather onto a piece of paper ..."

He was telling of a woman who knew that foundrymen had cast their names into Vulcan's right arm in 1904. She knew this secret because her grandfather—one of those men—had told her the story while she sat on his knee. She was at Vulcan Park to view the pieces on the ground before they were hauled to Robinson Iron for repair. She was there, nearly 100 years after those craftsmen had made Giuseppi Moretti's vision a reality, to see the name of her grandfather that had remained hidden inside the statue's arm for most of that time.

That woman—like most long-time Birmingham residents—has a bond with Vulcan. And now Yoder, this recent transplant to the city, has a bond with the work of art as well.

"I'm an unlikely person (for the Vulcan project) because I never set foot in the city of Birmingham until the summer of 1995," he says. "I was involved in the historical society. The consensus was that someone needed to come from the corporate business community. I was the only person standing. I had less credentials as far as being from here and knowing the history."

Turns out that this senior executive vice president and general counsel for AmSouth had more credentials than he realized.

"I moved here from Pittsburgh (another steel town much like Birmingham)," Yoder says, straightening his tie. "Moretti lived there for years and his works are scattered around there and they take them for granted. They have no clue. They have statue after statue in public parks. Moretti did these huge panthers for Pitt (the University of Pittsburgh).

"His studio there is now a tile store. I returned to Pittsburgh for a friend's 50th birthday. On a Saturday morning I went into this tile store and saw a small statue of two cherubs holding a ball. It was done by Moretti. I introduced myself and told (the business owner) about Moretti and he looked askance at me."

That statue is now on loan to the Birmingham Museum of Art.

"I have this unique bond with Moretti," Yoder says. "He lived in Pittsburgh longer than he lived in Alabama. I didn't know those statues were made by Moretti until I came here and worked with Vulcan."

And worked with Vulcan he has.

Under Yoder's leadership the Vulcan Park Foundation, founded in October of 1999, raised the money needed to get the statue back on its pedestal. Today, Vulcan is back on Red Moutain and the park and visitors center is scheduled to open early in 2004. The foundation was in the unenviable position of having three jobs to do at once, Yoder says. It had to fix the statue, decide what to do with the park and raise the money.

"Normally the first two things would be decided and then we would be out raising money for it," he says. "We decided to create a visitor destination that people would return to. We wanted to maximize and put the visitors center at the crest of the hill so it would have views of the city. It is important for the park to make money, for people to use it for weddings, family reunions and business meetings.

"Fundraising was a challenge. We didn't reach this final decision on the park until six months into the process. I was heartened by the reception we got in the very early stages. They (the business community, government and individuals such as the McWane family) believed in Vulcan."

Later, as Yoder looked at Vulcan's repaired right arm with the re-cast spear at long last placed properly in the hand, he says, "The statue means more to me now than when we started. Vulcan is a way for people to recognize what is home.

"I moved my family here after 17 years in Pennsylvania and I want them to think of Birmingham as home. I think they will associate Vulcan with home."

Eric Essix

"My grandfather gave me my first guitar. It was the first time that I ever owned a guitar, after begging him for many months and him threatening not to get it if I didn't learn to play. There wasn't a whole lot of money in our family so it was quite an investment. I picked it up and he wanted me to learn some blues and gospel." Eric Essix is reminiscing.

Where did the music come from?

"I have to go back to the influence of gospel music which is very prevalent in this city. There is a church on every street conrer and the music that comes from those churches is really at the root of my musical experiences. I started singing at 7 or 8 in the Smithfield Seventh Day Adventist church choir. Singing in gospel choirs was my primary music experience."

Essix was born a child of the south, a native of Birmingham, Alabma during the turbulent 60's. "I don't remember a lot of the events that took place during that time," Essix recalls, "but I do remember music being an important part of my life at an early age.

"Aside from the gospel sounds I heard in church, The Beatles made the biggest musical impact on me as a child. I was fascinated by their guitars, those incredible songs and the whole image that they projected. I thing that's when the love affair with the guitar truly began."

The first jazz record he ever heard was Wes Montgomery's, *California Dreamin*. "I began to teach myself how to play by copying licks from Al Green, Stevie Wonder and Jackson 5 records," Essix says. "In 1973, I joined my first group called the Harmonettes, and at 13 began playing gospel music in churches around Birmingham."

Essix's first professional opportunity came several years later when he co-founded a jazz fusion quartet called Souvenir and began playing venues around the south. When the group broke up after three years, he produced a solo record called *First Impressions* that landed him a deal with Los Angeles based jazz label Nova Records.

The record made a national impact, but it was *Second Thoughts*, his follow up release on Nova, that created a real presence for Eric on what would later be called "smooth jazz" radio with a song called "Come September."

After graduating from Boston's prestigious Berklee College of Music in 1993, Eric released *Third Degree Burn* featuring a band consisting of his fellow classmates. Touring nationwide for two years as Eric Essix & Modern Man, the band performed intelligent compositions, with intense muscianship and a powerful stage presence. The tour was documented with a recording called *Eric Essix & Modern Man, LIVE!* In 1994.

When the band members called it quits, Eric signed with Tribute/Diadem Records and released *Beautiful Music: Guitar*, an album of origianl solo guitar compositions and a compilation album called *Just Like You*.

"When my son Miles was born in 1995, I channeled all the emotions I was feeling into my music and produced a record I called *Small Talk*," Eric says. The project was later picked up and released by Ricky Schultz at Zebra Records and topped the smooth jazz radio charts with the single, "For Real." Today his son is really interested in making films. "I bought him a video camera for Christmas. He's going to enter his first film in the Sidewalk Film Festival next year. He's hired me to do the score."

In 2000 Eric returned home to his roots with the release of *Southbound* on Zebra which produced a top 14 jazz radio single with the classic "Rainy NIght in Georgia."

"The intent was to do a record that clearly spoke to my early musical influences with compositions that had strong connections to the South in some way," Eric explains.

"I want to continue to make music that reflects a love for my homeland and infuse more elements of gospel, blues and soul music, as well as jazz, into my sound.

"My ideal scenario as a musician is to continue to play music live. I always come back to wanting to perform in front of people and get that immediate response and to also do music for television and film."

VESTAVIA HILLS
Beautiful Neighborhoods, Award-Winning Schools

A picture-post-card wooded area on the summit of Shades Mountain with sweeping vistas of the Appalachian foothills first attracted the attention of a former Mayor of Birmingham in the 1920s. George Ward purchased 20 acres on the crest of the mountain as the site for a home he built there in 1925 on the style of the classic Greek and Roman temples that he had grown to love during his frequent trips to Italy and Greece. He named his creation Vestavia, a combination of "Vesta", the Roman goddess of the earth, and "via", Latin for "by the roadway."

In the 1940s, the attractive mountaintop area was laid out as a subdivision to accommodate approximately 1,000 persons. The City of Vestavia Hills was incorporated in 1950, and, over the next half century, acquired a reputation as one of the Birmingham area's most desirable places to live. Today, the city has a population of over 30,000 people, making it the third largest municipality in Jefferson County.

In addition to its beautiful neighborhoods and award-winning homes, the city's school system, ranked as one of the best in the state, has served as a major catalyst of the city's growth and a primary attraction to prospective home buyers. Several of the schools in the Vestavia system have been recognized as "National Blue Ribbon Schools of Excellence." The system's quality of education services have been cited in *The Wall Street Journal, Redbook, Fifty Fabulous Places to Raise Your Family*, and other publications.

Vestavia's students have been at the heart of this luster. The high school's math team has placed first in national competition in 11 of the last 13 years, and the debate team has seven national championship trophies. Vestavia High averages 19 National Merit Finalists annually, and in 2002, the school's graduating seniors were awarded more than $7 million in scholarships to a wide range of national colleges and universities. The high school's athletic teams consistently rank among the top finishers in Jefferson County, with 48 state titles and one national championship in baseball in the school's trophy case.

Such an award-winning student body obviously reflects a top notch faculty. Vestavia teachers at the elementary, middle, and high school levels have garnered considerable spotlight with numerous regional and national awards, which led the city's Strategic Planning Team to cite Vestavia's school system as the "city's greatest asset."

Dr. Charles McCallum has been proud to call Vestavia Hills his home for the past 36 years. When he was elected mayor of the city in 2000, he brought the same management style to his position as Vestavia's chief executive that he relied on for six years as the president of UAB. His philosophy of including as many of the talented people around him as possible in the business of running the city has met with the same level of success that characterized his term of office at UAB.

"Citizen involvement has been the key here," McCallum states. "We are fortunate in Vestavia Hills to have a tremendous pool of talent from which to draw for volunteers to serve on the numerous committees that we have created in this city. Harnessing and directing that talent from the huge number of doctors, accountants, engineers, architects, bankers, attorneys, and developers who reside here has not only saved the city a significant amount of money, but it has also created a community spirit here of which we are very proud."

That teamwork and community involvement led to the design and construction of the full service Vestavia Hills Community Playground in 2002. A group of dedicated intergenerational volunteers pooled their individual talents and came together to raise the money, lay out and plan the facility, and complete the construction of the playground in a single week.

During his first years in office, McCallum has focused on expanding the number and scope of those committees. They now number 14, ranging from those charged with promoting economic development and education to others dealing with transportation issues and senior citizen services.

McCallum has also placed emphasis on expanding the city's economic base, which had eroded, to help support the numerous municipal services that have resulted in the quality of life enjoyed by the city's residents. What was originally a bedroom community in the 1940s has become a vibrant area boasting a variety of business and professional services.

The commercial heart of Vestavia Hills is the 390,000 square feet of business and office space being developed along U.S. Highway 31 which runs through the center of the city. In addition, the Liberty Park development just off Interstate 459 is adding another 30,000 square feet of high quality space for offices and businesses. In 2002, the residents of Cahaba Heights voted overwhelmingly to be annexed into Vestavia Hills, adding more than 100 businesses and over 7,000 residents to the city.

They are all watched over carefully by the city's police and fire departments and emergency response personnel. Vestavia Hills also operates its own system of municipal courts, public works department, building inspection services, engineering department, library, and parks and recreation board.

"The Vestavia Hills Chamber of Commerce has been instrumental in working with city leaders to bring business to our city," states Liz Ramsey, former executive director of the Chamber. "During the past ten years, the Chamber has helped to increase commercial activity by compiling a Business Start-Up Kit to help anyone interested in opening a business in Vestavia. We have also made available a list of retail properties for sale and for lease, and worked with developers in the location of new

A future musician works on his craft at the recently constructed community playground, while other youths enjoy their new skate park.

shopping centers. The Chamber has also partnered with SCORE, the Service Corps of Retired Executives, and the Small Business Center at UAB to advise business owners on how to make improvements to their existing operations and to provide valuable information on how to start new businesses."

Diversification of the social fabric of Vestavia Hills has also been a strong focus for Mayor McCallum. The city involves hundreds of people from its broad based ethnic heritage in community events such as its International Food Festival, Dogwood Festival, I Love America Day, and Christmas parade.

"Another of our goals is to be more involved in the overall planning activities for the Birmingham metro area," McCallum notes. "We have a monthly meeting of the Mayors of Hoover, Mountain Brook, Homewood, and Vestavia Hills to discuss transportation issues, public services, environmental issues, water services, and others as they relate to the over-the-mountain communities. In addition, we want to help promote the area's key attractions, such as the Birmingham Museum of Art, the McWane Center, the Alabama Symphony, Civil Rights Institute, Botanical Gardens, etc. to our residents. Locally, we have a long-range development plan for Vestavia Hills that focuses on planned, controlled growth designed to enhance the quality of life here. It calls for additional neighborhood parks, sidewalks, bike paths, and senior citizen services. All of us in Vestavia Hills are very excited about making this a great metropolitan area, and we are working closely with regional and metropolitan development boards and Region 2020 to make our entire metropolitan area a better place to live and work. We will make the Birmingham and Jefferson County area one of the most outstanding areas in the country. Working together with the considerable human resources available to us, there is nothing we can't accomplish."

UNIVERSITY OF ALABAMA
AT BIRMINGHAM
Touching Lives

In just three decades, the University of Alabama at Birmingham has evolved from a promising medical center and urban extension program into the largest single employer in Alabama, one of the nation's most respected universities and a world leader in medical research and health care delivery. By every measure, UAB is thriving, and plans already underway insure continued growth that will benefit every life that UAB touches: in the classroom, by the bedside, in the community, and beyond.

The visionaries that built UAB didn't believe in limitations, as the university's meteoric rise to the forefront of medical research proves. They saw the university as a means to move the state forward, beginning in Birmingham, a city that was beset by social strife and a flagging economy.

Their vision paid off. Today UAB is one of the nation's top 20 universities in support from the National Institutes of Health and among the top 30 in federal research and development expenditures. University Hospital routinely ranks among the best in the *U.S. News & World Report* listing of the nation's best hospitals, and their peers in disciplines from AIDS to women's health and internal medicine to pediatrics consider UAB's physicians among the best in the country.

As it grew, UAB became the catalyst that helped transform Birmingham from a city whose economy was tied to the failing steel industry into a center for biomedical research, engineering, and finance unparalleled in the Southeast. From a few blocks on the city's Southside, UAB has grown to encompass 77 city blocks. Its economic impact in the Birmingham area has reached nearly $2.5 billion, and it employs more than 16,000 people.

A key driver in UAB's success is a tradition of interdisciplinary partnerships—in particular, joint programs and 80 university-wide centers bridging the medical center and academic units. The university's comprehensive program for commercialization of faculty research and technology transfer is recognized as a national leader. New companies in computer and biomedical technology and pharmaceuticals occupy its high-tech business incubator. The university's ambitious plans for programmatic growth and expansion of interdisciplinary biomedical research efforts herald not only enhanced academic prestige for UAB, but significant economic promise for Birmingham and Alabama.

In 2001, UAB dedicated the $37 million Hugh Kaul Human Genetics Building, just months after the announcement of the mapping of the human genome. The Kaul Building is the centerpiece for research and treatment of patients with genetic diseases at UAB. The new 340,000 gross-square-foot Shelby Interdisciplinary Biomedical Research Building began construction in 2002 as part of a plan to double UAB's

research space to more than 1.4 million square feet over the next decade. This expansion will create an estimated 3,400 jobs as hundreds of millions of additional dollars flow to UAB's research program and will boost an ambitious plan to move UAB's School of Medicine into the top 10 in NIH funding by the year 2010.

UAB Hospital is hard at work on a $275 million expansion and renovation project. The new 850,000 square-foot facility, scheduled for completion and occupancy in 2004, will house a greatly expanded emergency department, private intensive care rooms, and large surgical suites outfitted to support the latest technology, such as robotics and minimally invasive surgical techniques.

With 136 degree-granting programs, UAB fulfills its commitment to the discovery, dissemination, and application of knowledge through its schools of Arts & Humanities, Business, Dentistry, Education, Engineering, Health Related Professions, Medicine, Natural Sciences & Mathematics, Nursing, Optometry, Public Health, and Social & Behavioral Sciences.

UAB provides superior, affordable education to some 16,000 students who are attracted to one of the South's most exciting and diverse institutions, where more than 90 percent of the faculty hold terminal degrees. Its distinguished faculty excels in teaching, scholarship, and research with an interdisciplinary focus, earning nearly $400 million a year in competitive contracts and

grants. Having so many of the world's leading researchers on faculty means UAB undergraduates get the opportunity to work with them on cutting-edge research, some as early their freshman year —an opportunity found at few universities in the world.

UAB also fosters a nurturing environment for this changing student body. The campus master plan calls for the "greening" of a central quadrangle area, the addition of a campus recreation center, and more on-campus amenities for students.

UAB also adds to the city's great sporting tradition. UAB fields 17 intercollegiate teams as a Division I member of the NCAA and founding member of Conference USA. In recent years, Blazer football has twice finished second in the conference; women's basketball and men's soccer have competed in NCAA tournament play; and the nation's top-ranked collegiate golfer hailed from UAB.

UAB also is an important part of the city's cultural landscape. UAB's elegant Alys Stephens Center is home to the Alabama Ballet and the Alabama Symphony Orchestra, and brings other nationally and internationally known artists to Birmingham, from the National Symphony Orchestra to Roberta Flack. The Center's four venues also showcase the UAB departments of Music and Theater as well as UAB's own professional theatre company in residence, The 13th Street Ensemble. The UAB Music Department offers jazz, pop, classical and gospel

concerts by its performing groups, as well as choral and opera productions.

In addition to its role in education and health care, UAB continues to build on its strong tradition of partnering with the city, the state, and the Southeast to work for community betterment, economic growth, and service to the people of Alabama. Working with local K-12 school systems, UAB developed a number of initiatives that have improved new teacher training, enhanced classroom resources and provided much-needed science and math programs. Several initiatives also are underway in the city's oldest and most underserved neighborhoods, bringing together university and community resources to improve housing, education, health, crime prevention, and transportation.

UAB also enjoys strong support from the corporate community and the citizens of the Birmingham area. The Campaign for UAB is the largest fund-raising effort ever undertaken by an Alabama university. Publicly announced in 1999, the campaign approached its $250 million goal so rapidly that within a year, the target was raised to $350 million, and UAB was rapidly nearing the new goal well before its target date. That community members, business leaders, and foundations view UAB as a wise investment is evident in the widespread and generous response to the Campaign. Almost 40,000 donors have contributed, including 57 gifts of $1 million or more.

(L-R) The UAB Honors Program, housed in the newly renovated Spencer Honors House, provides gifted and highly motivated students with an intimate, innovative, and challenging interdisciplinary course of study. Blazer basketball is just one of 17 intercollegiate teams UAB fields as a Division I member of the NCAA and founding member of Conference USA. Some 16,000 students are attracted each year to UAB, one of the South's most exciting and diverse institutions. Its distinguished faculty excels in teaching, scholarship, and research with interdisciplinary focus, earning more than $400 million a year in competitive contracts and grants.

141

UAB HEALTH SYSTEM

Medicine That Touches The World

Recognized worldwide for its excellent patient care and groundbreaking research, the UAB Health System has supported the remarkable growth of the University of Alabama at Birmingham—and the expansion of Birmingham's economy—since its roots were first formed in the 1940s. The visionary leadership that nurtured the young medical center remains the hallmark of the Health System today, as it continues to evolve in step with the swift changes taking place in healthcare delivery. The Health System now boasts one of the nation's premier academic medical centers, along with a growing network of clinical facilities.

FACILITIES

The centerpiece of the UAB Medical Center is the 908-bed University Hospital, a nationally known teaching hospital and Alabama's major tertiary-care facility. The existing hospital will be replaced with an all-new facility in 2004. In addition, The Kirklin Clinic® at UAB has, in less than a decade, become Alabama's premier center of specialty outpatient care, offering services in over 30 specialties and housing more than 700 physicians. Also, Alabama's only eye specialty hospital, the Callahan Eye Foundation Hospital at UAB, is home to internationally known eye surgeons and research programs.

In 2001, the UAB Health System and the Children's Health System established CWH, a non-profit alliance promoting closer cooperation between the two partners. Children's Hospital is the primary teaching facility for UAB's Department of Pediatrics.

In 2002, an agreement in the Bessemer/Hoover/Vance area created UAB Medical West, a 300-bed, full-service community hospital.

RESEARCH

By blending the best minds in medicine with a superior academic setting, the UAB Health System has created an environment that promotes research and discovery. Grant support has doubled at the University every decade since its founding, from $18 million in 1969 to almost $400 million today. Thousands of study projects involving an army of researchers are expanding the frontiers of medical knowledge, from gene therapy as a possible cure for cystic fibrosis to a preventive vaccine for AIDS, to islet cell transplants as a cure for juvenile diabetes.

Since its foundation in 1972, the UAB Comprehensive Cancer Center has made fundamental discoveries in the nature of the disease, helped develop innovative approaches to combat it, and touched thousands of people across the state and region with prevention, diagnosis, and treatment programs. In 2000, the Center received a $13.8 million grant from the National Cancer Institute to establish a breast cancer Specialized Program of Research Excellence (SPORE), placing UAB among the nation's leaders in research and treatment of cancer in women. Today, UAB is the only institution in the nation with SPORE grants for both ovarian cancer and breast cancer. In 2002, the Center received one of the first two brain cancer SPORE grants in the nation.

Likewise, UAB has become internationally recognized as one of the finest academic medical centers for the research and treatment of diabetes, rheumatoid arthritis, cardiovascular disease, stroke, digestive and kidney diseases, and many other conditions.

THE REWARDS THAT MATTER

UAB continues to be awarded prestigious honors and credentials for its high quality patient care.

In 2002, the American Nurses Association named University Hospital a "nursing center of excellence" and

awarded it the elite Magnet hospital certification. UAB is the first and only hospital in Alabama to earn this certification, presently granted to only 55 of 5,500 hospitals nationwide.

For over a decade, UAB has been the only Alabama medical center to be consistently included in *U.S. News & World Report's* listing of *"America's Best Hospitals."* UAB earns high marks for programs such as rheumatology, cardiology and cardiac disease, cancer, nephrology (the structure, function, and diseases of the kidneys), gynecology, hormonal disorders, (enocrinology, diabetes, and metabolism), pulmonology (the treatment of respiratory disorders) rehabilitation, and otolaryngology (ear nose and throat).

In recent years, University Hospital has also received the Alabama Quality Award, measuring customer commitment, innovation, reliability, and sensitivity to employees and the community.

COMMUNITY SERVICE

Recognizing the fact that the responsibilities of a world class medical center do not end with providing exceptional healthcare and conducting groundbreaking research, the UAB Health System has made community outreach programs an integral part of the organization's mission. The System has underscored its commitment to the community by making the highest quality healthcare conveniently accessible.

Primary and specialty care are available at neighborhood locations throughout the Birmingham metro area, including The Kirklin Clinic® at Acton Road, the UAB Geriatric Health Center at Mount Royal Towers retirement community, and UAB Health Centers at Bessemer, Hoover, Hueytown, Inverness, Moody, Parkwest, Tannehill and Vance.

EYE TO THE FUTURE

The UAB Health System is keeping an eye sharply focused on the future. In the summer of 2000, ground was broken on the new University Hospital, a $275 million, technologically advanced diagnostic and treatment facility with a patient-friendly design making care more efficient and accessible. The public has been invited to become a partner with the UAB Health System in the hospital's comprehensive fund-raising campaign. Volunteers and financial supporters will help bring good health and hope to thousands of patients and their families. Complete information on becoming a partner is available at 205.975.0838.

A PARTNERSHIP FOR LIFE

Not only has it changed lives through the provision of superior healthcare, the UAB Health System has also contributed to the Birmingham area through the thousands of job opportunities it has made available, the construction and renovation projects that have renewed and re-sculpted the city's Southside, and the re-investment of its revenues into additional services to benefit area residents. In addition, the University's world renowned research initiatives have led the way in unlocking secrets to the treatment and prevention of cancer, heart disease, stroke, diabetes, and other diseases.

The outlook for healthcare in Alabama has never been brighter. With unique people and programs, knowledge, and compassion, the UAB Health System continues to strengthen the bonds between patient and doctor in a true partnership for life.

Facing page, clockwise: The Kirklin Clinic® at UAB houses hundreds of physicians in over 30 specialties. UAB researchers continue to expand the frontiers of medical knowledge. University Hospital is a Magnet certified "nursing center of excellence." The Kirklin Clinic® at Acton Road delivers comprehensive cancer care in a convenient neighborhood setting. UAB Medical West delivers primary and specialty care to the area's western communities.

Right: UAB operates the state's only adult Level I Trauma Program and is home to one of only two Comprehensive Head Injury Centers in the nation.

Below: The system's hub of activity, the new University Hospital will open in the summer of 2004.

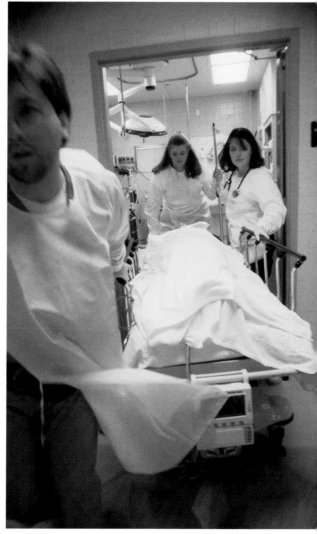

143

Marian McKay Rosato

Her back to a window in a small, classy suburban restaurant, Marian McKay Rosato is singing. Night is falling outside. A guitarist and a bass player flank the thin, blonde singer sheathed in a classy black dress, her hands embracing a microphone. Eyes closed in a dreamy world of her own, Marian sings as the soft summer night turns romantic.

> "Moonlight and magnolia, starlight in your hair
> All the world, a dream come true
> Did it really happen, was I really there
> Was I really there with you.
> "We lived our little drama
> We kissed in a field of white
> And stars fell on Alabama...
> Last night"

Stars Fell on Alabama is Marian's favorite song. "It's just very dreamy and mystical, and it's about romance and finding that one special someone and having a moment that was timeless and will just go on forever," she says.

Music, the songs of others and her own voice, soft yet strong, informs every fiber of her world. And it has from the time she was a child. She remembers the music her father played when she was a girl.

"He just loved big band music, and my mom and dad met in high school, and they followed the big bands...They liked to dance. I always heard my dad singing along to it. He had a nice voice. So then the words captured me. Somehow they were there, and I knew those words. Because his music was always playing. So somehow a chord was struck."

Marian has been in Birmingham since the 1970s, when she and her brother Mike and her partner Gary started Charlemagne Record Exchange. After 25 years, the little store, with the vast musical catalog, knowledgeable salespeople and business partners who love what they do, thrives in a second-floor walk-up in Five Points South.

"I think there is a network of people that have either discovered or have yet to discover that there are unique kind of places in the city, that make Birmingham unique. And a lot of times, you don't really know about them, but you learn from a friend. And it's something that's off the beaten track, something that's not your generic record store...and there are just people who are crazy enough to try and do something like this and be involved in music in this way."

The store brings Marian close to music every day, but it is in performance that the music speaks through her.

"The first time I heard Billie Holliday, I was probably in my 20s, and I just thought that was it. That was the music that...something about her style, and then of course the songs that she chose. From there, I started listening to jazz and developed a love for what she and the songwriters from that era wanted to portray.

"When I hear it, when it's capturing your thoughts, and it's painting pictures in your mind, to me it brings a sense of romance. It's almost spiritual the way they put together the message they're wanting to convey and the emotion. It's timeless. It will always paint that picture for me, emotionally"

Marian sings a few times a month at different clubs, restaurants or events.

"It's wonderful that there are so many great musicians in Birmingham that have been doing this style of music twice as long as I have. So I've just been very fortunate to have been nurtured and supported by some of the wonderful, fine musicians who have thought they heard something in me that they want to accompany. That's a great honor and a great privilege that I've been overwhelmed by."

In front of a microphone, she seems plugged into something at once ephemeral like starlight, yet intimate as a kiss.

> "My heart, beat like a hammer,
> My arms wound around you tight,
> And stars fell on Alabama ...
> Last night"

IMAGING BUSINESS MACHINES

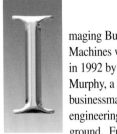

Imaging Business Machines was founded in 1992 by Gary Murphy, a Birmingham businessman with an engineering background. From the very beginning, Murphy set out to manufacture and market color scanners that go beyond taking photographs of pieces of paper. While engineering a revolutionary scanning platform capable of capturing intermixed documents at a fast throughput rate, the company pioneered a number of new technologies that have set the standard for high end document imaging.

Imaging Business Machines' signature product is the ImageTrac ® Scanning Platform, a high-speed, high-capacity machine that converts paper documents into color, grayscale, and bitonal images.

The industry was quick to recognize the benefits of Imaging Business Machines' technology. Only two years after the company was launched, an Australian airline began using the ImageTrac scanner, forerunner of the ImageTrac II, to capture color images of airline tickets. Since then, ImageTrac scanners have become an airline industry standard, capturing images of over 1.5 million passenger tickets per day.

Today, the ImageTrac Scanning Platform is employed across several industries in a variety of complex applications, such as wholesale lockbox, tax returns and payments, passport applications, document archive, pharmaceutical, remittance, airline tickets, accounts

receivables, test scoring, and order entry. Many of the country's largest

banks use the ImageTrac platform to capture color images of forms, checks,

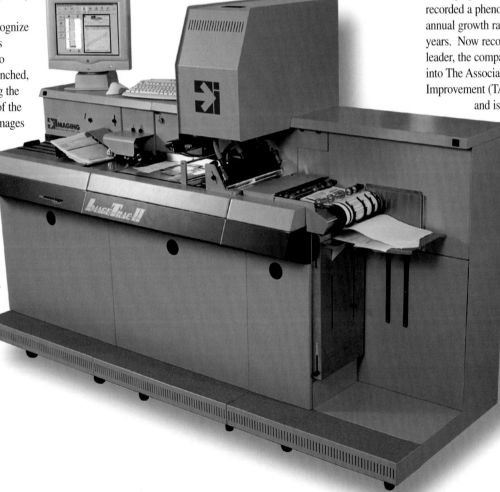

envelopes, and other documents. Customers in the U.S. and in 24 countries around the world include Melon Bank, the U.S. State Department, Bank of America, KLM Royal Dutch Airlines, Combined Insurance, and Merck-Medco. Alabama customers include AdvancePCS, Alabama Department of Industrial Relations, Imaging Systems Company, U.S. Airforce Historical Research Agency, and the U.S. Department of Treasury.

Imaging Business Machines is headquartered in Birmingham where it maintains a corporate office along with a research and development center in Liberty Park. Irondale is home to the company's newly expanded manufacturing plant. The company also has offices in Dallas, Texas, and Konstanz, Germany.

Imaging Business Machines has recorded a phenomenal 30 percent annual growth rate over the past five years. Now recognized as an industry leader, the company has been inducted into The Association of Work Process Improvement (TAWPI) Hall of Fame, and is a recipient of the Best of AIIM award from the Enterprise Content Management Association. Local honors include receiving the "Best in Business" and "Fast Track" awards from the Birmingham Business Journal.

NELSON BROTHERS, INC.

A Commitment to Customer Safety and Service.

In the early 1950s, Dugan Nelson was working as a welder with crews following construction projects around the Southeast. While living in Parrish, Alabama, he struck up a conversation with a man who ran a coal mining operation. The man spoke of the need among surface miners for an alternative to the nitroglycerine-based dynamite that was widely used at that time for blasting through earth and rock to extract the coal lying beneath. Dugan piqued the interest of his brother, Olen, on the need to fill this niche, and in 1956 they launched Nelson Brothers, an explosive manufacturing company relying on the less expensive and more stable ammonium nitrate to produce the products needed by the mining industry. Almost a half century later, the company the two brothers founded has developed a global reach, exporting to 17 countries around the world.

The company, now headquartered on Lakeshore Drive in Homewood, maintains a product development lab at its original location in Parrish along with plants in Alabama and Wyoming and operations centers in West Virginia, Kentucky, Oklahoma, and Virginia.

"We're located in the major coal producing areas," explains Bill Nelson, who, along with his brother, Tony, now run the business founded by their father and their uncle. "We sell directly to the major coal mining companies in this country, and we export raw ingredients worldwide."

Bill, who serves as the firm's CEO, joined the operation in 1971 after graduating from Auburn University. Tony, the president of the company, came onboard seven years later. Each brought a strong desire to expand and improve the family business. They wasted little time in pursuing those goals.

Under their leadership, the company in 1981 developed and integrated a new emulsion technology and began operating an emulsion plant that became a model for similar operations worldwide. Other pioneering efforts over the years include breakthroughs at their quality control laboratory that increased the shelf life of their products tenfold, and the introduction of water-resistant products that allowed customers to take high-cost dynamite out of boreholes. Other company-sponsored innovations and technological advancements have impacted the industry through the introduction of new products and services, reduction of raw material costs, and increased manufacturing efficiency.

"All this has translated into savings that we've been able to pass along to our customers," relates Tony Nelson. "We're now involved in several joint ventures that will give us the strength to expand our markets and continue to grow in the future. Most importantly, it allows us to remain focused on what we do best — provide our customers with personalized services and professional products, helping to ensure their success and growth."

Nelson Brothers' customer list now includes four of the top five coal producers in the United States. Demand for their products and services has led to a growth in the company's employment rolls from the initial two brothers in 1956 to approximately 450 people today.

Because of the inherent risk in the manufacturing and application of explosives, safety remains today the overriding issue at Nelson Brothers that it was when Dugan and Olen first donned their hard hats almost 50 years ago. That original hard hat worn by Dugan Nelson is on display in the company's conference room, serving as a constant reminder of Nelson Brothers' commitment to safety, customer service, and the highest quality products for their customers.

Dugan and Olen Nelson are shown here with two industry innovations, bulk ANFO and new water resistant cartridges. Nelson Brothers, 40 years later, continues to innovate—improving product performance for its customers' use.

THE BANC CORPORATION

Providing Cost-Effective Financial Solutions

After enjoying his retirement for only 15 months, James A. Taylor was glancing through *The Birmingham News* in July of 1997 when a disturbing headline caught his eye. The John Hand building, one of downtown Birmingham's historic landmarks, was slated to be sold at auction after years of languishing in vacancy and neglect and sliding into a state of disrepair. Taylor resolved to purchase the storied old building and breathe new life into the structure rather than allow part of Birmingham's history to be forever lost to the wrecking ball.

"I told my wife I was going to buy that building and put a bank in it," Taylor relates.

Taylor, a native of Fayette, Alabama, had moved back to Birmingham in 1987, having lived here during the 1960s. He retired nine years later from a successful career in banking. The uncertain future of the historic building and the challenges of establishing and growing a new financial institution headquartered there intrigued him to the point of re-entering the professional world.

Only 63 days later, Taylor had purchased the building and assembled a group of investors who raised $26 million to purchase a bank in Warrior, Alabama, just north of Birmingham. After securing regulatory approval, Taylor moved the operation into the John Hand building, and opened the doors to The Bank on July 1, 1998.

Additional acquisitions were quickly lined up, and Taylor became the chairman of the newly formed *The Banc Corporation*. In its brief four year existence, the holding company has recorded phenomenal success. It now lists $1.4 billion in assets and is the seventh largest bank in Alabama. The Banc Corporation has also expanded its footprint, now operating 21 locations throughout Alabama and 14 in the Florida panhandle. The Corporation provides commercial banking products and services to over 52,000 consumer and commercial customers in both states. The Banc Corporation stock is publicly traded on the NASDAQ exchange.

"Our success has been due to the careful acquisition model we've followed," Taylor states. "Rather than just buying a bank, we've gone to a

select number of financial institutions and asked them to partner with us. Local leadership is retained, and the individual presidents are empowered to make decisions relating to the local banks. We're able to provide our customers with the services of the larger, regional banks, while still retaining the personal touch. We continue to achieve our goals by listening to our customers, understanding our markets, and providing cost-effective financial solutions."

The new look that The Bank brought to Birmingham's financial community also resulted in a new look for the John Hand building. The completely renovated, 21-story, 155,000 square foot building has played a major role in the revitalization of Birmingham's Central Business District.

The Bank's offices are spread over three floors of the building with other floors available for future expansion. The building's prime location on First Avenue and 20th Street North was instrumental in attracting some of Birmingham's major names in business and professional services and convincing them to establish their headquarters there. Spacious loft apartments on the upper floors have drawn people looking for a prestigious residential address in near proximity to their downtown business. Luxurious interiors, security, and incredible views are just some of the few amenities drawing prospective residents to the building.

The top two floors are occupied by the Birmingham Athletic Club, a premier health club ensconced in an incomparable atmosphere of rich wood interiors, extensive wine cellar, massive humidor, complete business office, and members' lounge.

The renovated building has turned heads across the country, including that of *The New York Times*, which carried a third of a page story on the startling transformation.

"The purchase and renovation of the John Hand building had probably more impact on the redevelopment of downtown Birmingham than any other single event," noted Michael Calvert, the president of Operation New Birmingham.

Photo: M. Lewis Kennedy, Jr.

Newly remodeled 3rd floor entrance.

148

EASTERN HEALTH SYSTEM, INC.

Eastern Health System, Inc. (EHS), the parent organization for three of the Birmingham area's premier healthcare facilities, traces its roots to a group of physicians and business leaders who founded East End Memorial Hospital in the East Lake area in the 1940s. After four decades of expansions and additions, the facility relocated in 1985 to the new Medical Center East. The hospital became the flagship facility of EHS, formed that same year. Its three hospital facilities—Medical Center East in Birmingham, Medical Center Blount in Oneonta, and St. Clair Regional Hospital in Pell City—offer community platforms for inpatient and outpatient services, and a variety of related programs.

Medical Center East is a 282-bed facility offering an impressive list of inpatient and outpatient health and medical services, and the highest level of sophisticated diagnostic and treatment technologies. With an active medical staff of over 200 physicians in 65 specialties, Medical Center East offers premier programs in Primary Care, Orthopaedics, Obstetrics, Cardiovascular Care, Cancer Treatment, and Emergency Care, as well as comprehensive services in Diabetes, Endoscopy, Continence, Same Day Surgery, Digestive Disorders, Bariatric Surgery, and Sleep Disorders.

EHS opened Medical Center Blount in Oneonta in 1999. The 40-bed hospital offers advanced services for medical, surgical, and intensive care patients, and a full range of outpatient services that serve as a model for the future of healthcare delivery. The medical staff's dedication to meeting the growing health and medical needs of Blount County is evidenced in the hospital's expanding list of specialized services, including Advanced Trauma, Oncology, Cardiology, Orthopaedics, Pediatrics, and Women's Health.

St. Clair Regional Hospital in Pell City entered into a unique operating agreement with EHS in 1995 to offer individuals in St. Clair County a full range of comprehensive healthcare and medical services. The 82-bed acute care facility provides skilled inpatient care, full outpatient and diagnostic services, home healthcare, primary care clinics, and a multi-specialty physician facility. The facility's medical staff includes more than 100 physicians in 19 medical specialties with enhanced capabilities ranging from nuclear medicine to cutting-edge bone densitometry.

"Eastern Health System, Inc. will continue to enhance the health, well-being, and quality of life for the people in the communities we serve," states Robert C. Chapman, FACHE, the organization's president and CEO. "We will accomplish our mission by adhering to the shared values of integrity, accountability, leadership, responsibility, and excellence."

Realizing that enhancing the quality of life for both individuals and the community extends far beyond the standard medical environment, EHS is involved in a number of programs and outreach services that meet the needs of patients and their families. A series of community-based primary care clinics ensures both quality and convenience, and home care programs at all facilities provide skilled services after hospitalization. Services to enrich the lives of the elderly and handicapped include a residential independent and assisted living facility, a handicapped and elderly apartment complex, a long term care facility, special programs in Respite Care and Adult Day Care, and a transportation service to medical appointments. Additionally, through its Family Practice Residency Program, the System works to provide trained physicians for the future.

Unified under Eastern Health System, Inc., all of these programs and services work together to ensure a broad continuum of care for the residents of the Birmingham metropolitan area.

Medical Center East is the flagship facility of Eastern Health System, Inc. formed in 1985. Its three hospital facilities — Medical Center East in Birmingham, Medical Center Blount in Oneonta and St. Clair Regional Hospital in Pell City — offer community platforms for inpatient and outpatient services, and a variety of related programs.

Dr. Lawrence Pijeaux

Dr. Lawrence Pijeaux stopped in front of the replica of a 1950s-era bus during a tour of the Birmingham Civil Rights Institute that he runs. A smile came over his face and he told a story.

"I'm a product of the Civil Rights movement," he said. "I sat behind screens on buses and graduated from a segregated school system."

Then, laughing, he explained that he became one of the first African American bus drivers in his home town.

"I went from riding in the back of the bus to driving it. I'd pull up to the bus stop and some white people would see me and wouldn't even get on the damn bus."

So, this educator who spent most of his years in schools says his job as executive director of the Civil Rights Institute "has special meaning in part because I see how far we have come. I can see the growth my people have made.

"As it relates to chronicling the history of the Civil Rights movement, there is no better place than here. It is important to have this institution on what we finally call Holy Ground (on 16th Street across from the 16th Street Baptist Church and Kelly Ingram Park). This is a national treasure. That's why this job is so special to me."

Dr. Pijeaux is at first formal. But later, during a tour of the institute, a sly sense of humor and an interesting viewpoint emerges.

"We were struggling for our rights when we came here in shackles," he said, standing in front of a dirty water fountain with a sign above that read 'colored.' "The fight for equality is a constant thread in our country.

"In the North there's a tendency to overlook racism. Whether we like it or not, it's been confronted here in the South. In the South we have struggled with equality in the forefront of our everyday life. In other parts of the country where I have lived racism is alive and well, but subtle."

As the tour continues, images of Martin Luther King Jr. and Fred Shuttlesworth pop onto screens and appear on walls. Voices from the past ring out. Dr. Pijeaux points to the jail cell door behind which Dr. King was incarcerated in Birmingham. "That bench was the actual bench in the cell," he said. "It was donated anonymously by the daughter of a police officer."

Dr. Pijeaux's job isn't just about history. He is proud of the Civil Rights Institute and its economic success.

"Right now the Institute has to function as a corporation," he said. "We are a business. Our product is the permanent exhibition."

"The art museum is willing to exhibit works of art from its collection here because we meet the standards of climate control and security. That's significant. We've been identified by the Alabama Bureau of Tourism as a tourist destination. That is significant because it will clearly support the idea that we have a positive impact on the city."

He talks of having the original copy of the Declaration of Independence at the Institute.

"18,000 people saw that document here," Dr. Pijeaux said. "It brought people from around the state to see our facility for the first time.

"People usually think of a renovated building and they are surprised when they see this magnificent facility. Word of mouth has really helped us. People can't believe how well maintained the facility is and how well they are treated by the staff. To have people compliment us on service is important. The way people are treated makes them become good will ambassadors."

"We have to operate like a corporation. However, we must be driven by our mission."

"This is a place where we can use lessons learned in the past to make a difference in the future," he said. "The Civil Rights Movement was really a human rights issue...We are dealing with human rights worldwide. That's in our mission.

"What we look at as racism is not black and white, it's green."

NATIONAL BANK OF COMMERCE

National Bank of Commerce is the lead bank of publicly traded Alabama National BanCorporation (ALAB). Alabama National's eleven bank subsidiaries in Alabama, Florida, and Georgia share in the same banking philosophy of localized decision–making and personalized service.

With headquarters in the historic Woodward Building in downtown Birmingham, National Bank of Commerce operates 16 branch offices in Jefferson, Shelby, and St. Clair Counties. At NBC, customers find personal and business banking services, wealth management, brokerage, mortgage loans, leasing, and insurance services. The bank's financial services are easily accessible through traditional branches, telephone banking, and the Internet.

"We don't sell products, we sell solutions," states Robert B. Aland, NBC's executive vice president. "The broad variety of businesses and services industries that make up the economy of Birmingham has created an excellent climate for business here. Our bankers focus on needs-based selling. We determine the needs of our business customers and help them select the right financial products and services to meet those needs. Integral to that process is recruiting, training, and nurturing key people and branch managers, which is what we strive to do."

"We offer the same personalized service to our individual customers," Aland continues. "NBC features numerous options for checking and savings accounts as well as loans, investments, leasing, and insurance services. We are proud to be a community bank offering the diversified products and services of a large regional financial institution."

John H. Holcomb III, the president of NBC and chairman of the board and chief executive officer at Alabama National BanCorporation, sees the institution's success rooted in its employees, directors, and management team. "ANB's success is attributable to outstanding employees operating in a customer-based environment," he noted in the 2001 Annual Report. "Another key has been the company's reliance on distributed decision making rather than a centralized approach. This fosters a sense of local ownership of decisions and performance, followed by local accountability for results."

NBC's operating philosophy has resulted in stability and growth. Assets grew to $1.3 billion by December 31, 2002, and a new office opened in 2002 to serve the rapidly growing Highway 150 area of Hoover.

2002 also proved to be a record-breaking year for Alabama National BanCorporation. Diluted earnings per share increased by over 20 percent over those of the previous year. Assets at December 31, 2002 grew to $3.3 billion, an increase of 16.6 percent over December 31, 2001.

The directors and management team of National Bank of Commerce and Alabama National BanCorporation are excited about the challenges and opportunities for growth in Birmingham and in the markets in which they operate. Taking an "owner's" view of reacting to those opportunities will further enhance share owner value and continue the institution's tradition of exceeding customers' expectations.

William E. Mathews, V, Robert B. Aland, John H. Holcomb, III, Richard Murray, IV, and Victor E. Nichol, Jr.

With headquarters in the historic Woodward Building in downtown Birmingham, National Bank of Commerce operates 16 branch offices in Jeffferson, Shelby, and St. Clair Counties. At NBC, customers find personal and business banking services, wealth management, brokerage, mortgage loans, leasing and insurance services.

LUCKIE & COMPANY

Disciplined Imagination.

Similar to the banyan tree whose roots are exposed above ground, the roots of Luckie & Company are clearly visible in the firm's headquarters offices on Lakeshore Drive. The vintage Smith Corona manual typewriter that Robert Luckie used when he launched the advertising business in 1953 is prominently

cialists, PR counselors and website designers has been seen across the country and around the world.

"We become a business partner with our clients rather than just a vendor," explains Tom Luckie, one of the firm's executive vice-presidents. "We provide a work environment where creative people can interact and share ideas that produce winning results for our clients. Our focus is integrity and producing value for our clients' adver-

 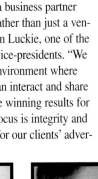 

Left to right: Smith Corona; Bob Luckie III; Tom Luckie; Ed Mizzell

displayed in a case in the foyer at the entrance to the firm's reception area. It serves as a visual reminder of the road the firm has traveled in growing from a small local advertising agency to one of the South's largest full-service communications, marketing, and public relations specialists.

While Robert Luckie remains involved with the business today, he has passed the reins to his sons and the talented management team that remains committed to the "Luckie Values" on which the company was founded a half century ago. Those 60 professionals work with clients to identify the goals they have for a particular project, outline strategic plans and initiatives designed to meet those goals, and then implement a program geared to producing quantifiable results. They have been successful for a diversified roster of local and national clients ranging from ACIPCO, Alabama Power, Blue Cross and Blue Shield of Alabama, Regions Financial Corp., ExpressOil to Bayer Advanced, Little Debbie, Papa John's Pizza, BellSouth, Ventura Foods, Mercedes-Benz U. S. International, U. S. Steel, and Colonial Bank. The work of Luckie strategic planners, creative spe-

tising dollars."

"It takes disciplined imagination to generate great results," said Luckie president Bob Luckie. "It takes discipline to find the best way to communicate to target customers, and the imagination to bring a creative solution to every facet of the job."

Luckie advertising campaigns and strategic public relations initiatives have translated into successful bottom-line results for their clients. They have also led to the company being recognized in the national and international arenas, most recently on the French Riviera. Luckie & Company was one of only two U.S. companies and the only Alabama agency to win a Media Lion Award among the 17,000 entries at the 2002 Cannes Lion Advertising Festival in Cannes, France in June.

Ed Mizzell joins Bob and Tom Luckie as part of the management team that will lead Luckie & Company into its next half century of growth and service to its clients. The leading edge technology that their staff utilizes today to create their award-winning campaigns may one day be displayed alongside the old Smith Corona typewriter in the Luckie & Company office of the future.

HAND ARENDALL, L.L.C.

Delivering Solutions to Difficult Problems.

Six decades of experience and a proven track record of successfully representing a diverse list of clients have made Hand Arendall one of the leading providers of legal services in Alabama. Organized in 1941, the firm currently lists 65 attorneys with expertise in all areas of traditional civil practice.

"From the outset, this firm was founded on the principle of delivering constructive, reasonable, and cost-effective solutions to difficult problems," says Roger Bates, a member of the firm. "Our client relationships are based on providing the highest quality, uncompromising legal services in a professional environment utilizing the finest resources available."

Hand Arendall's credentials include experience in virtually all areas of civil litigation, with over half of the firm's lawyers devoting their practices primarily to litigation. They regularly handle cases in state and federal forums in the southeastern United States, and have successfully litigated cases throughout the country. The national manufacturers, banks, medical facilities, insurance companies, and governmental entities. All have turned to Hand Arendall for the highest quality legal services in a timely and cost-effective manner. Each case and project is staffed with the goal of achieving success for the client with maximum efficiency.

The firm's corporate and business

Hand Arendall, one of the largest law firms in Alabama, currently maintains offices in Birmingham, Mobile, and Foley. Hand Arendall attorneys are licensed to practice law in a number of Southeastern states and the District of Columbia. They are frequently called upon by out-of-state law firms from throughout the country to serve as local counsel in a diverse

Six decades of experience and a proven track record of successfully representing a diverse list of clients have made Hand Arendall one of the leading providers of legal services in Alabama. Organized in 1941, the firm currently lists 65 attorneys with expertise in all areas of traditional civil and business practice.

firm's practice extends to all areas of the dispute resolution process, including trials, appeals, mediation, and arbitration.

Hand Arendall attorneys utilize a sophisticated computer network and litigation support system to manage their efforts. They also have the capability to go on-line directly with their clients.

That client list now includes a broad range of national and inter-

lawyers focus on handling all types of financial and corporate transactions, including the creation, maintenance, and reorganization of business entities; financing for both borrowers and lenders; bank formations and bank regulatory compliance issues; public and private securities; and governmental offerings. Tax, pension, and employee benefits lawyers advise businesses, not-for-profit institutions, and individuals.

array of legal issues.

"We're known for the long-term relationships we have established with our clients," states Roger Bates. "A reputation for integrity and achieving success for the client helps build the trust necessary to develop and sustain those relationships. We look forward to continuing that tradition of trust."

THE ELMER & GLENDA HARRIS
EARLY LEARNING CENTER OF BIRMINGHAM

Managed by Auburn University, the Center is directed by Dr. Byran B. Korth and Dr. Robbie B. Roberts, Assistant Professors at Auburn University.

In 1995, a unique partnership of business, government and education leaders brought to downtown Birmingham a new concept in early education for children. The public-private initiative, originally known as the Birmingham Early Learning Center, was the first project of the Birmingham Urban Revitalization Partnership, Inc. Designed to help revitalize economically distressed areas of the Magic City's urban core area, the Center operates as a state-of-the-art learning facility serving over 200 children from six weeks to six years old.

The Revitalization Partnership initiated a city-wide campaign to obtain corporate sponsorship to help launch the project. Corporate partners purchased child care spaces for their employees. Other partners provided scholarships for children of low-income families, as well as funding for outreach efforts and parent education.

The Department of Human Development and Family Studies in the College of Human Sciences at Auburn University manages the Center. Its two directors, Drs. Byran Korth and Robbie Roberts, hold Ph.D. degrees, and head a staff of 55 teachers and administrative personnel.

The Center is accredited by the National Association for the Education of Young Children, the nation's largest organization of early childhood educators. Only about five percent of all child care programs nationwide have met the rigorous standards for this accreditation. Yet, given the high standard of care and education offered, tuition remains competitive with other centers in Birmingham as a result of the corporate sponsorship.

"We have a four-fold mission: to provide quality education and care for young children; support and conduct research; educate college/university students; and work collaboratively with the community," states Dr. Byran Korth, Director of Children's Programs. "We offer a developmentally appropriate curriculum designed to help children develop social, emotional, cognitive, and physical skills. In addition, we serve as a research facility where professionals from around the nation come to study issues relating to childhood development and family relationships."

"We also have training and outreach missions," states Dr. Robbie Roberts, Director of Teacher Training and Outreach. "The Center provides observation and internship opportunities for hundreds of college students each year."

Outreach activities also include parenting education, as well as training for teachers and directors of other Birmingham metro centers. The Center serves as a mentor site for 25 metro area centers as part of a quality child care improvement program.

The facility is located on 14th Street and Seventh Avenue North in the heart of Birmingham's historic Civil Rights District. The name was changed in 2002 to the Elmer & Glenda Harris Early Learning Center of Birmingham to honor the couple who played such an important role in obtaining corporate sponsorship for the building of the Center.

Each of the 16 classrooms is equipped with developmentally appropriate materials designed to expose children to math, literacy, science, and art in an interactive atmosphere that promotes fun while learning. The rooms are staffed with teachers holding degrees and professional credentials in child development or early education. Color security cameras are located in each classroom and the inner courtyard playgrounds, and can be viewed by parents through a monitoring station located in the building's lobby.

The Center has become a model program showcasing what can be accomplished through the collaborative efforts of business, higher education, and government. Dozens of educators from around the world toured the facility when it hosted a National Science Foundation funded conference on the Transition from Childhood to the Workforce. The center was also featured on the NBC Nightly News.

"We are pleased to be providing these services to children and families of Birmingham," Dr. Korth relates, "and to raising the standards for quality child care in this country."

AMERICAN CAST IRON PIPE COMPANY

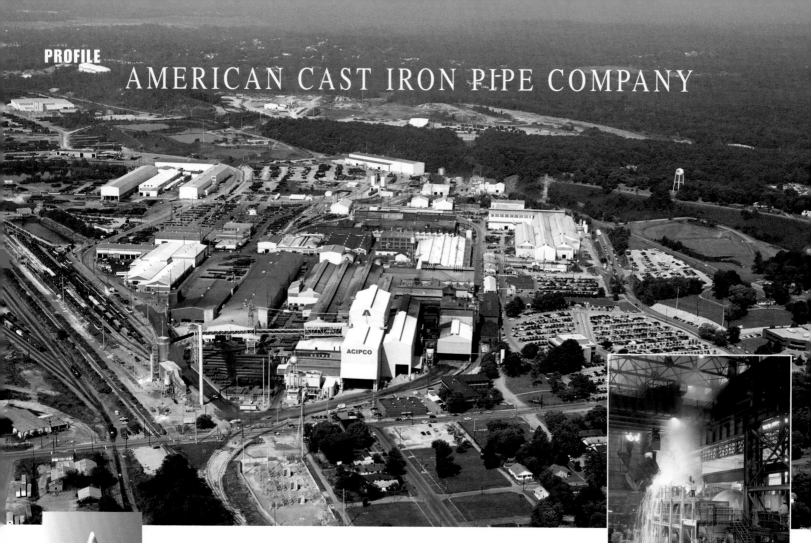

American Cast Iron Pipe Company (ACIPCO) has been a major player in Birmingham's economy since the company was founded in 1905, helping establish the Magic City's early reputation as the industrial center of the South. As one of Birmingham's oldest companies, ACIPCO has grown to become the largest manufacturing employer in the city and the largest individual iron pipe casting plant in the world.

Each day, more than 2,000 tons of ACIPCO's diversified line of products are produced for the waterworks, capital goods, and energy industries. The privately held company markets worldwide a wide range of ductile iron pipe and fittings, valves, pumps, centrifugally cast steel tubes, electric resistance welded steel pipe, and spiral-welded steel pipe.

The company's corporate headquarters and principal manufacturing facility, which employs almost 2,400 people, are located on a 2,000-acre site in Birmingham with almost 60 acres of plant under roof. ACIPCO

subsidiaries and district sales offices are in various locations across the country.

Pioneering new technology and continuously improving and upgrading its production methods have been the hallmarks of the company since its inception. ACIPCO's early work with ductile iron pipe led to the basic design theories from which national standards were established, and that tradition endures today. ACIPCO has remained on the cutting edge of technology and processes for its industry, launching major facility improvements in the steel pipe and ductile iron pipe plants. These include a new spiral-welded steel pipe plant, construction of the world's largest furnace of its kind for melting foundry iron; and installation of a full-scale scrap metal recycling plant for supplying raw materials and contributing to environmental stewardship.

In addition to setting standards for efficiency, ACIPCO has also led the way in the development of human relations in the workplace. John Eagan, the company's first president, believed that the 'Golden Rule' should be as important in business as in everyday life. He introduced a number

of policies considered revolutionary in his day—a medical plan and health-care facility for ACIPCO employees, retirees, and their families; a safety program; home building plan supported by company loans; company pension plan; improved racial relations; and others.

Eagan's legacy continues today. ACIPCO operates as a beneficial trust with both employees and customers as beneficiaries. ACIPCO Health Services utilizes more than 60 health-care professionals to provide medical and dental care to more than 10,000 employees, retirees, and their families at the company's on-site clinic. In addition, the 5,000 square foot Eagan Center for Wellness offers employees and their families a complete on-site fitness center with aerobics, cardiovascular, and strength conditioning equipment.

A result of these employee benefits has been an average length of service among ACIPCO employees of an impressive 20 years. Another is the company's listing six consecutive years on Fortune magazine's *100 Best Companies to Work For in America*. ACIPCO is the only pipe manufacturer to ever receive the honor.

ACIPCO has been a major player in Birmingham's economy since the company was founded in 1905, helping establish the Magic City's early reputation as the industrial center of the South. As one of Birmingham's oldest companies, ACIPCO has grown to become the largest iron pipe casting plant in the world.

PROTECTIVE INDUSTRIAL INSURANCE COMPANY

An Emphasis on Personalized Service

ne of the oldest African-American owned businesses in Alabama traces its roots to the son of a former slave who saw a need and sought to fill it. In the 1890s, Charles Morgan Harris left school after completing the sixth grade to enter the business world. He began training as an embalmer, and in 1899, he joined forces with his sister to open the Davenport and Harris Funeral Home. Harris' son joined him in the business in the 1920s, and they launched the Protective Burial Society, the precursor of Protective Industrial Insurance Company.

The elder Harris found that there was a pressing need in the African-American community for quality burial insurance. He and his son began by offering this service to families who paid the weekly or monthly premiums in cash to agents who canvassed the community on a door-to-door "home service" basis. In the 1950s, the company expanded its scope of services to include industrial insurance policies with higher benefits. Protective Industrial now offers traditional whole life and term products in addition to the burial policies on which the company was founded.

"We continue to emphasize the personalized service on which we built our reputation," said James C. Harrison, Protective's president and CEO. "Our founder identified a traditionally under-served market, and offered a service to fill their needs. Over the years, we have expanded our list of insurance products to better serve our customers. We focus on providing the ultimate in personalized service to the people who put their trust in us. Protective Industrial was founded on integrity, and we have never strayed from that principle. In over eight decades of operation we have never missed a payroll or failed to pay a claim."

Over 80,000 customers around the state have sought the peace of mind that comes from relying on Protective Industrial Insurance Company. The company is headquartered in Birmingham, but its representatives work as agents in markets including Mobile, Montgomery, Tuscaloosa, Anniston, Selma, and Decatur. The company's success is a result of the service provided by those representatives and the strong, conservative management team that has focused on consistently delivering quality service at a reasonable price.

Harrison cites a number of challenges that he faced when he assumed the company's helm in 1995. He began by assessing the resources of Protective Industrial and focusing on how to operate more efficiently. Several satellite offices were closed, and personnel were re-trained to work as independent agents in the markets served.

The results were impressive. Shareholder value has tripled in the seven years that Harrison has guided the company's growth.

"We plan to continue to expand our range of services and the quality products we offer," he notes. "We're also exploring the possibilities of moving into markets outside Alabama. We'll continue the careful, conservative growth policies that have served us well in the past."

THE METRO GRILL

A Gourmet American Grill

In March of 2001, the latest addition to the list of premier white table-cloth restaurants in the Birmingham area opened its doors to discerning diners. The Metro Grill, located in the Brookwood Village complex on Lakeshore Drive, is a gourmet American grill featuring casual fine dining and live entertainment.

"We were voted 'Best New Restaurant' in the Birmingham Weekly Readers' Poll in 2002, and among the top three restaurants overall in Birmingham," says Rick Tuttle, the restaurant's general manager. "We're extremely proud to have been so honored in such a short period of time. It tells us we've filled a niche in this area for providing excellent food and service in a unique setting."

Open for lunch on weekdays and for dinner Monday through Saturday, the Metro Grill tempts diners with a wide variety of dishes, each prepared with an unwavering commitment to quality.

The luncheon menu, served from 11 a.m. until 2 p.m., consists of appetizers, salads, and main courses ranging from hickory grilled beef tenderloin and Carolina trout to vegetable lasagna and roast black Angus sirloin sandwiches.

Nighttime brings out a different array of epicurean delights. Guests can begin their culinary experience with appetizers of roast sweet peppers, sautéed crab cakes, duck confit, cornmeal fried soft shell crab, and other delicacies. A crisp salad of iceberg lettuce or fried egg salad makes an excellent second plate. Evening entrées include a number of items for which the Metro Grill has become widely known. Signature Gulf Coast

seafood dishes include grilled day boat black grouper and Destin cobia. Meat lovers have applauded the pork tenderloin, veal chop, hickory grilled

spring lamb, and the pork tenderloin. Other favorites include the duck l'orange and pan roasted stuffed chicken.

Whatever entrée the diner chooses,

Whatever entrée the diner chooses, the Metro Grill has the perfect wine to complement the meal. The restaurant's extensive cellar features dozens of labels with an emphasis on the French Rhone wines. The waitstaff is trained to be attentive, not intrusive. Each stands ready to offer assistance in recommending the right wine to accompany the meal. Full bar service is also available.

the Metro Grill has the perfect wine to complement the meal. The restaurant's extensive cellar features dozens of labels with an emphasis on the French Rhone wines. The waitstaff is trained to be attentive, not intrusive. Each stands ready to offer assistance in recommending the right wine to accompany the meal. Full bar service is also available. For those special occasions and private parties, the Metro Grill offers complete catering services.

Those with a sweet tooth have learned that the chefs have a number of belt-loosening creations that are as tempting to the eye as they are to the palate. The most difficult decisions after a meal are selecting from the home baked bread pudding with bourbon créme Anglaise; flourless chocolate tort; raspberry crisp; or strawberries soaked in Grand Marnier with Polenta cake.

The Metro Grill has also achieved a reputation as an exciting entertainment venue. A jazz pianist regularly provides background music for diners from seven until ten p.m. Monday through Saturday. In addition, the adjoining stage, dance floor, and back bar rocks Thursday, Friday, and Saturday nights beginning at 10:30 with the sounds of nationally acclaimed musical groups and the best of local talent. The dance floor remains crowded until the wee hours.

Birmingham diners were quick to discover the Metro Grill soon after the restaurant opened. The fine dining, comfortable atmosphere, and quality live entertainment they found there has kept them coming back.

SLOSS REAL ESTATE GROUP

Redefining the City's Future

Members of the Sloss family have been helping to transform the skyline of Birmingham since the 19th century when Colonel James Withers Sloss founded the giant furnaces on First Avenue North that forged the Magic City's future in iron and steel. Over a century later, the Colonel's great-great granddaughter serves as president of a company that continues to redefine the city's future through a wide variety of urban renovation and construction projects.

Cathy Sloss Crenshaw is the president of Sloss Real Estate Group, a multi-disciplined real estate firm headquartered in Birmingham. Her grandfather, A. Page Sloss, founded the company in 1920, and her father, A. Page Sloss, Jr., served as company president for many years before becoming chairman of the board. They also work tirelessly for the revitalization and enhancement of Birmingham's unique commercial districts, believing that the city itself is important to and provides identity for the entire metropolitan area.

Their work began in the Lakeview district, where the company spearheaded a public/private initiative that created a master plan for the redevelopment of the 36-block area. It includes Pepper Place, where Sloss Real Estate has renovated 11 buildings to transform a group of abandoned warehouses into Birmingham's premier design center. Pepper Place also includes a Farmers' Market, theater, and restaurants, and has been featured in magazines and on television regionally and nationally as an example of significant urban redevelopment.

Other ventures include renovation of the former *Southern Living* Building and its neighbor, the quarter-million-square-foot First Commercial Bank Building. Both were redeveloped into Class A office space. The former Rust Building became Ridge Park, offering one of the finest views of downtown Birmingham in the city Ridge Park played a major role in the $100 million reinvestment into the surrounding Highland Avenue area. These and other projects have earned Sloss numerous awards for design, construction, landscaping, and preservation.

While a number of the most recognized features on Birmingham's skyline bear the Sloss Real Estate Group signature, the newest jewel in the company's portfolio is One Federal Place. The 11-story building, jointly developed by Sloss and Atlanta's Barry Real Estate Companies, added 300,000 square feet of Class A office space, new retail businesses, and a pocket park and fountain to downtown Birmingham. It also attracted Bradley Arant Rose & White, Alabama's largest law firm, to the 19th Street and Fifth Avenue North location. The $50 million glass and granite structure is the largest downtown office construction project in over a decade. Plans to redevelop the Old Federal Reserve building on the same block are also underway.

In November, 2000, Sloss Real Estate Group, Inc. and its partner, Integral Properties, were awarded the Hope VI Project. Demolition began in February, 2002, on six blocks of public housing known as Metropolitan Gardens. Twelve city blocks are included in the Hope VI master plan, which will offer lofts, townhouses and flats, parks, schools, offices, and retail space. A. Page Sloss expresses optimism about the potential for Hope VI to "change the way people feel about visiting and living in downtown Birmingham."

"Birmingham has always been a great place," Cathy Crenshaw adds. "Our extensive tree cover, varying topography, and beautiful historic buildings are something everyone should be proud of. We're happy to be a part of the ongoing work of creating community in this wonderful city."

Left: Pete Sloss, Sloss Real Estate Chairman of the Board, and Cathy Sloss Crenshaw, President, enjoy the Pepper Place Saturday Farmer's Market. Below: The Ridge Park Building in front of the Birmingham city skyline. Above: The view from Sloss Real Estate Group's offices in the Ridge Park Building. Above top: Ridge Park's entrance.

LOWRY, STERLING & THOMAS, LLC

The name Lowry has been associated with quality printing and print services in the Birmingham area for almost a century. Starting in 1904 as a small regional printer, the company has grown into a full-line communications and specialty products provider. Their experienced staff is able to analyze a customer's needs and develop, from design to fulfillment, a product targeted to meet them. Lowry serves many of the largest and most prestigious commercial and institutional customers in the Southeast including the University of Alabama at Birmingham, University of the South, Auburn University in Montgomery, the Birmingham Regional Chamber of Commerce, the National Bank of Commerce, and Covenant Bank.

"With the traditional print communication provider, there is only one set of capabilities, one set of equipment, and expertise in only one area of production. The Lowry approach," according to Executive Vice-President Gordon Sterling, "is to find the most efficient and cost effective source of print services through a consortium of suppliers. And since in today's world, ink on paper is not the only method of communication, Lowry is active in CD duplication, website design, and promotional products. They also provide packaging, delivery, and mailing services for a wide variety of customers."

Throughout its history, Lowry has specialized in unique and challenging projects. For over 20 years Lowry has produced, packaged, delivered, and provided security for a variety of testing and evaluation programs for the education community. Customers include the University of Alabama, the University of Alabama at Birmingham, the State of Alabama, and various testing and evaluation companies throughout the nation.

With the growth of the Internet, Lowry has recently branched out to provide promotional products that can be ordered online. Over 600,000 advertising items, designed to include the customer's logo and message, are available. The products range from inexpensive novelty items to top-of-the-line awards or appreciation gifts. Lowry's services in this area include researching the best source and/or venue for a particular promotional effort. Personalized greeting cards, letterheads, business cards, labels and envelopes are also available and can be quickly and economically ordered via the computer. Staying true to its roots, Lowry still provides high-quality process printing of everything from brochures to coffee table books and periodicals.

"We've taken the heritage of quality built by Lowry Printing over the last 100 years," says Bob Thomas, President and CEO, "and moved into the twenty-first century with an ever-evolving array of products and services not available from the traditional commercial printer."

Above: Bob Thomas, president, and Gordon Sterling, executive vice president, of Lowry Sterling & Thomas, LLC. Below: Sterling and Barry Mize check a proof on the press.

COLONIAL BANK

Just over 20 years ago, Colonial Bank, a subsidiary of The Colonial BancGroup, Inc., became part of the financial landscape of the South as a full service bank eager to provide a full range of financial services to its customers. The mission of the bank's founders was to maintain a community bank focus while offering all the services and products of the largest mega-banks.

A glance at Colonial's track record over those years indicates that the people who have guided the bank have not only met, but exceeded the goals of the founders. Colonial BancGroup's assets have soared dramatically from $166 million in 1981 to close to $16 billion today. The 21 Colonial Bank offices in the Birmingham region now report assets of almost $800 million. Close to 200 people are employed at Colonial offices in the Jefferson, Shelby, Tuscaloosa, and Walker County area.

"We've done this through carefully studied acquisitions, steady internal growth, and a second-to-none team of banking professionals serving our customers," says Jack Naramore, the president and CEO of Colonial's Birmingham region. "We've stayed our original course of offering a full range of quality services and financial products while retaining our 'community bank' focus. Many of our staff members have come to us from other banks in the area. They appreciate our friendly work environment and our streamlined operations which is free of much of the cumbersome bureaucracy that identifies many other banks. Our operations are streamlined allow our managers to make decisions and move quickly. The quality of our employees and our dedication to customer service are what separate us from other banks."

In recent years, Colonial BancGroup has strategically expanded its presence in Alabama as part of a long-term strategy of sustained, controlled, qualitative growth. The multi-state holding company now lists more than 270 full service offices in Alabama, Florida, Georgia, Tennessee, Texas, and Nevada. More than 50 community banks have been acquired and merged into Colonial Bank, integrating them into a structure that contributes to Colonial's community banking philosophy while achieving corporate synergies and efficiencies. Over the past five years, Colonial has concentrated on further expansion from its base in Alabama into markets in Florida, Georgia, Nevada, and Texas which are expected to grow faster than other areas of the country.

Colonial's banking professionals will be welcoming these new customers with an expanding range of services to meet their ever-changing needs. Business and individual customers can now avail themselves of Colonial's cash management services, wealth management products, international banking, electronic banking, and other solutions to financial needs.

"Colonial Bank has had a significant impact on the Birmingham region in the past," Naramore points out, "and will continue to be a major player in the region's future. We are one of the largest residential construction lenders in the market. We'll continue to invest in quality assets, and remain active in developing new strategies, services, and products to better serve our customers. The long-lasting relationships we've established with the people who have put their trust in us will remain the cornerstone of Colonial's success in this community and in the other markets we serve."

Personal service to those communities is also a high priority for Colonial Bank's employees, and it begins at the top. Jack Naramore stays active in a number of civic programs ranging from serving on the Metropolitan Development Board, Leadership Birmingham, and the Birmingham-Southern College Athletic Foundation Board to coaching Little League baseball and softball in Vestavia. Colonial Bank is a proud supporter of the Bruno's Memorial Classic, United Way, City Stages, and other community and charitable events.

FRANK S. BUCK, P.C.

Frank S. Buck, attorney,
represents clients in diverse cases, and concentrates his practice
in plaintiff's personal injury law.

As the son of a family practice physician growing up in Ionia, Michigan, Frank S. Buck knew that he did not want to follow his father's lead and enter the medical profession. His passion from the time he was a youngster was to become an attorney.

After obtaining his bachelor's degree at Michigan State, Buck attended Samford's Cumberland School of Law in Birmingham. He remained in Birmingham after graduating from Cumberland in 1975, and opened a law practice where he could serve the people in this region.

In general practice for his first few years, Buck is now widely known as a plaintiff's personal injury attorney with a proven track record of prompt, successful settlements for his clients. He now concentrates his efforts on automobile, trucking, and railroad accidents; wrongful death cases; apartment/rental fires; wrongful prescriptions; defective products; and on-the-job injuries. Licensed to practice in Alabama and Florida, Buck has successfully represented clients throughout the Southeastern states.

After being headquartered in the City Federal Building for 20 years, Buck moved in 1995 into an historic Prairie Mission-style home on Birmingham's Southside that he has been renovating to its original style of the early 1900's. Decorated by Buck with a large collection of period antiques, the building is listed by the Jefferson County and Alabama Historical Commissions.

Now almost three decades old, Buck's practice is defined by a large percentage of referral business. "This is probably the sincerest compliment I can get," he notes. "It means that my clients were pleased enough with my service that they recommended me to their friends and family when legal assistance was needed. Building relationships is the most important part of being successful in this business. We have worked very hard for our clients over the years, and are pleased that they are comfortable in recommending us to others."

Buck's practice includes one other associate and five legal assistants. He offers free consultation and home appointments when clients are unable to come to the office. Buck also publishes a quarterly newsletter with information, updates, and news pertaining to his areas of practice.

Because the legal profession is in a perpetual state of change, Buck maintains an ever vigilant eye on the industry to remain on the cutting edge. He does this through continuing education above and beyond what is required annually for attorneys to remain licensed.

Fair. Fast. Efficient. These three characteristics are the basis for any successful law firm, and have been the cornerstones on which Frank S. Buck has built his successful practice.

COMPASS BANK

The will to provide an unmatched level of customer service and consistently exceed customer expectations has defined Compass Bank as a financial institution that continues to outperform the industry. Over the past two decades, the company has expanded its footprint dramatically, entering some of he highest growth and economically diverse markets in the Western states.

Compass Bank, a subsidiary of Compass Bancshares, a Birmingham-based financial holding company, has $23 billion in assets and operates more than 300 full service banking offices in Alabama, Arizona, Colorado, Florida, Nebraska, New Mexico, and Texas. Compass is among the top 40 U.S. bank holding companies by asset size, and ranks among the top earners of its size based on return on equity.

While the recent slowing of the national economy and continued economic uncertainty created a headwind for many businesses and financial institutions, Compass has proven its resiliency. The company's earnings per share continued a climbing pattern, now in its 14th consecutive year. Dividends per share have increased for 21 consecutive years.

"We continue to believe that generating consistent growth in earnings is the best way to ensure that long term value is created for our shareholders, and we will continue to focus on the fundamentals that brought these results," states D. Paul Jones, Jr., Compass' chairman and chief executive officer.

Locally, the 2,500 employees of Compass Bank staff 21 conveniently located retail branch offices and three operations facilities. The company's team of financial professionals offers a full range of services in four primary business lines—retail banking, corporate banking, asset management, and insurance.

The personalized service commitment of its bankers, combined with the latest in technology infrastructure, have become the hallmarks of Compass Bank. Each Compass associate operates along a simple business axiom ñ treat every customer the way you would want to be treated. Whether consulting with a company's top executives on interest rate management or long-term plans for the company, Compass professionals know that business flows from connecting with customers and meeting their financial needs with innovation, personal interest, and a commitment to providing a superior level of service.

That connection has vaulted Compass to the Forbes Platinum 400 list of America's best companies. It has also led to a place on Keefe, Bruyette, & Woods Honor Roll for the past five consecutive years as one of the country's 13 best performing banks over the past 10 years.

"Compass has been a recognized leader in the industry because of our long-standing commitment to our customers," says Randall L. Haines, the bank's regional president. "We know that offering financial solutions and working as partners with our customers sets us apart from other financial institutions. We look forward to the future with enthusiasm and optimism as we continue to serve the needs of the customers in our markets."

Randall L. Haines, Compass Bank's Alabama Corporate Banking Executive and Birmingham City President (left), and bank customer John Stein, Chairman and Chief Executive Officer of Golden Enterprises, Inc. at Golden Flake's Birmingham facilities.

Compass is located in:

AL	GA
AZ	NE
CO	NM
DC	TN
FL	TX

▲ Loan Production Office
● Cities With Bank Offices
Ⓒ Company Headquarters

Charles Ghigna

Charles Ghigna's world is different than ours. It's full of rhymes and giggles and pudgy cheeked children whose laughs are as bright as the sun in the windows of his Homewood home.

His mustache lifted as he smiled. The crow's feet grew at the corners of his bright eyes. "I'm more inspired here, more at home," he said. "I can look over the tree tops behind the house and hear the children's voices from the church."

If you have a child younger than 15, there is a good chance you have seen Ghigna, a tall, trim man who more often than not is wearing a shirt with a Walt Disney logo on the pocket. That's because "Father Goose" has been writing children's books of verse for Disney and other national publishers for more than 10 years. Ghigna is ever-present, reading poetry and talking with children all over Birmingham and the country. He has 50 speaking engagements a year.

Ghigna lives in a comfortable brick home on a sidewalk-lined street. On his Jeep is a vanity license plate that reads "PA GOOSE" after his 1994 book of children's poetry entitled Father Goose. He writes in an attic room with neat filing cabinets, a roll-top desk and a typewriter. In the cabinets are poems and books and ideas.

Eating lunch at the Great Wall restaurant on this sunny day, Ghigna talked of his success, of watching his son Chip grow and about the pleasure of unleashing his imagination for a living.

"He (Chip) has this amazing gift," Ghigna said. "Every morning he gets up and thinks he can conquer the world. He helps me see the little boy in me. That's when I do my best."

Then: "The most important thing in life is hope. You get up early in the morning and you have hope. You have to have competitiveness to have hope."

That competitiveness was important to Ghigna early in his career when he was struggling for recognition. He was teaching at the Alabama School of Fine Arts and writing "serious" poetry when he began to search for another market.

"I don't apologize for any of that (writing children's poems). I paid my dues for years in the children's magazines. Friends say 'Gosh, you got lucky,' but that's not the case. I wrote for that market for 10 years. I went to the library and read those magazines. I studied them."

Getting published was difficult at first, but eventually he began to know some of the editors. One of those editors at Disney is now his agent in New York.

"The fact that I was not in New York made it difficult," he said. "I have a really good agent in New York now. Almost none of the New York publishers will look at unsolicited manuscripts."

Ghigna no longer has a problem selling projects to New York publishing houses. He has just finished the third in a series of math books for Random House and he has signed a contract with Simon & Schuster to write three books. He worked all summer on a book of poems for "boys who hate poems. It is a book of poems on sports and other themes of interest for teens." He also will have a book published for Halloween in 2003 called *21 Spooktacular Poems*.

Writing, in the end, is a business. And Ghigna knows that more than most. But that smile, those crow's feet, that childlike excitement in his voice transcends the business. Ghigna is not a businessman.

It was another lunch at the same Chinese restaurant a half dozen years ago when he said, "This could all go away as quickly as it came. If it did, I would still be a writer."

Isabel Rubio

Isabel Rubio's tiny office in a beautiful old dark corner on the third floor of the Southside Baptist Church is a clutter. A black and white photograph of Andy Warhol stares from a bulletin board filled with notes and colorful, scenic posters in Spanish. A big toy tarantula hangs from a string behind her head.

The office is busy, much like its occupant. The phone rings constantly; more often than not Rubio answers in English, "Good morning, HICA," and then breaks into light-speed Spanish.

"We're the point of contact for Latinos in the community," says the executive director of the Hispanic Interest Coalition of Alabama. "Think of plopping yourself in Uzbekhistan and what you would need. We had a woman show up at our door in labor. They get their keys locked in their car and don't even know how to call a locksmith."

On this cold, overcast day Rubio is handling the office alone. She is giving directions to an interpreter going on a job, reminding him to return a form to HICA.

"The language barrier is huge," she says. "We need to make the public aware of the need for interpreters. And Latinos need to understand that they have the right to ask for services."

The radio is tuned to the UN debate about Iraq.

"All of that," Rubio says, pointing to the radio, "depends on interpreters. Even when we all speak the same language we misunderstand each other. Throw in another language and think about it. Interpreters have to be trained.

"I don't do that. I can get by, but you do not want me interpreting for you if you're bleeding. You would be in trouble. The community needs folks who are bilingual, but also trained. Being an interpreter is a profession. We have access to about 50 interpreters."

While she is not a trained interpreter, it was Rubio's confidence in her skill with Spanish that led her to found HICA two years ago.

"This is what I'm supposed to be doing," she says, leaning forward on the cluttered desk. "Things that never made sense to me before in my life now make sense."

Rubio explains that her maternal grandfather was a Mexican who came to this country. She was made aware of her Latino heritage from her mother, who died when Mrs. Rubio was young.

"Then two years ago I met a Mexican woman who was dying of cancer and I had the honor of being with her at the end," she says. "That gave me confidence in my ability to handle the language. I keep a picture of the woman here. That experience gave me the confidence to go forward with this."

Rubio had been working in social services in Birmingham for eight years when she had that experience. She says that helped her realize a calling to recognize her heritage and to use her skill to aid the growing Latino community in Birmingham.

"I didn't grow up seeing myself as a Latino," she says. "I've always been proud of my Latino heritage, but didn't consider that a big part of my life. Identity is a fluid thing. I definitely identify myself now with my Latino heritage. I realize now that I was taking steps my whole life that led me in this direction."

That direction is HICA, which provides information on resources, services and interpreters. Rubio's coalition has established interpreter services and published the first edition of a community resource guide in Spanish. HICA also trains bilingual candidates to interpret in the medical, social service and judicial areas.

"Latinos are going to be a permanent part of this community," she says. "People want to be here because this country is a great place to be. Ninety percent of the folks who come here, come here to contribute. They take a chance to come here. They come here and things happen, they happen."

Rubio took a chance as well.

"Stepping out to do this... The funding is always insecure," she says. "It's very overwhelming. The public doesn't realize there are just two of us here in this office. But it'll come."

Then, "People don't realize how simple it is to help."

THE COLLATERAL FAMILY OF COMPANIES

Improving the Lives of Individuals and Families

For seven decades, the family of companies founded by W.T. Ratliff has been engaged in virtually all aspects of real estate lending, investment, brokerage, property management, and financial services. The Collateral Family of Companies, owned today primarily by Mr. Ratliff's descendants, continue to play a leading role in improving the lives of individuals and families in the market areas the company serves.

NEW SOUTH FEDERAL SAVINGS BANK

Robert M. Couch
President and CEO
New South Federal Savings Bank

The history of New South Federal Savings Bank is firmly rooted in the origination and servicing of single family mortgages. That activity continues to account for the lion's share of the bank's business today.

With one full service deposit branch office in Birmingham and 40 loan production offices in 13 states, the bank's lending activities are funded primarily through customer deposits in CD's, IRA's, and Money Market accounts. Depositors are attracted from all 50 states as well as several foreign countries through listings in web-based rate charts and newspapers, direct marketing activities, and through deposit brokers.

New South is the largest thrift and the sixth largest depository institution, based on asset size, headquartered in Alabama. The bank enjoyed a banner year in 2002, including record loan production in a number of asset categories. New South was recognized as the top mortgage lender in Jefferson and Shelby Counties of Alabama for the fourth year in a row.

"Our people, our products, our attention to details, and our focus on customer service have contributed to our success as a mortgage lender," says Robert M. Couch, the bank's president and chief executive officer. "These are just some of the reasons that we are ranked as the top mortgage lender in our local market. For an institution of our size, it's important that our products and services are innovative and competitive. We offer over 100 mortgage products to enable us to serve the needs of virtually any borrower. Our deposit offerings are very competitive, routinely showing up in national rate listings, and attracting deposits from all 50 states. That's quite an accomplishment for a bank with just one deposit branch."

COLLATERAL MORTGAGE CAPITAL, LLC

Dave Roberts
President and CEO
Collateral Mortgage Capital, LLC

This privately owned commercial mortgage banking firm is the largest in Alabama and ranks 34th among lenders nationwide, according to a recent Mortgage Bankers Association survey. Now boasting a multi-billion dollar servicing portfolio, the firm remains headquartered in Birmingham with offices throughout the country.

Collateral Mortgage Capital provides financing for all types of commercial and multi-family real estate on a national basis. The firm represents life insurance companies, pension fund advisers, commercial banks, and Fannie Mae and Freddie Mac, the two quasi-governmental agencies in the home ownership and rental housing finance business. The company is also an active lender through FHA-insured loan programs and is the exclusive correspondent for its affiliate, New South Federal Savings Bank. Collateral pursues lending opportunities for apartments and a variety of commercial developments, such as office buildings, shopping centers, healthcare, and industrial property.

Founded in 1933 primarily as a residential mortgage banking firm, the company shifted its focus toward multi-family and commercial real estate in 1990, shifting single family residential mortgage origination to New South Federal Savings Bank. President and CEO Dave Roberts helped re-shape the company's direction. Beginning with a handful of employees and a portfolio under $25 million, the company reached the $1 billion mark in 1997 and the $2 billion plateau only three years later. In 2001, Collateral closed loans amounting to almost $900 million while revenues grew by over 69 percent. The company's commercial servicing portfolio grew 65 percent from $2.012 billion at the beginning of 2001 to today's $4.2 billion.

"With a multi-billion dollar servicing portfolio for over 60 investors, Collateral is embarking on a long-term strategy to build a strong national platform for our multi-family and commercial real estate lending activities that will serve both our borrowers and investors well," said Roberts. "Collateral highly values these relationships and our growth will remain guided by our philosophy of creating superior value for our customers while providing service that is unmatched within the industry."

SOUTHLAND NATIONAL INSURANCE

Dennis Painter
President and CEO
Southland National
Insurance Corporation

Based in Tuscaloosa, Alabama, Southland National Insurance Corporation has been active in advance funeral planning since 1988. Southland is a legal reserve life insurance company focusing on pre-need services to its funeral home customers. The Company's experienced professionals provide consultation and assistance on an individual basis.

Southland's policies and programs are designed for the pre-need market, and provide value, integrity, and performance. Marketing programs are professionally produced to enhance the client's image and assist in their pre-need efforts.

Southland's insurance products are among the finest in the pre-need industry. Pre-need funding plans are available in Single, Three, Five, and Ten Pay Options with immediate or graded death benefits. Southland provides a complete portfolio of Final Expense Plans processed on a simplified underwriting basis to the increasing number of funeral homes offering final expense products to their customers. The Company also offers trust funded

funeral plans that provide additional options and flexibility for funeral homes. The Company has the capability, if allowed by applicable law, to convert a current trust account to insurance. Marketing alliances with major casket companies provide Casket Protection specified on pre-arranged funeral plans funded with Southland National policies. Through New South Federal Savings Bank, Southland National offers funeral homes an attractive At Need Funeral Finance Program with convenient payment options of up to five years.

"We have grown from a company with a single funeral home customer in 1988 to one of the region's premier providers of insurance and financial services today," states Dennis Painter, the company's president. "Our success is a result of our strength in relationship building, our exceptional service, and our offering of value added services to our customers."

COLLATERAL BENEFITS GROUP

Kent Howard
Executive Vice President
Collateral Benefits Group

The newest member of the Collateral family, Collateral Benefits Group (CBG), was launched in 2001, building upon a 20-year heritage of administrative services in the benefits arena. Its vision is to provide associations and employers with voluntary and employer-sponsored benefit programs developed to the individual requirements of their members or employees.

CBG does this by offering a broad spectrum of benefits. These products and services are tailored to fit the client's specific needs. In some instances we have created unique programs when traditional offerings did not offer the required flexibility. Finally, we strive to deliver them with truly superior customer service and attention to detail.

More than 120 of the state's leading organizations have turned to Collateral Benefits Group for benefit assistance, including the 92,000 member Alabama Education Association, Baptist Health System, and the Drummond Companies.

JEFFERSON COUNTY BOARD OF EDUCATION

A celebration in Linn Park in 1988 marked 100 years of public education in Jefferson County. From a circuit riding teacher on horseback over a century ago, public education in the county has evolved into the Jefferson County Board of Education — operator of the second largest school system in Alabama in terms of student enrollment.

Over 41,000 students attend classes each day in 60 schools in the Jefferson County system. Each school in the system is fully accredited. Since 1985, six Jefferson County schools have been honored by the U.S. Department of Education with the national "Blue Ribbon" status. The Board today administers a budget in excess of $250 million.

"From the board level to the individual school sites, our focus in Jefferson County is to promote excellence in education," states Dr. Bobby Neighbors, the superintendent of the Jefferson County Board of Education. "We achieve that through administrative leadership, quality teaching, and proven student achievement."

Providing a quality education and preparing all students for tomorrow's world remains the mission of the Board. That job begins each school day when 405 buses travel a total of more than 15,000 miles carrying students to elementary, middle, and high schools throughout Jefferson County. The drivers have an exceptional safety record.

School cafeterias serve 29,000 students daily, 6,000 of whom eat breakfast as well as lunch at the schools. The excellent management that has characterized the system's Child Nutrition program has resulted in over a half million dollars in new equipment and furniture for the cafeterias and dining areas of many schools in the 2002-2003 school year. The system has been given high marks from the Federal Coordinated Review.

When their classroom work begins, students receive instruction from a dedicated team of teaching professionals intent on the total development of each child. Resource specialists help teachers stay current on computer hardware, software, and the growing resources of the Internet in bringing the world into the classroom. Since 1992, these specialists have helped Jefferson County teachers receive almost $3 million for technology, math, and science enrichment.

The Board instituted an award-winning Teacher Assistance Teams (TATs) program in its 60 schools to assist teachers in formulating instructional alternatives and strategies to serve students in the regular classroom.

The Board's Library Media Services Department was recently rated as exemplary by the State Monitoring Team for outstanding programs, professional development activities, and support for library personnel. The Department sponsors the only month-long Family Reading and Library Links for Success programs in Alabama.

Character education is an integral part of the instructional program in Jefferson County schools. Students from across the district participate in a county-wide essay competition during "Character Education Month," and an annual recognition program to recognize students displaying exemplary character is held each October.

The system's Staff Development Department is a firm believer in the principle that teachers who are life-long learners are better teachers. Professional development opportunities to keep teachers apprised of current best practices in all areas of education are available to Jefferson County teachers. Training in the particular content of all disciplines, workshops in classroom organization and management, instruction in methods of implementing various teaching strategies to address the needs of diverse learners, and a host of other seminars and study groups are available on a regular basis.

Fourteen staff professionals and over 400 teachers serve more than 6,000 physically and mentally challenged students and almost 1,800 gifted students through exceptional edu-

Far left: Former Leeds Elementary teacher Dr. Betsy Rogers (holding book) served as Alabama Teacher of the Year for 2002-2003. On April 30, 2003, she was named National Teacher of the Year, the first Alabama teacher ever to receive that honor. The announcement was made by President George W. Bush and First Lady Laura Bush in a Rose Garden ceremony. Dr. Rogers will travel all across America and the world in 2003-2004 carrying the message of equity in public education. She is shown here reading a holiday story to Deane Stephen's (right) second grade class at Greenwood Elementary School.

Below left: The JefCoEd Public Education Foundation sponsors the STAR Mentor Program through which National Board Certified teachers mentor application candidates through the process to become certified. At Concord Elementary, two mentors work with six candidates during the year-long application process: (Front, L-R) candidates, Debra Williams, Teena Williams, Katsy Sellers, Amanda Stone, (Back, L-R) Candy Boissel, Susan Mahaffey and mentors Sherry Baltscheit and Angela Forsyth. National Board Certification is the national standard for excellence and professionalism in teaching. Jefferson County is a leading Alabama school system in numbers of NBCTs.

Below right: This iron sculpture signifies students joining hands in learning. It marks the site of the Jefferson County Schools Central Office, 2100 18th Street South, on the corner across from Vulcan Park. The sculpture was designed by JefCoEd Career Technical welding instructor Robert Withers at Minor High School.

ACKNOWLEDGEMENT
This profile on the Jefferson County Schools System was made possible by the JefCoEd Public Education Foundation, in partnership with these area supporters: Barge Waggoner Sumner & Cannon, Sunbelt Builders, Roy F. Bragg, Ned Paine, Gary C. Wyatt, Inc., Alabama Gas, Giattinia Fisher Aycock Architects, McCauley Associates, Inc., Lane Bishop York Delahay, Inc., Jones-Williams Construction, Southern Carpet & Hardwood, Davis Architects, Harris & Associates Architects/Planners, and Alabama Art Supply.

cation. Jefferson County was the first school system in Alabama to offer the International Baccalaureate program. This two-year curriculum, recognized as the world's most rigorous academic program for high school students, is one of only 23 such programs in the Southeast and 400 in the world.

The students' day also includes opportunities for instruction in the arts. The system's Arts Department offers visual arts, speech/theatre arts, band, choral, elementary music, and several county-wide arts events annually for students. Those include a Music Festival, Elementary and Secondary Botanical Gardens Arts Exhibits, Marching Band Jamboree, and Poetry Festival. The Shades Valley Theatre has been recognized as one of the premier theatre programs in the state, representing Alabama at the International Festival in Lincoln, Nebraska for two consecutive years. In 2002, theatre students were awarded over a million dollars in scholarship money.

The Jefferson County Board of Education also operates one of the largest athletic programs in Alabama. All Jefferson County students in grades K-8 receive daily physical education with a certified physical education teacher. Students can participate in 15 different sports. Since 1954, over 54 State Championships have gone to schools in the Jefferson County system, which has produced such stellar athletes as Bo Jackson and Charles Barkley.

Schools in the Jefferson County system remain active even after the bell marking the end of classes in the afternoon. The Community Education program offers extended day programs and enrichment classes to children and adults in the community. In addition, 25 of the system's schools feature child care programs in which more than 1,200 children are enrolled.

The results of the system's many innovative programs, outstanding teachers, and focused leadership have been impressive student achievement. In recent years, Jefferson County's students have ranked ahead of the state average in ACT testing. In addition, the system leads the state by five percentage points in the number of students passing the highs school basic skills exit exam. Each year, the system produces eight to ten National Merit Scholars. Last year's graduating seniors garnered almost $26 million in college scholarships.

The Jefferson County Board of Education is on track to continue these impressive numbers. The New Construction Department is directing the most ambitious building program in the system's history. Four new schools have been added to the system, and 28 existing facilities will receive new classrooms.

In 1991, the Jefferson County Schools Public Education Foundation, Inc. was established as a funding resource for a variety of programs designed to benefit Jefferson County schools, teachers, and students. Early on, the Foundation developed a system-wide fundraiser, School Coupons (originally called Kids Count). That very successful fundraiser is now shared with neighboring school systems and generates up to $1 million annually for area schools and education foundations. At the close of the 2002 campaign, over $8 million had been raised for local education through School Coupons.

A primary focus of the JefCoED Foundation is teacher support, advancement, and retention. Much emphasis is placed on first year teacher development and on spotlighting the excellent work of the system's most outstanding teachers. A groundbreaking mentor program has been established in conjunction with the National Board for Professional Teaching Standards. That candidate assistance program helps Jefferson County remain a state leader in the number of Board Certified teachers on staff.

"Through the hard work of dedicated teachers and the leadership of experienced administrators, Jefferson County schools are accomplishing great things in public education," Dr. Neighbors notes. "We are proud of our efforts, and delight in the accomplishments and successes of our students."

Alan Hunter

Work and play. There really isn't much beyond that. To Alan Hunter the juxtaposition of these two central human conditions has created the synergy for much that has been exciting and energizing about his life.

Alan Hunter was one of MTV's five original VJs, along with Martha Quinn, J.J. Jackson, Mark Goodman and Nina Blackwood. Last August the network celebrated its 20th anniversary, and Alan talked to CNN about getting older.

"Hey, I eat my Wheaties. You get older, and you get a little healthier actually, so I'm doing good. I had a great '80s, had a terrific '90s. I got two lovely kids, and now I have a production company doing. We're independent feature films. So MTV was sort of a departure for me."

After years in New York and L.A., he came back home to Birmingham to find a creative renewal and bottle it after a fashion in the Southside entertainment and creative office complex, WorkPlay. He and brother Randy operate Hunter Films, a company making commercial and feature films, with offices in the WorkPlay complex. Hunter Films' *Johnny Flynton* was nominated for an Academy Award in 2003 for Best Short Film. Although it didn't win the Oscar, the exposure has placed Hunter Films and Birmingham on the map.

Alan Hunter created WorkPlay with his three brothers. Hugh, Alan, Randy, and Blake Hunter joined forces to found WorkPlay, a new multimedia complex on Birmingham's Southside. Located under the same roof is a cabaret-style theater, a sound stage with state-of-the-art production capabilities, digital recording suites, and office space designed to attract creative-driven tenants.

Brother Randy had been working as a musical recording artist, and was familiar with the nuances of that industry. Hugh was a commercial photographer. Alan had experience in acting and television show hosting in New York and Los Angeles, while Blake had a head for business.

"It was a collaborative effort that drew on all our strengths," Alan explains, "and we had always entertained the notion of being in business together. There is a great deal of artistic talent in the Birmingham area, and we felt the city has a lot to offer the film and entertainment industry. We definitely felt that we wanted to locate in the heart of the city, especially in this section of Southside which is developing into a arts district. The galleries, shops, and theater at the Pepper Place and the clubs and restaurants in the Lakeview District are all close by. Our goal was to serve as the catalyst bringing all this together."

Christening their vision WorkPlay, the brothers touched all the bases in creating a cutting edge facility that is poised to become one of the most unique entertainment complexes in the country. The former warehouse was gutted and completely re-designed and re-built to accommodate each of the activities housed in the building.

The WorkPlay Theatre is a 250-seat cabaret-style room designed to showcase an eclectic schedule of local, regional, and national entertainers. No seat is farther than 50 feet from the stage. State-of-the-art lighting, sound, and acoustics, ensure the musical and theatrical talent on display will be enjoyed under optimal audio-visual conditions. Independent movie screenings and lectures, as well as musical and theatrical talent, will be scheduled for the Theatre. A full service lobby bar compliments the Theatre, which will also be available for corporate and private functions with turnkey options that include catering, full technical production, and event coordination services. Ticket sales and reservations, a schedule of events, and a seating chart are available on their website at www.workplay.com.

WorkPlay Studios were designed with musical inspiration in mind. Two 48-track digital audio recording suites and three isolation rooms will facilitate original and commercial work, sound design, and post-production activities. Both control rooms are fully interfaced with the Theatre to allow for a perfect live recording and broadcasting environment. The Studios is available for hourly, daily, and weekly rental.

The 5,250 square foot WorkPlay Sound Stage is unique to Alabama. Available for film, television, and commercial production, the Sound Stage offers an isolated acoustic environment as well as a 30-foot fixed light grid with sub-grids. Private offices, dressing rooms, showers, green room, storage areas, canteen, and drive-in access make the facility a film producer's dream.

"I had worked in the television and film industry in Los Angeles where there are numerous facilities like this," Alan relates, "but we didn't have one in Alabama. We wanted to offer filmmakers a top-flight sound stage with all the amenities here in Birmingham. We'll be making films here that will have the potential for worldwide distribution. Two feature length film projects are currently underway. We're hiring, casting directors, and raising capital right now. It's an exciting time for the film production industry in Birmingham."

Wes Chapman

In 1984, a 19-year-old named Wes Chapman, raised in rural Union Springs, Alabama, set out for New York City to compete for a spot in the elite American Ballet Theatre. He had reason to be confident: After graduating from the Alabama School of Fine Arts, Chapman had already spent two seasons with the Alabama Ballet. He felt ready.

When he arrived in New York, he first auditioned for the New York Ballet and won a spot there—which was a coup, because he hadn't studied at the company's ballet school.

Then, the next day, during auditions for American Ballet Theatre (ABT), he found himself in a preparatory class with Mikhail Baryshnikov, who was then the company's director. Now he was beyond nervous; nothing could have prepared him for that moment. "I was mortified," he recalls.

Baryshnikov offered him the spot. Chapman's only question: Do I have time to go home and pack up my things?

It was the start of a long and definitive mentor-protégé relationship between the two men. Chapman traces much of his professional success, as a dancer and now as artistic director of the Alabama Ballet, back to that moment.

"I feel like he discovered me that day," Chapman says. "I know he needed a dancer to fill a spot, so I was in the right place at the right time. But I always had this feeling from him that I was one of the dancers that he had discovered to promote the company and his vision of the way he saw ballet."

Wes Chapman has been consistently praised for his "elegance and fine-scaled classicism" in a wide variety of roles with the American Ballet Theatre.

His talent, however, does not end with performance. He joined the Alabama Ballet in 1996, and has directed the Birmingham-based company to a new level of professional-ism and created a fresh enthusiasm for dance in the Birmingham community.

In February of 1998, Chapman received the Distinguished Career Award from the society for the Fine Arts, and organization based at the University of Alabama.

A native of Union Springs, Alabama, Chapman began his training at the age of nine at the Montgomery School of Ballet under the direction of Emily Caruso.

At only 13, the prestigious American Ballet Theatre accepted Chapman into their summer program and only three years later he began training at the Alabama School of Fine Arts. In 1983, Chapman graduated from ASFA with the highest honors, the Prix d'Excellence de Dance and the Duane Dushion Award.

After performing one season with the Alabama Ballet, Chapman accepted an invitation from Mikhail Baryshnikov to dance with the American Ballet Theatre.

It did not take long for Chapman to move up in the ranks of this world-renowned company. In 1987, the native Alabamian was promoted to Soloist and two years later was appointed Principal Dancer.

At the Alabama Ballet, Chapman has transformed a struggling regional company into a powerhouse of artistic expression, while bringing new works and new audiences to the art of ballet.

TIMBERLINE GOLF
AND RESIDENTIAL COMMUNITY

Just 30 minutes from downtown Birmingham, nestled in the rolling hills and verdant valleys .of Shelby County, is the newest addition to the burgeoning list of the Magic City's premier golf attractions. Timberline Golf and Residential Community is a semi-private golf facility located just off I-65 at Calera.

Timberline is the golfer's 'golf club.' Focusing solely on golf allowed the developers to allocate all their resources on creating the type of quality golfing experience associated with the finest private courses.

The course, designed by 1976 U.S. Open champion Jerry Pate, plays to par 71, a full 6,841 yards from the back tees. Pate combined his design expertise with Mother Nature's incomparable handiwork to create one

of the most interesting and varied landscapes in the area. The area's big timber and huge hardwoods gave rise to the course's name.

"Jerry Pate obviously has close ties to the Alabama market, and we knew he would design and build us a quality golf course,' says Timberline's developer Larry Clayton. "People know his name, and we were very impressed when we went to look at some of his other courses."

From a flat, low-lying plain, the course winds into hills and rolling terrain that varies with every hole. With four par fives and five par threes, Timberline offers enough challenge for the skilled golfer while remaining a very playable course for the high handicapper.

To complement the golf course, a 10,000 square foot rustic-style club house is planned. Practice facilities include three putting greens, two

bunkers, and three large teeing areas.

Semi-private memberships are available to individuals and businesses, as well as a daily fee for the public. Tee times are available by calling 205.668.7888.

One of the most unique features of Timberline is the full gauge railroad that runs through the course. Once used to haul timber, the Heart of Dixie Railroad now operates sparingly as a tourist attraction lending a touch of history and nostalgia to the setting.

Timberline Golf and Residential Community encompasses some 300 acres and includes more than 160 residential lots. The property, marketed by RealtySouth, was designed as single family and garden homes built around the championship golf course. Owners can select from the provided floor plans or bring their own.

"We're the only semi-private golf course between Birmingham and Montgomery, and are very conveniently located off the I-65 corridor," says Linda Mann, Timberline's sales and marketing director. "We are very attractive to golfers within a 50 mile radius. We feel that we have a beautiful, player-friendly course that has mass appeal."

Those masses appeared on July 8, 2002, at Timberline's grand opening. Civic leaders, media, and representatives of local chambers of commerce joined golf enthusiasts to 'tee off' the sparkling new facility that is destined to become a very popular golf destination as well as a premier residential community.

BIRMINGHAM-JEFFERSON CONVENTION COMPLEX

In the heart of downtown Birmingham, just a stone's throw from a number of the city's premier cultural attractions, municipal and county government offices, the Birmingham International Airport, and the state's largest hotel, is the Birmingham-Jefferson Convention Complex. A multi-purpose facility featuring an exhibit hall, meeting rooms, arena, concert hall, and theater, the BJCC serves as a magnet drawing hundreds of cultural and sports events, as well as conventions, trade shows, and meetings to our area each year. Since its opening in the 1960s, the BJCC has come to be known as one of the South's best meeting and convention values.

The BJCC features all the facilities necessary to secure its position as Alabama's foremost entertainment and convention complex:

- 220,000 square feet of space in the Exhibition Hall

- 100,000 square feet of space in 74 meeting rooms
- 10-story, internationally acclaimed Medical Forum
- 19,000 seat Arena
- 3,000 seat Concert Hall
- 1,000 seat Theater
- Alabama Sports Hall of Fame

With almost a quarter million square feet of exhibit space, the massive Exhibition Hall can accommodate over a thousand 10' x 10' exhibit booths. Connections for electricity, water, telephone, data, and compressed air are available, along with many natural gas outlets as well.

Almost two million visitors each year pass through the doors of the Exhibition Hall attending trade shows, exhibits, religious group meetings, and other special events. As many as 28,000 attendees at a time have participated in national and regional events held at the facility. Its capabilities have attracted such conventions and expos as the Citgo BASSMASTERS Classic, Women of Faith, National Association of Black Journalists, and the Alabama

Oilmen's Association. The facility has also been the site of two Presidential visits in the past year.

In addition to trade shows and exhibits, the BJCC is also a very popular venue for meetings and seminars. Meeting planners across the country have made this a multi-billion dollar industry nationwide, and are increasingly taking a closer look at Birmingham as a host city for their events. More than 100,000 square feet of space for those meetings are available in 74 separate rooms, each equipped with state-of-the-art audio-visual equipment.

The versatility of the Arena is reflected in its schedule of events. Musical performances by superstars such as Cher, the Eagles, Jimmy Buffet and Bruce Springsteen; world-class athletes with Champions on Ice; and the Ringling Brothers and Barnum and Bailey Circus are just some of the headliners that have drawn local fans as well as out-of-state visitors.

The Arena is also home to the

Steeldogs, Birmingham's home team in the arena football2 league. Other major sporting events hosted at the Arena include first and second round NCAA Men's Basketball Tournament and preseason NBA games. Seating capacity at major sporting events is 17,000, and the facility can be configured to accommodate up to 19,000 for performances.

The Concert Hall has been acclaimed by performers and critics alike as among the most acoustically perfect halls in the world. The 3,000 seat facility features the latest in fiber-optic audio-visual systems providing almost any high-tech capability required by meeting planners. The spacious, yet intimate hall is home to the Birmingham Broadway Series and host to a range of other performances such as the Alabama Symphony Orchestra.

Ballets, small plays, operas, and concerts have found a gracious home in the 1,000 seat Theater. In addition to hosting these events, the facility serves as the home for the

Birmingham Children's Theater, the largest children's theater in the country in terms of attendance and number of performances. With a national reputation for excellence, the Birmingham Children's Theater has brought the excitement of live theater to hundreds of thousands of school children across Alabama, the Southeast, and the U.S. With its remote site teleconferencing capabilities, the facility is also ideal for business meetings, product launches, and new product training.

In 1992, the Medical Forum Conference Center opened at the Convention Complex and made instant headlines. A comprehensive diversity of design utilizing fiber-optic signal distribution, satellite uplinks and downlinks, wireless response pads, translation capabilities, and closed circuit television monitors make the Forum a unique resource for medical education and professional seminars. A 270-seat tiered auditorium is the center of this remarkable interactive educat ion complex.

Rounding out the list of attractions at the BJCC is the Alabama Sports Hall of Fame, a sparkling facility housing memorabilia from the state's honored athletes and sportsmen and women.

Complete catering services are available for functions at all the Convention Complex facilities.

Connected by a covered walkway to the BJCC is the Sheraton Birmingham Hotel. Alabama's largest and most recognized hotel, the Sheraton offers luxury accommodations in over 700 guest rooms, along with complete business and meeting facilities in the heart of Birmingham's Central Business District. A complete range of amenities, guest services, and restaurants and lounges makes the Sheraton the lodging facility of choice for business as well as vacation travelers.

Meeting planners have also found much to like at the Sheraton Birmingham. The hotel offers 315,000 square feet of meeting and exhibit space as well as a 25,000 square foot ballroom, the state's largest.

"We have become a significant player in attracting conventions, trade shows, concerts, and sporting events," says Frank Poe, the executive director and chief executive officer at the BJCC. "It is our mission to provide a top-notch complex and pull in events that have a positive effect on the quality of life and economic activity of Birmingham."

Poe and his staff work closely with the Greater Birmingham Convention and Visitors Bureau to do just that. Their efforts have resulted in the BJCC anchoring what is now a $1 billion per year hospitality industry in the Birmingham area. More than 16,000 people are employed locally in the provision of hospitality services.

"Birmingham is now being looked at as a destination in itself rather than just a city along the road to somewhere else," states Jim Smither, president of the Greater Birmingham Convention and Visitors Bureau.

To encourage even more meeting planners and exhibitors to continue to look at Birmingham as a destination and a site for their functions, the City of Birmingham is studying the possibility of a major expansion to the BJCC. Funded in part by lodging tax, the expansion would allow Birmingham to remain competitive with other cities in the Southeast in attracting conventions, meetings, tourists, and possibly additional major league sports events. Studies are currently underway evaluating the economic impact on the area of increasing the size and scope of the facilities at the BJCC.

Birmingham has much to be proud of. The Birmingham-Jefferson Convention Complex, perfectly positioned in its proximity to restaurants, the cultural district, the airport, and Interstate highway access, remains near the top of the list of attractions that add a touch of magic to the Magic City.

With the downtown skyline as its backdrop, the BJCC is Alabama's foremost entertainment and convention complex. The BJCC is conveniently located just five minutes from the Birmingham International Airport and within walking distance of the cultural district, financial center and restaurants. The state's largest hotel is adjacent to the complex.

Remon Danforah

"To sell a suit is easy, but to groom a man is more demanding." On the basis of such a principle, Remon Danforah has built one of Birmingham's most stylish men's clothing shops.

Remon Danforah's grandfather had a friend in the clothing business in Ramallah, 10 miles north of Jerusalem. Remon started working in this tailor shop when he was five years old. The shop was tiny, with three employees making custom-made suits.

Remon did simple alterations, then began making men's suits. "I grew up there, working in that tiny shop."

In 1973 Remon was 16. He had a sister living in Birmingham, and a deep, burning desire to succeed. He traveled to the United States, arriving on a Thursday. That Saturday he went to see the owner of Robert Tailoring Company. Without speaking a word of English, he made a "me work" pantomime, sewing with an imaginary needle and thread pulled through the air. He started working that Monday, earning $55 a week.

He began working extra hours, doing alterations at night. Within two years of his arrival, he opened his own alteration shop with a $50 sewing machine. Remon laughs now as he recalls sitting in his new shop on the first day thinking: "Lord have mercy, what did you do, Remon?"

A year and a half later, Remon opened a slightly larger shop where in addition to doing alterations he began selling men's clothing. That small shop located across the street from John's Restaurant 14 years ago was the modest beginnings of what is now a truly first-rate men's clothing store which simply bears his name: Remon's.

People like Remon Danforah and it's obvious that Remon likes people. People are everything to him. "There's no business without relationships. Knowing your product and enjoying what you do, makes you the best at what you do." Remon is genuine.

"My job now is to create a complete image for my customers," Remon explains. "Because my background is in tailoring, I am abe to offer my clients a superior level of expertise in selecting the proper clothing and achieving a perfect fit. There are many stores that can sell you a designer suit or sports jacket, but the most important thing is the fit and service after the sales transaction has long been completed. My clients are confident that the clothing they purchase from me will fit them perfectly. They also know that the garments will be tailored at no cost forever, regardless of whether the customers gain or lose weight over the years. I've also learned that people also want to meet the person whose name is over the door, and that's one of the reasons I'm almost always here."

Remon prides himself in meeting the sartorial needs of some of Birmingham's most visible business and professional men with some of the world's finest clothing.

The shelves and clothing bars are filled with exceptionally beautiful clothes from some of the most venerable designer names around: Hickey Freeman, Pal Zileri, Mabro, Zanella, Borrelli, Cole-Haan, Michael Toschi, and Robert Talbott. To complete the look, he offers his customers an impressive array of ties, cufflinks, and eclectic accessories.

Remon travels to New York City several times each year to personally select new and unique items for his inventory, and to keep his finger on the pulse of the constantly-changing fashion industry.

In addition to his many customers, plenty of passersby stop and wave at Remon through the broad and ever-changing windows of the store now located on the corner of Third Avenue and Richard Arrington Jr. Boulevard.

There is nothing casual or impersonal about Remon's relationships with his customers. Their ultimate satisfaction ensures his own. It's no wonder that many of them never shop anywhere else. His commitment to serving them well is reciprocated through their loyalty to him.

CULINARD

The Culinary Institute of Virginia College

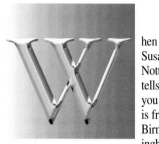

When Susan Notter tells you she is from Birmingham, her delightful accent immediately identifies her as a product of the city in England rather than from Birmingham, Alabama. When she left her hometown years ago, she probably never imagined she would find herself living and working in another city of the same name in the United States. Fortunately for those of us in the Magic City who love good food and its artful presentation, Notter brought her extensive culinary skills, along with her infectious enthusiasm, to Birmingham to found the Pastry, Baking, and Confectionary Arts Program at Culinard, the Culinary Institute of Virginia College.

Culinard provides a comprehensive culinary education through a delicate weaving of world-class cuisine with art, science, history, geography, social diversity, and global awareness. Students are taught culinary skills and techniques that will help them savor the world's finest foods, while, at the same time, savoring life itself.

The Institute offers two outstanding programs: one in Culinary Arts and the other in Pastry, Baking, and Confectionary Arts. Both provide the foundation, skills, and knowledge essential in developing successful careers within the hospitality industry.

Notter was lured to Birmingham, Alabama from Maryland where she had been co-owner of an international school of confectionary arts. At home in the kitchen since she was ten years old, she received a degree in hotel management, catering, and institutional operations from a culinary school in England before working and studying in Germany and Switzerland. It was there amidst oceans of chocolate and intricate pulled-sugar designs that she honed the skills that led her to become a much sought after instructor and guest chef. She now lists demonstrations, seminars, and guest appearances in restaurants from Singapore to Sri Lanka and on cruise ships throughout the world. She has also co-authored books on pulled and blown sugar.

"I met Jill Bosich, the dean of culinary education at Culinard, when she and I were members of the Culinary Olympic Team," Notter relates. "She contacted me about coming to Birmingham to found the

bakery and pastry program here. Very few schools in the country offer a program such as this. We begin with the fundamentals of cooking and intermediate kitchen skills. Basic culinary skills are an asset to the pastry chef, offering more job opportunities and a greater understanding of the business. The student then progresses through bakeshop and pastry to advanced patisserie. Candy making and decorative centerpieces make up the last of the nine quarters required for an associate degree. An Occupational Associate degree was first offered to graduates of the Culinary Arts program in October of 2000. The first degrees in Pastry, Baking, and Confectionary Arts were conferred in April, 2002."

The foundation of the school's curriculum are the institutional kitchens and bakeshops that represent a progressive stage in the training of a culinarian. The specially designed kitchens allow for small groups of students to have simultaneous hands-

on training in the full range of kitchen tools.

Those of us with a penchant for sweets can sample the handiwork of Notter's students at The Bakery at Culinard, located on Vulcan Road in Homewood just down the street from the Virginia College campus. The 5,000 square foot facility, on which Chef Notter assisted in the design, doubles as a training facility as well as a charming, fully operational bakery and coffee shop. Patrons can watch a wedding cake being expertly decorated, browse the attractive display cases featuring eye-popping desserts, pick up a loaf of fresh baked bread and other bakery goods, and unwind with a cappuccino from the European-style bistro. Guests can choose from indoor seating or a spot on the outdoor patio. Catering services are also available for any size event.

The Bakery is located next door to 195 Mizan Plaz, the Institute's acclaimed restaurant featuring progressive American cuisine ranging from the American Southwest to Southeast Asia to the south of France. This is where students apply the skills they have acquired from their intense classroom work into the actual creation of international menus as part of their advanced food preparation classes. These menus are then offered to the public at the restaurant.

The menu, which changes regularly, includes lunch and dinner suggestions beginning with appetizers, soups, and salads all the way to entrees of pasta dishes, seafood, chicken, steaks, and chops. The restaurant also offers a selection of fine wines from its extensive cellar, along with complete bar service. A separate dining room is available for private parties, as is off-site catering complete with impeccable service.

For those who want to learn how to prepare fine food, but are not pursuing a career as a professional chef, Culinard offers a series of non-credit classes. Cooking, baking, and wine courses are taught by the Institute's own renowned chefs with lively classroom demonstrations and tastings. Classes include instruction in sushi cooking, Mediterranean cuisine, seafood specialties, heart healthy cooking, and elegant desserts.

One of the principles on which the Culinary Arts and the Pastry, Baking, and Confectionary Arts Programs at Culinard were founded suggests that life's possibilities are endless when one learns from the right instructors. To that end, the Institute has assembled some of the finest chefs in the area who have joined Susan Notter on the faculty. This dedicated team of culinary professionals has developed one of the most comprehensive culinary instruction and training programs available anywhere.

Financial aid is available to those who qualify, and assistance is offered in locating housing for out-of-town students. Morning, midday, and evening classes are offered to accommodate work schedules. The Institute's career services department offers assistance in job placement, but local restaurants have sought out the schools' graduates sometimes even prior to their completion of the course work.

"Part of the great joy of this is seeing the instant gratification that our students receive from learning the art of cooking," Notter explains. "Our program is designed so that the student is part of the process from beginning to end. They learn to assemble the ingredients, prepare their creations, and serve them correctly. My goal is to visit my students years from now when they own their own restaurants."

Left page: Chef Notter adding the finishing touches to her wedding cakes. The bakery at Culinard serves up rich and tasty desserts, like the raspberry tart.

Right: The bakery offers breakfast, brunch and desserts and pastries in a unique contemporary setting. Below: Diners can unwind on the beautiful outdoor patio.

LIMESTONE SPRINGS

Finding a Dream Home.

The rolling hills and valleys of the Appalachian Mountains serve as a stunning backdrop for a strikingly beautiful 800-acre community centered around a spectacular golf course. And the pristine setting is just a short drive from downtown Birmingham.

Limestone Springs near Oneonta in Blount County features one of the most beautiful mountain golf courses in the country with a wide range of available homes and home sites surrounding the course. *Golf Digest* magazine recently named Limestone Springs as one of the top 10 upscale course designs with unrestricted walking (4 1/2 stars) in the nation, and also ranked it among the top five courses in Alabama. *Golf Week* rated it the number one course in the state. The award-winning 18-hole golf course was sculpted by former U.S. Open winner Jerry Pate, one of the nation's foremost architects of championship golf courses. Limestone Springs easily measures up to the demanding standards expected of a Pate-designed course.

The semi-private facility offers golfers one of the most exciting golf club memberships in the country. Benefits include:

- Full, Corporate, Junior, Out-of-Town, and Sports memberships are available
- Members are not subject to operating deficits or capital assessments
- Club charging privileges
- Exclusive use of member's designated parking areas
- Free and unlimited use of practice range
- Designated member only warm-up area
- Member's rate for Limestone Springs golf cottage rentals
- Reciprocal privileges at other Honours Golf facilities
- Full use of swim and tennis facilities
- Fourteen-day advance tee times

The benefits, however, extend far beyond the signature golf course. Members and their guests enjoy full use of all the club's amenities, including unlimited access to Limestone Springs' sprawling clubhouse and fully equipped locker rooms, spectacular mountaintop swimming pool, workout facilities, and lighted tennis courts.

Many have found their dream home at Limestone Springs. The large wooded home sites sit between scenic limestone bluffs, valleys, and streams. Miles of hiking and mountaintop nature trails are just steps away. Residents of the community also have access to one of the region's finest school systems. The development is marketed by RealtySouth, a leading name in residential real estate in Alabama.

For anyone who loves the community's unique combination of world-class golf, outdoor activities, and refreshing tranquility, the Limestone Springs Golf Cottage is the next best thing to living there. Located within walking distance or a cart ride from the clubhouse and first tee, the fully furnished cottage features four spacious bedrooms and baths; comfortable living, dining, and meeting areas; and computer data ports with Internet access. An exceptional facility, the Golf Cottage is available for rental on a nightly, weekly, or longer basis.

As a member of the Limestone Springs Golf Club, members can tee it up at other Honours Golf courses, including Kelly Plantation in Destin, Florida; Rock Creek in Fairhope, Alabama; Peninsula Golf & Racquet Club in Gulf Shores, Alabama; Highland Park in Birmingham; The Slammer & The Squire at the World Golf Village in St. Augustine, Florida; and The King & Bear at the World Golf Village in St. Augustine. Being added in 2003 will be Farmlinks in Fayetteville, Alabama and Reunion Golf and Country Club just outside Jackson, Mississippi. "Limestone Springs fits well into the Honours Golf program," says Bob Barrett, the CEO of Honours Golf. "We strive to be the best in all the markets we serve. All courses that bear the Honours brand are courses of exceptional quality and design, and that is exactly what people have found at Limestone Springs."

The friendly staff at Limestone Springs invites all to drive the short 45 minutes from Birmingham to experience what many have already discovered. Limestone Springs offers residents and golfers one of the most exceptional experiences in country living lifestyles and championship golf just minutes from the conveniences of the city.

BIRMINGHAM WATER WORKS

Serving Your Community, Preserving the Environment

One of the most heavily used of our natural resources, water is expected to be there, always clean and pure, whenever we turn on the faucet. The customers in the service area of the Birmingham Water Works, which includes Jefferson, Shelby, Walker, St. Clair, and Blount Counties, use almost 100 million gallons of water every day. The Birmingham system is the largest in the state of Alabama, and one of the largest in the United States.

"City water" did not exist in the days when Birmingham was a brash youngster forging its future in iron and steel. At the time of the city's birth and in the early boom days of the 1870s, people obtained their water from wells or from street vendors. Well water, however, was not always good, nor reliable. The water obtained from vendors, drawn from a spring near Avondale, was exposed to surface contamination as it was peddled around town on ox-drawn carts and sold for 25 cents a barrel.

Recognizing the need for a municipal water system, the Elyton Land Company constructed a pumping station in 1872, drawing water from Village Creek. Water from the system first flowed on May 13, 1873 to customers in the downtown area all the way to Morris Avenue.

Continued growth of the city, however, soon exhausted the water available from local creeks, and the newly formed Birmingham Water Works Company looked south for expansion. Over the next several years, a new pumping station was built on the Cahaba River, a reservoir was constructed on Shades Mountain, and filtration plants were put into operation.

A milestone in the history of the Water Works was the change in ownership that occurred in 1951. Revenue bonds created an independent, public corporation to operate the system, and the Birmingham Water Works Board was born. The subsequent creation of bedroom communities throughout Jefferson County and the rapid growth of the suburbs led to additional demands for water. The Birmingham Water Works responded, leading to expansion of service to communities

in Walker, Shelby, St. Clair, and Blount Counties.

In 1988, the Board received national recognition for its water quality. "We now have the distinction of being one of the top five water systems in the entire country," notes Anthony Barnes, the chairman of the Birmingham Water Works Board. "Our water consistently meets or exceeds government regulations for quality and safety. The Birmingham Water Works has gained national recognition for performance, efficiency, and reliability. This operational efficiency allows us to deliver high quality water at rates well below the national average to customers throughout our service area."

Raw water from any of the system's water sources has a long road to travel before it arrives sparkling and clear from the taps in our homes and restaurants and the water coolers in our offices. Even the most pristine looking water from streams, rivers, and mountain lakes can harbor legions of microbes and bacteria eager to set up an all-you-can-eat buffet in our stomachs. In the early 1990s, the Water Works committed over $2 million to construct

EnviroLab, a complete laboratory facility staffed with chemists and technicians and outfitted with highly sensitive, state-of-the-art instruments to perform multiple tests on water samples to ensure the supply meets the standards set by the Environmental Protection Agency. As stringent as those standards are, the Birmingham Water Works has raised the bar even higher. Where EPA guidelines require quarterly testing in certain areas, Water Works' policy stipulates conducting these tests on a monthly, and, in some cases, weekly basis.

"The Birmingham Water Works is recognized as one of the best systems in Alabama," states Joe Power, former chief of the drinking water branch of the Alabama Department of Environmental Management, the agency designated to oversee state drinking water standards. "They have been a real leader in upgrading their facilities to meet current and future water requirements. This has resulted in their ability to provide extremely high quality water at low prices to their customers."

The Birmingham Water Works took another huge step to upgrade its system and move it into the new mil-

lennium when it installed a Supervisory Control and Data Acquisition (SCADA) system in 1997. The $6 million state-of-the-art program consists of a series of distributed control systems connecting 134 sites including treatment plants, raw water pumping stations, tank sites, pressure reducing stations, etc. to a Central Operations Room and Emergency (CORE) recovery command center. With its ability to control the distribution of millions of gallons of water each day, the CORE is the heartbeat of the water system.

Recognizing that water is a critical key to economic development, the Water Works has established the provision of an adequate supply of water for business and industry as one of its top priorities. Protecting that water supply, especially in critical watershed areas, is even more important. For that reason, the Birmingham Water Works has enacted an aggressive watershed protection policy, not only to minimize the environmental impact of construction in watershed areas, but also to protect our water sources.

The Water Works Board of Directors are local business and community leaders with expertise in

various areas that comes together to form a congruous governing body. Anthony L. Barnes, Chairman of the Board, is president and broker of Barnes & Associates, PC REALTORS®, and Jordan Frazier is an acclaimed automobile dealership owner. Jim Lowery is mayor of the City of Fultondale and past president of the Jefferson County Mayors Association. David Herring is a retired bank executive and a former Birmingham City Councilman. McDaniels Johnston is a retired banker with expertise in finance and strategic planning.

The general manager, Mike Vann, a 26-year veteran of the utility, heads the senior management team. Mr. Vann, was appointed to the top position in 1999. The other members of the management team include Ronald Mims who heads Corporate Communications, Randall Chafin is over Operations and Technical Services while Mac Underwood guides Finance and Administration. "Our philosophy has been to exceed rather than to just meet the federal and state guidelines for clean, safe water," Vann states. "This is evident in our participation in the Partnership for Safe Drinking Water, a

program that consists of water systems which have established goals far more stringent than EPA regulations. We have met this goal even in the midst of the drought of 2000 and the widespread damage caused by that year's tornadoes."

"We also focus on operational efficiency. Surveys have shown that the costs of operating our system are among the lowest in the country. However, our metropolitan area is growing, and we continue to plan for the future and keep pace with that growth. We continuously evaluate our system operations and service so that our area will never experience the water shortage situation that many cities now face. We intend to stay ahead of the city's growth, not try to catch up with it," Vann further stated.

In 1887, W.A. Merkel, chief engineer of the Cahaba Pumping Station stated, "—it is through the foresight and understanding of the Birmingham Water Company that the city has never been without sufficient water supply." This statement continues to be the challenge and mission for the Board in the new millennium as it focuses on serving its customers and preserving the environment!

Top: The SCADA system is a state-of-the-art program that connects 134 sites to a Central Operations Room and Emergency (CORE) recovery command center. With its ability to monitor water source levels each day, the CORE is the heartbeat of the water system.

Middle (From L-R) Birmingham Water Works Board members and executive staff are Mac Underwood, R. Randall Chafin, Director David Herring, Director Jordan A. Frazier, Chairman Anthony L. Barnes, Director The Honorable Jim H. Lowery, Director McDaniels A. Johnston, Michael O. Vann, General Manager, and Ronald A. Mims.

Bottom: EnviroLab manager, Desiree Alexander instructs Birmingham elementary students on her daily tasks, water treatment and operations at the Birmingham Water Works.

John Bright Fey

For the past 40 years, John Bright-Fey has been a student, practitioner, scholar and teacher of classical Chinese arts and letters; classical Chinese medicine; Northern Shaolin Kung-Fu Arts; classical styles of T'ai Chi Chuan; and a variety of other traditional Chinese health, exercise and martial disciplines.

The dragon of classical Chinese culture is a powerful symbol of creativity and its transformative possibilities. Bright-Fey honors this tradition and his own lineage in his Blue Dragon Academy, which he opened here in 1990.

Here students at all levels of training and expertise come to study and tap into the amazing reservoir of knowledge and experience which is the passion and life's work of John Bright-Fey.

At this time on a weekday morning there is no one at the Blue Dragon Academy, which sits in a nondescript strip shopping center in Hoover. Bright-Fey is sitting in the front office area of the academy-behind are a corridor lined with pictures and awards and a large room with a matted floor where classes are taught. He is quietly talking about the contemplative mind in today's society—a topic that is not nearly as common coffee shop conversation fodder as Bright-Fey wishes it was.

In Chinese mythology the Blue Dragon was the library beast, he slept in the clouds and answered questions. On this quiet morning in Hoover, Bright-Fey is doing the same.

"I teach a body-mind philosophy. My entire life I've studied how body and mind work together to create movement-physical, creative movement.

"People live life as if their mind, body and spirit were separate, when in fact they are not," Bright-Fey says.

Born in Louisiana, Bright-Fey has lived in many areas of the country, but he moved to Birmingham in 1990, and it felt a lot like coming home.

"I never met people more open minded. If someone has a good idea, people will come out of the woodwork and help. This city is an amazingly resilient and flexible place," he says.

Bright-Fey's and the Blue Dragon Academy's mission is simple: Bring contemplative movement and health exercise to the general community.

"Life should get bigger, brighter, more interesting and funnier every day. We teach techniques and philosophies that allow that to happen," he says

"We have a way we see ourselves inside and it is different from how we really behave, which is mechanical, habitual. Dissonance is the difference between the inner self and the outer life, outer self. Resolve that difference because dissonance can rattle a life apart."

John Bright-Fey's work in the traditional Chinese health, exercise and martial disciplines helps people find the connections between their outer and inner lives—wherever that connection may lie.

It allows people to do battle with themselves, the inner demons of depression, doubt, fear and insecurity. A poet and author, Bright-Fey has developed a comprehensive approach to contemplation and discipline he calls the New Forest Way. They are tools designed to help us live life the way we really want to.

"Look in a child's eye and take full measure of his laughter. If you don't know how, I'll show you how."

AmSOUTH BANK

The Relationship People

On the first business day of January 1873, a Swedish seaman-turned-businessman named Charles Linn opened the doors to the financial institution he founded that would become the First National Bank of Birmingham. From that day, little more than a year after Birmingham itself was incorporated as a city, the financial institution that grew to become AmSouth Bank has never wavered from the characteristics that defined it at its inception:

■ Principled leadership

■ Superior performance

■ An unwavering civic commitment

AmSouth's leaders over the years recruited and built a dynamic management team that ranks today among the best in the industry. They guided the growth of the bank to become a holding company known as the Alabama Bancorporation in 1971. As such, it acquired 20 affiliate banks during the next decade. In 1981, the institution's name was changed to AmSouth to better reflect its expanded scope and service, and it became the first bank holding company in Alabama to be listed on the New York Stock Exchange.

AmSouth today is one of the largest and strongest financial institutions in the Southeast with $44 billion in total assets. The company operates 600 branch offices and more than 1,200 automatic teller machines in Alabama, Florida, Georgia, Mississippi, Louisiana, and Tennessee. AmSouth has acquired a reputation for building its business by building relationships, a philosophy that emerges as a natural extension of the bank's basic values.

AmSouth's professionals begin with understanding a customer's goals and objectives. They then outline a financial blueprint for meeting those individual needs. The ultimate goal, a long-term relationship with the customer, is a result of the successful implementation of financial programs designed to meet the customer's needs,

whether it's a college education, home ownership, a business expansion, or a host of others.

AmSouth offers its customers a varied array of high quality financial products and services. Dozens of options in personal banking, small business banking, commercial banking, wealth management, and investment services ensure that AmSouth can meet its customers' needs with solutions tailor-made for their specific situations.

Along with helping customers realize their dreams, AmSouth bankers focus on delivering an unparalleled level of service. That service begins with six basic values:

■ Do more than is expected

■ If something's wrong, make it right

■ Make time for people

■ Improve someone's life

■ Make a difference

■ Do the right thing

The relationships that helped AmSouth's customers succeed have also resulted in the bank's continued success. A $10,000 investment in company stock at the beginning of 1996 was worth $23,718 by August 2002, 45 percent greater than the growth of the S&P 500. In 2001, the bank's dividend yield outpaced most alternative investments, and was a primary reason that Barron's ranked AmSouth among 29

Birmingham's City Center is home to AmSouth Center, the bank's headquarters and one of several AmSouth facilities in the Birmingham region. More than 4,200 of AmSouth's 12,000 employees work in and around Birmingham.

companies best positioned to outperform the broader markets.

"Our mission of building relationships isn't just how we approach customers, it sets the course for how we work with the community," said C. Dowd Ritter, AmSouth's chairman, president, and chief executive officer.

"We lead by example, whether in charitable contributions or employees volunteering their time. That makes us a better company, and it makes Birmingham a better place."

AXCAN PHARMA
AXCAN SCANDIPHARM

Founded as Scandipharm, Inc. in 1991 in Birmingham, Alabama, the Company initially targeted under-served medical markets such as cystic fibrosis, chronic obstructive pulmonary diseases (COPDs), and certain subsets of HIV/AIDS and cancer. In August 1999, Scandipharm was acquired by Axcan Pharma Inc., a leading North American pharmaceutical company in the field of gastroenterology.

Axcan Pharma was established in 1982 by current president and CEO, Léon F. Gosselin. Since its inception, Axcan has focused on a single specialization on which to build its reputation—gastroenterology. This singular focus has allowed the Company to leverage its resources hence maximizing its effectiveness in building enduring relationships with health authorities and medical practitioners in the U.S. and Canada.

In addition to the name change to Axcan Scandipharm, Scandipharm's union with Axcan Pharma has involved the successful merging of products, services and resources. Axcan Pharma's strong research, clinical testing, and product development portfolio, coupled with Axcan Scandipharm's solid U.S. sales and marketing team, have allowed the two companies to operate in perfect synergy. This synergy has also provided a distinction from specialty pharmaceutical companies that focus solely on the distribution of products and offers potential licensors the prospect of rapidly expanding the potential market for their products.

Today, Axcan Pharma and Axcan Scandipharm are working hand-in-hand to become a multinational leader for disorders linked to gastroenterology. In 2002, 88 percent of the Company's business was generated from North American sales.

The Company's principal activity is the marketing of gastroenterology-related pharmaceutical products and services including active ulcerative proctitis, liver disease, esophageal cancer and cystic fibrosis. Despite the relatively high number of patients suffering from gastrointestinal diseases and disorders, there are only about 9,500 gastroenterologists in North America. Since the Company markets specialized products to a relatively cohesive community of physicians, its sales force is able to reach this market more easily than pharmaceutical companies with a product portfolio targeting a more diverse range of diseases. And, since the causes of most gastrointestinal diseases are unknown, most treatments currently available provide relief from symptoms rather than a cure. Therefore, users of Axcan's products tend to be chronic patients who remain under the care of a physician for a prolonged period.

All activities underscore the Company's single, well-defined Mission—to improve the quality of care and treatment of patients suffering from gastrointestinal diseases and related disorders by providing effective therapies, products, and specialized programs that meet the needs of patients and their caregivers.

Axcan is one of the few Canadian pharmaceutical companies with a U.S. sales and marketing organization. Its U.S. corporate office remains in Birmingham, Alabama. Axcan's common shares are listed on the NASDAQ National Market under the "AXCA" symbol and on the Toronto Stock Exchange under the "AXP" symbol.

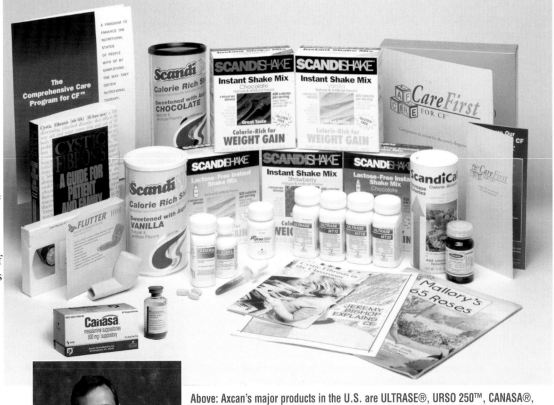

Above: Axcan's major products in the U.S. are ULTRASE®, URSO 250™, CANASA®, PHOTOFRIN®, and VIOKASE®. The company also markets a broad line of nutritional supplements and patient-focused programs.

Left: David W. Mims, Executive Vice President and Chief Operating Officer

LEVAND STEEL & SUPPLY

Birmingham's reputation in the early twentieth century as "the Pittsburgh of the South" convinced the leaders of Levand Steel & Supply Corporation in the early 1980s to look to the Magic City as a location for one of the company's trading offices. The company, founded by the late Jack J. Levand in Ohio in 1934, specializes today in ferrous products ranging from steel scrap to large steel castings. Levand's products are now handled from offices in Birmingham, Los Angeles, and Baltimore to customers throughout the United States and around the world.

Chris Metcalf, a 42-year veteran of the industry, was tapped by another company in the mid-1970s to relocate to the South from his native England. Metcalf, who proudly traces his family's roots to 14th century England, came to the United States in 1976, and opened the Levand office in Birmingham five years later.

"The early 1980s were a depressed time for the steel industry in America," Metcalf relates, "and we were not well known in the South. We had to create a plan to increase our market share in the Southeastern states. We were well established in the Northeast, the Midwest, and on the West Coast, and worked hard to make ourselves better known in this region."

Metcalf and his staff quickly launched a multi-faceted approach to improving the company's name recognition in the South. Knowing that they faced serious challenges in competing with firms long established in this area, they focused on personalized service to their clients, and were available, as they are today, 24 hours a day, seven days a week. They also began selling British and German manufactured metallurgical instruments for the aluminum foundries and the recycling industries.

Their efforts paid off. Levand Steel & Supply's Birmingham office now is a principle shipper of products each month to a diversified list of customers.

Metcalf also points to the founder's penchant for diversification as a reason for the company's steady growth over the years. Moving into the mining sector proved to be an effective strategy. Levand Steel & Supply now owns three iron ore mines in California, a gypsum and Agricultural lime mine in Brazil, and other mining interests in the Western states.

A second successful venture established by the company's founder was in the expansion into the production of fabricated counterweights ranging in size from those used in small excavators all the way up to 600-ton units required on large earth moving shovels. Levand now directly and indirectly supplies approximately 60 percent of the counterweight fill used in this country and overseas.

Another start-up division specializes in the manufacture and worldwide shipment of austenitic manganese steel and martinsitic alloy steel castings, ranging in size from 100 to 39,000 pounds.

Even with this diversification, Levand Group continues to handle major tonnages of basic feed materials, including steel scrap/by-products, used in the steel, foundry, cement, and fertilizer industries each month. These products are shipped by truck, railcars, barges, and bulk cargo ships.

"We're only a six-person office here," Metcalf states, "but we've worked well as a team. Our investment in computers and the latest technology has been instrumental in fueling our growth over the years. Our commitment to customer service and our diverse range of operations will help us maintain a sound footing in the future."

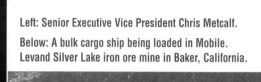

Left: Senior Executive Vice President Chris Metcalf.
Below: A bulk cargo ship being loaded in Mobile.
Levand Silver Lake iron ore mine in Baker, California.

WASHINGTON GROUP INTERNATIONAL

Integrated Engineering, Construction and Management

Washington Group International is a leading international engineering and construction firm headquartered in Boise, Idaho. With more than 35,000 employees at work in 43 states and more than 30 countries, the company offers a full lifecycle of services as a preferred provider of premier science, engineering, construction, program management, and development in 14 major markets. These markets include energy, environmental, government, heavy civil, industrial, mining, nuclear services, operations and maintenance, petroleum and chemicals, process, pulp and paper, telecommunications, transportation, and water resources.

Washington Group International serves its clients through six business units well positioned to emphasize their competitive advantages and contribute to the company's long-term growth:

Infrastructure. This unit provides public and private clients a preeminent constructive force with the experience, reputation, management, and skilled professionals needed for heavy civil construction projects. Performing as a general contractor or in joint ventures with other contractors, the unit has extensive experience in projects ranging from hydroelectric facilities to tunnels and bridges.

Energy and Environment. The Energy and Environment unit specializes in long-term operations and management processes at U. S. Department of Energy nuclear sites, and is also a major supplier to other public and private clients. Engineering, construction, analytical, management, and operations services are provided for highly hazardous materials and process facilities.

Mining. With more than 50 years in the mining industry, Washington Mining serves the metals, precious metals, coal, minerals, and minerals processes markets. Providing clients with competitive and efficient services, such as contract mining, technical and engineering, and equity participation has been the hallmark of this operating unit.

Industrial/Process. This business unit is a powerful, single source provider of quality engineering, construction, operations and maintenance, and logistics services to a wide range of markets and Fortune 500 clients who are seeking a partner to support their expansive programs around the globe.

Defense. Washington Defense serves promising markets focusing on chemical weapons demilitarization, weapons destruction in Eastern Europe, waste handling and storage, threat analysis and mitigation, and others.

Power. Washington Power is a premier player in the entire power business from engineering, construction and operations, and maintenance perspectives. The unit, which has a strong base in nuclear and fossil, provides leading turnkey capabilities in new generation, particularly in independent and merchant power plants, and has a strong service business.

Washington Group International has had a presence in Birmingham since 1905. The company, located at Inverness Office Park, now lists almost 1,200 employees in the Birmingham metropolitan area.

"Washington Group International is committed to industry-leading quality performance that adds value for our clients, sustains profitability for shareholders, and cultivates growth for our employees," states Jimmy Parker, the president of Rust Constructors, a Washington Group affiliate. "We deliver quality services ranging from small conceptual studies for a pulp and paper company to design, procurement, and construction of a grassroots auto plant to demilitarization of biological or chemical weapons for states in the former Soviet Union. Washington Group combines the strengths of legacy companies, including Badger, Catalytic, Ebasco, Litwin, MK Ferguson, UE & C, and Raytheon to name a few. The combination of these heritage organizations has created one of the largest international engineering and construction firms poised to meet the challenges of a dynamic world economy."

With more than 35,000 employees at work in 43 states and more than 30 countries, the company offers a full lifecycle of services as a preferred provider of premier science, engineering, construction, program management, and development in 14 major markets.

Jasmine Reyes

"I'm trying to make her understand that she has to go by your rules and not just go by what God says..."

Jasmine Reyes was talking on a cell phone to a Department of Youth Services employee, making arrangements for a Latino woman to work with the department and for the Latino woman to meet DYS workers and surrender her baby until they could appear in family court. The woman had a problem with an abusive husband and the DYS was concerned about the child's safety. Reyes, who was interpreting, jumping from Spanish to English and back again, was comforting the Latino woman and was working with both sides for a resolution.

"That has been going on all day," she says, putting her phone back in her purse. "We have emergencies like that. I'm so used to interpreting and translating because I do it all the time. It's important to learn to interpret for these people."

Reyes, coordinator of En Español, often works 12-hour days handling individual crises while trying to create a network of Spanish-speaking physicians, medical translators and targeted youth services to help the growing Latino community gain access to proper medical care.

On this cold, sunny day she sits in a comfortable leather chair in a quiet, modern conference room at the Birmingham Regional Chamber of Commerce waiting for a committee meeting to begin. But Reyes' work often is done in homes or emergency rooms or health clinics.

"I think America is so political," she says. "These are human beings. Healthcare is important. How would the politicians feel if they got sick and didn't have insurance because they were undocumented?"

"The Latino community is exploding in the Birmingham area. There are at least 70,000 Latinos living here now. These are often uninsured and unrepresented people. We are trying to work with doctors, trying to create a network of physicians. Affordable healthcare is crucial."

Reyes is interested in more than just healthcare, however. She is working to develop Hoover House as a place for the Latino community to receive a wide range of services, including employment.

"We are trying to work something out that everyone will benefit from, workers and employers," she says. "We would know their skills and would work out a system to send people to jobs that match their skills."

Reyes has a special passion for her job. Before coming to Birmingham she moved from Puerto Rico to Massachusetts so one of her two sons could receive treatment in Rhode Island for an unusual form of epilepsy.

A single mother, she raised her sons in New England where they both still live with Reyes' three grandchildren. She was a teacher in Puerto Rico and used those skills in a job for the YMCA in Rhode Island. It was a job at the YMCA that brought her to Birmingham.

"I'm happy. What I most enjoy is helping people and empowering people. To see them grow and go on with their lives, that's what I love doing.

"It's wonderful living in Birmingham. It's a nice city and I've met some wonderful people. I dance Salsa when I'm not at work. I teach Salsa and I work with youth to help them get applications ready for college. I also mentor three children on the weekend. I'm busy, I'm booking."

This energetic, excited woman is a walking advertisement for the Latino community.

"A lot of people have reservations," she says. "What are we going to do with the illegals? If they are criminals deport them. For the most part, Latinos are responsible, accountable people. When we say we're going to be there, we'll be there."

So, where will Reyes be in the coming years?

"I'm going to stay in Birmingham. I love Birmingham. I have a lot to do and I have to finish what I started."

Dr. Henry Panion, III

Behind the control board in a recording studio; behind a keyboard at the piano; behind the conductor's stand on the stage of a symphony hall, Henry Panion looks above all things supremely comfortable.

It's in his smile, perhaps; or the interplay of his hands with the music.

Some may know Dr. Henry Panion III for his participation in recent albums from Stevie Wonder (Conversation Piece, Natural Wonder), on which he served as arranger and conductor. As a composer, his works have been performed by several of the largest symphony orchestras in the United States.

He's also arranged for Aretha Franklin and for recordings for The Winans, New Jersey Mass Choir and Babbie Mason.

Dr. Panion is Professor of Music at the Music Department of The University of Alabama at Birmingham, which offers degrees in Music Technology and Music Business (www.music.uab.edu).

Henry Panion, III, Ph.D., holds degrees in music education and music theory from Alabama A & M University and Ohio State University, respectively. He is most known for his work as conductor and arranger for superstar Stevie Wonder, for whose performances and recordings he has led many of the world's most notable orchestras, including the Royal Philharmonic, the Bolshoi Theater Orchestra, the Birmingham (England) Symphony, the Orchestra of Paris, the Melbourne (Australia) Symphony, the Rio de Janeiro Philharmonic, the Ra'anana Philharmonic, the Nice Symphony, the Gothenberg Symphony, and the Boston Pops Orchestra. The two-CD set Natural Wonder features Dr. Panion conducting his arrangements of many of Stevie Wonder's award-winning, chart-topping songs with Stevie and the Tokyo Philharmonic. Other artists for whom Dr. Panion has had the opportunity to conduct and/or arrange include The Winans, Chet Adkins, Dionne Warwick, and Aretha Franklin.

Dr. Panion's own works for orchestra are programmed by orchestras throughout North America and by many of this country's major orchestras, including the Cleveland Symphony, Philadelphia Orchestra, Detroit Symphony, Baltimore Symphony, San Francisco Symphony, Symphony Nova Scotia, and the National Symphony. A selected list of other orchestras performing Dr. Panion's works include San Antonio, Columbus, Charlotte, San Diego, Louisville, North Carolina, Indianapolis, Arkansas, Jacksonville, Alabama, and the former Birmingham Metropolitan Orchestra, for which he served as Music Director from 1995-1997.

As a producer, composer, arranger, and orchestrator, Dr. Panion's work has produced two Grammy Awards, two Dove Awards, and a host of other national music awards and nominations. From 1994 to 2000, Dr. Panion served as chair of the Department of Music at the University of Alabama at Birmingham. Other honors included a 1995 Distinguished Alumni Award from Alabama A & M University and a 1996 Distinguished Alumni of the Year Award from the Ohio State University. He is the 1996 recipient of the Caroline P. and Charles W. Ireland Award for Scholarly Distinction and a 1995 inductee into the Alabama Jazz Hall of Fame. In 2000, the University of Alabama System Board of Trustees honored Dr. Panion for his many contributions to the field of music and bestowed upon him the distinguished appointment of University Professor.

MORESON CONFERENCING

High Quality, Cutting Edge and Timely Communications.

Mark Jackson faced more than the standard obstacles that line the traditional road to success in business. Jackson spent the first year and a half of his life in Children's Hospital in Birmingham battling asthma. Doctors told his parents he would be lucky if he lived to celebrate his fourth birthday. The same dogged determination that led Jackson to prove his doctors wrong led him to found Moreson Conferencing and guide it to its present position as the fifth largest conferencing provider in the United States with more than 20,000 ports available worldwide.

Moreson is now a global teleconferencing provider of high quality, cutting edge, and timely communications and information services to a variety of customers ranging from non-profit organizations to Fortune 500 companies. The company's conference calling products include live and archived audio, streaming, data sharing telephone, Palm Pilot, and Internet-enabled value-added services.

Employing the latest generation technology to its reservationless service has been a key to the company's success. Clients using Moreson's QuickCall service may now record their live conference, creating an archive of the meeting that may be retrieved from any touch-tone telephone in the world. The quick and easy procedure allows board members, sales staff, and other team members access to timely information they may have missed. It is particularly useful for training sessions on new services, legal use for documentation, or for allowing administrative assistants to check details of meeting minutes. It was especially useful to companies that rely on travel as a means of conducting business to return to normal in the wake of the events of September 11, 2001.

Mark credits his father, Carey Jackson, as he inspiration for much of his success. A retired naval officer and former U.S. Steel executive, the elder Jackson remains active as the president of his own company and a board member of a seminary in Louisiana. He was also instrumental in founding Lakeside Baptist Church in Birmingham.

Mark also followed his father's lead in service to his community. Though born in Birmingham, Mark Jackson based his Moreson Conferencing in Montgomery before moving part of the operation back to the Magic City in 2002. He now serves as a member of the Board of Trustees of the Birmingham Regional Chamber of Commerce, and was recently asked to join the Chamber's Birmingham Innovators Group (BIG).

The initiative sent over 100 business leaders to St. Louis to study that city's mass transit system, sports dome, and other amenities to determine which can be adapted to serve Birmingham. He has also been active in the political arena, campaigning for a number of candidates in national and statewide elections.

Every Friday morning since 1996, Jackson has sponsored a national Prayer Call that has served as an informal, non-denominational gathering of individuals that provides spiritual food for that business day, the coming weekend, and the following week.

Other activities have included joining Governor Don Siegelman and George Bush, Sr. in baiting fishhooks at a bass tournament to raise money for a Montgomery area school. In October, 2002, he served as one of three key chairs for the American Lung Association's statewide Asthma Walk.

"I am alive today because of the research results of the American Lung Association," Jackson notes. "It was a great honor to give back to an organization that has given me the opportunity to live a quality life, raise a wonderful family, and build a successful business."

Mark Jackson says, "Loyal employees make a company successful. Ours are the best in the industry. I should know, I work for them everyday."

MEDJET ASSISTANCE

Traveling With Confidence.

A serious illness or accident requiring critical medical attention is a chilling prospect to face at any time, but when the incident occurs far from home or in a foreign country, the scenario could have life-threatening consequences. MEDJET Assistance is an annual membership program for business as well as vacation travelers that provides for the transport of the member or the member's family to their home hospital or the hospital of their choice in a medically equipped and staffed jet.

Roy Berger, the president of MEDJET Assistance, points out how most people are unaware of how little is offered in a standard travel insurance policy and through protection offered through certain credit cards. Coverage on some policies states that air evacua-tion is authorized only if medically necessary, Berger states. Other companies accept responsibility only for taking you to the nearest, most appropriate hospital. If you are in a Third World country, that nearest, most appropriate hospital may or may not be adequate. You could still be left in a foreign country. What MED-JET Assistance offers to its members is comprehensive medical transportation to the hospital of their choice anywhere in the world.

In its ten years of operation from its headquarters at the Birmingham International Airport, MEDJET Assistance has built a membership base of approximately 50,000 clients throughout North America. Each travels with confidence, knowing that in the event of a medical emergency, a uniquely equipped aircraft operating as a flying intensive care unit with specially trained and experienced physicians and nurses will be dispatched for them. These aircraft, operated by MEDJET Assistance authorized affiliates, are fitted for cardiac and trauma life support and emergency and critical care medicine, as well as pediatric and neonatal care.

Stories abound of the benefits of carrying the MEDJET Assistance card, from a member who suffered a stroke in Abu Dhabi, one of the Persian Gulf emirates, to another who tore a hamstring on a dogsled expedition to the North Pole. These types of medical transports can carry a price tag of $75,000 or more. They were completely covered through the MEDJET Assistance program.

But the company provides comprehensive benefits for more than adventure travelers in remote regions of the world. MEDJET Assistance files contain hundreds of cases of average people on everyday vacations who were glad to have the MEDJET Assistance card in their wallet or purse.

MEDJET Assistance allows the traveler to be in control of his or her destiny with regard to medical treatment," notes Phillip Morris, the company's executive vice-president. "What we offer is inexpensive protection. For $195 a year for individuals or $295 for a family membership, people can gain the peace of mind that comes from being able to travel anywhere in the world knowing that if something happens, they will be immediately evacuated to their hospital of choice at no additional cost. MEDJET Assistance is the most comprehensive, least restrictive emergency travel assistance program available to the consumer today."

The company's talented management team is joined by a strong group of investors with ties to the worlds of aviation, finance, government, and real estate. They have combined their talent and resources to operate a service that has removed a major source of worry and "high anxiety" from the minds of travelers.

If you are in a Third World country, the nearest, most appropriate hospital may or may not be adequate. What MEDJET Assistance offers to its members is comprehensive medical transportation to the hospital of their choice anywhere in the world. Company executives Phillip Morris and Roy Berger offer vacationing or business travelers peace of mind.

BRADLEY ARANT ROSE & WHITE LLP

radley Arant has long been a driving force behind Alabama's economic development. The firm has participated in preparing and implementing state legislation on education, tax reform, tax incentives, and municipal finance. Lawyers from the firm have also served on committees to draft business and property laws, including the Alabama Business Corporation Act, the Alabama LLC Act, the Uniform Commercial Code, the probate code, and others.

Today, Bradley Arant is helping shape the state's core growth industries, including banking, construction, healthcare, and manufacturing, and has formed a business expansion team to focus on economic development and an emerging business and technology team to assist entrepreneurs and investors.

Bradley Arant represents a diverse client base of regional, national and international companies, including nearly 100 of the Fortune 500. The firm has industry expertise in manufacturing, construction, real estate, banking, financial services, energy, oil and gas, healthcare, venture capital, retail, technology, biotechnology, telecommunications, and insurance.

With a steadfast commitment to the highest standards of legal service, Bradley Arant attorneys are consistently selected for memberships in professional organizations that recognize outstanding lawyers. Bradley Arant has 23 lawyers who have been elected to nine of the American Colleges, and the firm has 48 partners listed in the 2002-2003 edition of The Best Lawyers in America. In addition, three of the firm's attorneys have served as law clerks to the Supreme Court of the United States.

HISTORY

Bradley Arant traces its beginning to a two-lawyer firm established in Birmingham in 1871. Since then, the firm has played a major role in transforming the city from a small industrial town to a thriving metropolitan community with a diversified economy.

Throughout its history, Bradley Arant has been led by prominent lawyers with exceptional credentials. Among its current and former partners are a United States Congressman, several Alabama and Birmingham Bar Association presidents, and two federal judges. From its inception, the firm has rep-

Far left: A 21st century firm with a 100 year tradition: pictured left to right Bradley Arant partners Nick Gaede, Linda Friedman, Beau Grenier (managing partner), Anne Yuengert and Mike McKibben, in the Lee C. Bradley, Jr. conference room.

Right: In the courtroom of the Honorable J. Scott Vowell, Bradley Arant litigators Rhonda Caviedes, Abdul Kallon, Arlan Lewis and Jimmy Gewin.

Below left: Full service representation: corporate associates and partners Robert Walthall, Cathy Chatawanich, Jim Rotch, James Childs, Dottie Pak and Susan Doss.

Below right: We treat some of our clients just like our own family: pictured left to right, Children's Hospital CEO Dr. Jim Dearth with Billy Moore, Bradley Arant partner Deane Corliss holding Morgan Scott, Chief Operating Officer David Kinsaul, Bradley Arant partner Michael Denniston, Chief Nurse Executive Supora Thomas and John Molen, another Bradley Arant partner.

resented major industrial, financial, transportation, and energy clients in Alabama and beyond.

With more than 190 lawyers, Bradley Arant is the largest law firm in Alabama and one of the largest in the region, with offices in Birmingham, Huntsville and Montgomery, Alabama; Jackson, Mississippi; and Washington, D.C.

PRACTICE AREAS

Bradley Arant's practice areas include the following: antitrust and trade regulation, banking and financial services, bankruptcy and creditor's rights, construction, employee benefits, energy, environmental, estate planning, governmental affairs, government contracting, general corporate, healthcare, intellectual property, international law, labor and employment, litigation and appellate litigation, mergers and acquisitions, municipal and project finance, real estate, securities, tax and industrial incentives, telecommunications, and white collar crime. A business expansion team comprised of lawyers from across various practice groups provides expertise to businesses moving to or expanding in Alabama, and an emerging business and technology team provides a comprehensive range of services to new and growing businesses.

COMMUNITY INVOLVEMENT

Bradley Arant is strongly committed to numerous community, civic, and charitable endeavors in the cities where its lawyers live and practice. Both the firm and its individual members contribute time and talents to local Adopt-A-School programs, homeless shelters, and public service organizations.

Representative of Bradley Arant's dedication to good citizenship is the Birmingham Pledge, a simple but eloquent commitment to racial harmony authored by one of the firm's partners. Congress and President Bush have recognized The Pledge, signed by over 70,000 people from around the world, with a resolution signed into law designating a "National Birmingham Pledge Week."

In addition, the firm provides pro bono services to indigent individuals, non-profit organizations, and matters of broad public concern. Bradley Arant is the only Alabama member of the Law Firm Pro Bono Project, which is sponsored by the American Bar Association and the Pro Bono Institute.

PUBLIX SUPER MARKETS

Where Shopping is a Pleasure

Publix Super Markets, one of the country's ten largest-volume super market chains, made its debut in Birmingham in 2002. Local shoppers immediately discovered the many reasons that Publix has become the largest and fastest growing employee-owned super market in the United States.

The first Publix store in the Birmingham area was opened in the former Delchamps location in Southgate Village in Pelham. Five stores will be open by the end of 2003 in the Greater Birmingham area. The Alabama stores will bring the total in the Publix family to over 700 located in Florida, Georgia, Tennessee, Alabama and South Carolina.

The company was founded with the opening of a single grocery store by George Jenkins in Winter Haven, Florida in 1930. Seven decades later, Publix has grown into a *Fortune* 500 company employing nearly 120,000 associates. Retail sales in 2001 topped $15.3 billion. A massive fleet of trucks depart daily from eight distribution centers and three dairy products manufacturing locations in Florida and Georgia delivering products to stores across the Southeast.

Anchoring the company's phenomenal growth has been its unwavering philosophy of pleasing the customer. The Publix management team understands that shoppers have a broad selection of super markets where they can shop. The Publix Guarantee states that Publix will never knowingly   disappoint their customers and "If for any reason your purchase does not give you complete satisfaction, the full   purchase price will be cheerfully refunded immediately upon request."

In addition, the company has been an industry leader in introducing a wide range of innovative services to make itself stand out from the competition. Following the trend to the Cyber highway, Publix introduced the convenience of online shopping to customers in many of its locations. Publix Direct, the company's online shopping and home delivery business, is being tested in parts of South Florida. Plans for the expansion will be revealed at a later date.

Other Online services include the Publix Prescription Refills program. With a few clicks of the mouse, customers can submit a request to refill a prescription at any time, day or night. The prescription will be ready for pick-up whenever the customer chooses.

Thousands have also taken advantage of other Publix consumer-oriented services. The company's Event Planning Guide was created to assist customers in the often-intimidating planning required to make special events truly special. Publix customers can select from a variety of functions, including picnics, graduations, birthday parties, retirements, sports events, and weddings, and find a selection of suggestions and helpful tips on making the event a complete success.

The Publix Moveable Feast program further underscores the company's commitment to serving as a partner in party planning. Customers can browse through an extensive selection of custom-made platters and trays to serve at weddings, business meetings, tailgate parties, or family reunions. The deli managers, master bakers, and seafood specialists at individual stores stand ready to assist in determining the amount of food needed, and presenting it in the perfect style to fit the occasion.

The Publix Deli offers platters of fresh fruit, vegetables and cheese, meats, deli salads, and custom-made sandwiches using bread baked at the store's own bakery. Endless combinations of meats, breads, and fresh condiments create sandwiches, subs, and the most delicious party foods for a quick lunch or a complete family dinner.

The award-winning professionals in the Publix Bakery work with customers to customize any cake they bake. Wedding, birthday, anniversary, sheet cakes, ice cream cakes, and others are available as the perfect complement to any occasion.

Aprons meal solutions is a service available online at www.Publix.com. It consists of nearly 200 recipes to assist customers in preparing memorable meals for friends and family. Imaginative recipes for palate-tempting seafood, poultry, Asian, Italian, vegetarian, Southwestern, homestyle, and other dishes are available.

Publix and its associates also excel in community involvement, volunteerism, and a commitment to the company's market area. The company annually honors a number of associates with the "Mr. George Community Involvement Award" for best exemplifying the characteristics that George Jenkins instilled in associates when he founded the super market. All are active in civic and charitable organizations, and winners receive a trophy, time off with pay, and a donation of $5,000 to the charity of their choice.

"Our founder, George Jenkins, believed in supporting the communities we serve," said Brenda Reid, community affairs manager for Publix. "Today his spirit still lives. At Publix we passionately support organizations focused on our children through education, youth sports, and feeding the needy. We give our time, money, and services to help make communities better places to live and work."

The philosophy which has always put the customer first has resulted in numerous first-place honors for Publix Supermarkets. In February, 2002, Publix was cited as the highest ranking super market for customer satisfaction for the eighth consecutive year. The ranking by the American Customer Satisfaction Index is determined through customer interviews measuring factors such as customer expectations, perceived quality, perceived value, customer complaints and customer retention.

"We're pleased with this year's score, especially because the ranking is based on actual customer experiences," said Publix spokesman Lee Brunson.

Publix also garnered for the fifth consecutive year a prestigious ranking on *Fortune* magazines "100 Best Companies to Work For." The ranking, determined by survey results from randomly selected employees, evaluates trust in management, camaraderie, and pride in the company.

"We're proud to receive this recognition from such a respected publication," said Publix CEO Charlie Jenkins, Jr. "This honor is particularly meaningful because it reflects the voice of our associates."

The super market business is considered by many to be among the most competitive in the United States. Publix officials realize that size alone will not determine their market share. The niche they have carved for themselves emphasizes quality, service, cleanliness, and a genuine feeling of warmth and friendliness on the part of Publix associates to every shopper in their stores. Not content to rest on its laurels, Publix constantly monitors the performance of its stores and its people to remain a leader in the industry.

ERNST & YOUNG

Business Insights and Essential Strategies.

n alliance forged between two successful companies led to the creation of Ernst & Young, one of the world's premier providers of professional services. The firm offers business insights and execution strategies essential today: auditing, accounting advice, tax compliance and planning, corporate finance transaction assistance, law advisory, and others.

Business leaders today understand the need to act with the best available knowledge and move forward with confidence in order to compete effectively. Ernst & Young professionals deliver value by showing clients how to improve their operating effectiveness and achieve their economic objectives.

A global leader in the provision of these services, Ernst & Young ranks among the top names in the industry. The company's 104,000 people operating from 670 offices in more than 130 countries around the globe have developed a network of strategic alliances designed to deliver solutions anywhere in the world.

Ernst & Young's Birmingham headquarters looks out over the city's skyline from high atop the AmSouth Harbert Plaza in the heart of downtown. The company was the first major national accounting firm to locate in the Magic City in the early 1900s. Since then, it has built an unsurpassed reputation for integrity and service. Whether a Global 1000 company or an emerging growth business, all have turned with confidence to Ernst & Young to provide the right services to help them meet their objectives.

"The approximately 200 professionals in the Birmingham office realize that we are in the client service business," states Karole F. Lloyd, the firm's office managing partner. "That remains our number one priority. The issues that are most important to our clients are most important to us."

The staff in Birmingham, as is true in each Ernst & Young office around the world, takes an account-centric, issues-oriented approach to problem solving. They work closely with their clients to identify pressing challenges, such as globalization or increased competition. Identifying industry issues and outlining strategies for growth and enhanced profitability are also key objectives.

The many players in Birmingham's broad-based economy, ranging from world-class healthcare providers and research institutions to entrepreneurial companies and finan-

cial institutions, each have unique needs. They also have industry-specific questions. What are the benchmarks of operational, financial, and competitive excellence? What are possible impacts of regulation, globalization, and consolidation? How will product life cycles, capital markets, technology, or geopolitics and economics affect the future? Ernst & Young specialists are ready and able to answer these and other questions critical to the growth of a business.

In addition to the typical accounting services offered by other firms, Ernst & Young offers advice and assistance in protecting a company's information technology assets from viruses, attacks and internal security threats; capital markets advice; tax-effective supply chain planning; compensation design; planning and post-merger integration advice; and more. The company utilizes its knowl-

edge management capabilities to offer high quality service. The company is continually developing new ways to capture and deliver insights and ideas to be used by its professionals worldwide to benefit the firm's clients.

A barometer for measuring the firm's success in delivering services and solutions is the revenue plateau of almost $10 billion it reached in 2001. Success at the local level is also evident. The Birmingham office has produced three of the firm's management committee members and a number of individuals who went on to hold national offices within the company.

"We've been an effective incubator for a great deal of home grown talent," Lloyd relates. "As a supporter of our educational institutions and a good corporate citizen, we're one of the leading recruiters of the top students from the colleges and universities in Alabama. We've collaborated often with the Birmingham Regional Chamber of Commerce to showcase the many amenities the Birmingham area has to offer."

In addition to the success the firm has achieved in recruiting some of the best people in the field, Ernst & Young has also earned high marks for retaining much of that talent by building an environment that fosters growth and promotes the development of new skills and knowledge. The firm has frequently been cited as among the best places to work by publications such as *Fortune* magazine, *The Sunday Times* in the United Kingdom, and elsewhere in the world.

"Ernst & Young has had a significant impact on the growth and development of the Birmingham area since the company first established a presence here," Lloyd states. "We have built professional relationships with some of the businesses we serve that go back 30, 40, and even 50 years. As a center for healthcare, financial services, and the retail, manufacturing, and entrepreneurial industry, the Birmingham area is poised to experience a great deal of growth in the future. We're very excited about Birmingham's future and the climate for business that exists here. It's a great place to live the dream."

Jay Barker

They were not 80,000 strong. They weren't screaming at the top of their lungs. They were not stuffing hotdogs in their mouths and washing them down with smuggled liquor. And none of them paid $30 a seat.

But this crowd of 200 or so who attended a free men's conference on a sunny Saturday at The Church at Brookhills meant as much to Jay Barker as any that screamed as he led Alabama to the National Championship in 1992.

Barker was the first speaker of the day, coming to the altar after a band played electric Christian music for about 20 minutes.

"It was awesome," he said to the crowd. "I walked up to the side of the building and felt like I was back in the locker room. I could hear the rumbling, the men talking.

"Running out in the arena is like your feet are walking on air and that's the way it should be here. People won't stand up and worship God, but on Saturday they're standing up and yelling Roll Tide or War Eagle. If you do that, then stand up and praise God."

After his talk, Barker relaxed for a moment in a small counseling room outside the sanctuary. Music boomed through the walls as he sat cross-legged. His intertwined fingers were locked around his right knee. The National Championship ring shone in the fluorescent light.

"It has always amazed me that people get that excited before a football game and then maybe drag to church," Barker says. "They don't have that same passion for Christ. Imagine people getting so excited about Christ that they tailgate two days before a church service."

He was at The Church at Brookhills on this Saturday to talk about Christian men being energized to serve God. Dressed in black pants and a gray long-sleeve knit shirt, this graceful athlete exudes energy. And he adeptly compares athletics with his life as a Christian.

"Having been an athlete helps with the preparation," Barker says. "The work ethic is important. The great thing about being in the spotlight is that you can get people's attention. Great accountability comes from being in the public eye."

He glanced down at the championship ring.

"I wear this for other people. They want to see it; it's a topic of conversation."

Barker unabashedly uses his considerable celebrity to preach and work to bring people to Christ. It's even evident in his line of work—a three-hour sports talk show on WJOX Monday through Friday.

"I planned on getting into coaching," he says. "That's still a desire. The Lord laid this job of being on the radio in my lap. There's nothing wrong with Christian schools and Christian vocations, but we can't isolate ourselves. We have a chance to point people to Jesus. No matter where you work, you have a chance to make an impact.

"I tell them (others on the talk show) to be real because I'm going to respond. You gotta be real with people. I believe Jesus did that."

Earlier, during his talk, Barker said he began to feel God's presence as a child in Chalkville. He was talking fast, moving, getting louder, getting excited.

He raised his voice and said "Ego means to Edge God Out. I get on the radio and people call up and say 'You're so good.' Do you know how hard that is when I know how bad I am? Sometimes I come to church and I look good, but the inside is dirty. You've got to get out and let God come in and clean you up.

"Our purpose is to glorify God. The key is you don't lack purpose if you go to any job and realize your purpose is to reach people for God. What God is saying is 'Have a passion for me and then you'll have a passion for people.'

"We're not special, we're blessed. We get to be a mouthpiece for what God's saying. You can have a great impact on the world because you are with people every day."

Then this celebrity, this star athlete, this favored son of Alabama called for people to come to the altar and praise God. This man who in his time as an athlete commanded the attention of thousands around the country, knelt and prayed for purpose and passion. He wiped tears from his eyes.

And 50 men knelt beside him.

REALTYSOUTH

A drive through almost any of the residential neighborhoods in the Birmingham area will feature glimpses of a familiar real estate sign that is almost as prevalent as the dogwood and magnolia trees that dot our landscape in the South. The oldest and largest real estate company in the state, RealtySouth is the predominant leader in Alabama real estate, currently responsible for listing and selling approximately 50 percent of all homes in the Birmingham area. The company's market share in some areas of the state exceeds 70 percent.

"RealtySouth continues to surpass the competition as a result of careful planning, technological advancements, sound business decisions, and recurring business from a client base that has come to trust the name of RealtySouth," states Tommy Brigham,

the company's chairman and chief executive officer. "We bring together more buyers and sellers with homes than any other company in Alabama."

With roots dating back to 1955, the company has been a familiar name in the Birmingham area. More than 1,200 sales associates serve the greater Birmingham area out of some 20 conveniently located RealtySouth offices.

The RealtySouth family of services is administered through three primary divisions—MortgageSouth, TitleSouth, and InsuranceSouth. MortgageSouth, one of the top five lenders in the Birmingham area, offers personalized mortgage services exclusive to the realtor client. TitleSouth plays an equally important role in the home-buying transaction, providing coverage against hidden defects, such as senility or competency on behalf of the seller, a forged signature on a deed, or a probate in process that discloses unknown heirs.

InsuranceSouth is a full-service independent insurance agency

focusing on personal lines property, casualty, and life insurance. The firm represents multiple top-rated insurance companies, such as Travelers, Chubb, The Hartford, and Progressive.

In August of 2002, RealtySouth further solidified its position as the leading name in real estate in Alabama. The company was acquired by HomeServices of America, Inc., the second largest full-service independent residential real estate brokerage firm in the U.S. based on closed transaction sides. A Berkshire Hathaway affiliate owned by billionaire entrepreneur Warren Buffet, the company operates in 15 states with a combined annual sales volume in excess of $33 billion.

"We look forward to having Alabama's largest brokerage firm join the HomeServices family of companies," said Ron Peltier, president and chief executive officer of HomeServices on announcing the

acquisition. "RealtySouth has been successfully built on organic growth, strategic acquisitions, and a commitment to providing a superior customer experience. The shared vision among all of our companies is to create and deliver an unparalleled customer experience throughout the entire home ownership life cycle."

Peltier's excitement was mirrored by Tommy Brigham. "We look forward to partnering with the HomeServices companies," he noted. "For more than 45 years, we have been delivering a tradition of excellence and innovation to our customers. HomeServices commitment to technology, with leading edge agent tools and innovative products and services for customers, will contribute to our future successes."

Above: RealtySouth CEO Tommy Brigham. At left: Company headquarters along Highway 280.

THE OWENS GROUP, INC.

he Owens Group, Inc., a comprehensive organizational development consulting firm founded by Dr. Linda G. Owens, is dedicated to leading progressive organizations to success with innovative solutions to their business needs.

Dr. Owens leads a highly motivated team of professionals in assisting businesses and organizations in enhancing the quality of life for their stakeholders. The firm offers specialized training and organizational interventions in areas such as diversity and multi-cultural awareness, coaching, leadership development, change management, and performance management in the U.S. and abroad.

Dr. Owens has developed a comprehensive library of training modules that can be combined into customized training programs uniquely designed to meet the specific needs of clients. Ranging in length from one to five days, these programs have been proven effective in numerous situations. Training is available in the value of diversity, the challenges and opportunities in managing diversity, shades of excellence, training for diversity consulting, and others.

A broad variety of businesses and organizations have sought Dr. Owens' services. Clients have included non-profit organizations and Fortune 500 companies such as IBM, AT & T, Alabama Power Company, the Internal Revenue Service, Delta Airlines, Miller Brewing Company, and a host of others.

Dr. Owens' strategy includes creating a comprehensive plan that fits a client's particular needs, setting clearly defined objectives, and measuring the achievement of these objectives at reg-

ular intervals. She incorporates diversity into an overall strategic plan, integrates it into all systems of the company, and makes it a line responsibility. She and her staff provide the awareness, leadership principles, and organizational change interventions necessary to create a work environment conducive to the growth and development of all employees, regardless of differences.

"Our success has been a direct result of our collaboration with our clients," Dr. Owens states. "I studied diversity academically at the doctoral level, applied that knowledge as an internal diversity consultant, and worked as an external diversity consultant for diversity consulting firms. That background, coupled with the cooperation of our clients, has made The Owens Group, Inc. the dynamic organizational development firm that it is today."

Organizational culture does not change by training alone. In addition to diversity training, The Owens Group, Inc. offers a broad array of products and services to assist organizations in their change initiatives including:

- Team building
- Consulting services
- Performance management
- Communication skills
- Cultural assessments
- Executive and professional coaching
- Customer relations development
- Leadership management
- Web-based training

Dr. Owens is also co-founder of HIGHER GROUND, a dba of The Owens Group, Inc. Through seminars, workshops, and special events, HIGHER GROUND maintains a focus on personal development and healthy relationships.

Dr. Linda G. Owens, founder of The Owens Group, Inc., a comprehensive organizational development consulting firm dedicated to leading progressive organizations to success with innovative solutions to their business needs.

Dr. Al Pacifico

The conference room was big and quiet, thoughtfully designed and lit. Equestrian art, colorful books on Spain and Latin American countries lined the shelves. *A History of Baseball* sat on a shelf with sculpture.

Among these expensive and beautiful gifts was a simple poem in a frame. A poem from a grateful parent.

"I know God was watching over him
...But in you He found his soldier
In you He planted a seed
A seed that grew and blossomed
Into a wonderful physician and man."

Dr. Albert D. Pacifico, internationally known physician and researcher and a pioneer in the field of American cardiovascular surgery, is that "soldier," that "wonderful physician and man," who gave a parent the greatest gift—a child's health.

All the art and books and beauty in the conference room in Dr. Pacifico's office are gifts from patients and their families. Gifts from people who flew across oceans to come to Birmingham and have skilled hands repair their damaged hearts.

Dr. Pacifico was born in Brooklyn, NY and he received his Bachelor of Science degree from St. John's University on Long Island. In 1964 he began his internship at the New Jersey College of Medicine in Newark and then traveled to the Mayo Clinic to study with internationally renowned Dr. John W. Kirklin. In 1966 Dr. Pacifico came to Birmingham with Dr. Kirklin where Dr. Pacifico spent several years working in physiology, studying the pathophysiology of heart failure during and after cardiac surgery.

"I went to Mayo because Dr. Kirklin was there and came here because he came to Birmingham (to become chairman of the Department of Surgery and director of the Division of Cardio-Thoracic Surgery at UAB)," Dr. Pacifico said.

"I stayed for many reasons: I would be part of his group, the potential growth of this medical center, the support provided by the institution and the organization of the Division of Cardio-Thoracic Surgery. (That organization) allowed a doctor to build a practice essentially independently."

"The policy here is independent practice where each surgeon has an opportunity to grow in accordance with his ability."

And Dr. Pacifico's practice has grown. He has worked to perfect a technique that cuts surgery times dramatically—often from 10 hours to less than two hours, 20 minutes—to increase patient safety, reduce hospital stays and return patients to normal lives through a shorter recovery period. Dr. Pacifico performs nearly half of the cardiovascular procedures at UAB—an average of 1,200 a year—achieving in a few months the number of surgeries that many other surgeons conduct in a year.

His skill was such that when then-UAB President Dr. Scottie McCallum needed heart surgery he called on Dr. Pacifico.

The chance to study and work with Dr. Kirklin brought Dr. Pacifico to Birmingham, but the area helped keep him here.

"I have enjoyed living here, that's why I stay," he said. "I've had many job opportunities in many places. I feel a bond with Birmingham and the medical center.

"Birmingham is a fabulous place. The people are nice and there are many cultural opportunities and it's a relaxing, quiet environment."

Dr. Pacifico has raised his family in Birmingham. He has a son who is a physician in Seattle, a daughter at Birmingham Southern and a 17-year-old son who is a senior at John Carroll High School.

"The people are nice, there are many cultural opportunities and it's a relaxing, quiet environment. I had bought a piece of property (at that time) in the boondocks—Indian Springs—and built a road to my house and loved it because it was in the country. In Birmingham you can still live in the country and be at a major medical center in 15 minutes."

Gaynelle Hendricks

"We didn't have any money. We used our savings and we used our limits on credit cards. My husband was able to sustain the family. I took no salary for the first year.

"Everybody worked. My husband was the janitor. I bought the food. I hired teachers because my expertise was best used running the business."

Gaynell Hendricks sat in her downtown office above her sixth Wee Care Academy day care and remembered the beginnings of what has become a thriving Birmingham business. Her office is a jumble of African art, computers and paper and somehow it all works together with Hendricks at the center in control.

She founded the company in 1988 out of a personal need. She had twins and wanted to work and be with the children at the same time. Today Wee Care Academy, which began as a small day care operation in space rented from the Birmingham Board of Education, now has six locations and manages seven daycares for the Birmingham Housing Authority.

"As I began to look for childcare I didn't see anything available that I liked, so I decided to open a day care center. My husband (Birmingham City Councilman Elias Hendricks), daughter and I threw out different names. My 12-year-old came up with the motto and my husband came up with the logo. I leased an old elementary school building in the Thomas Community. It grew in the first year and in the second year we bought the building."

"For that time in my life it was right. That had never been one of my career goals. At that time I just wanted to have one, but it took off."

Hendricks has a quick wit and a bright face. Her excitement is contagious, as is her smile. And her mind for business is immediately evident. The Tennessee native moved to New Jersey with her husband and used that time to earn an MBA with an emphasis on marketing from Rutgers.

"I like marketing. It really came in handy marketing Wee Care. I went by the book. I did my own ads, wrote the copy, did my own voice on the radio.

"People could hear that I was a mother. We would play the ad in the morning and in the evening when mothers were dropping off and picking up their children. We know it's smart now because it worked. You don't have to be an MBA to be smart about things and make them work."

This mother of three and wife of a city councilman knows plenty about "making things work." Gaynell learned a lot in Elias' hard-fought political campaign.

"The campaign was hard work. I was there every day for six or seven months running the campaign. Once we got in it, we had to win. We had to pull out all the stops. We didn't have money, but we ran a smart campaign."

She points out that the campaign, like her business was a community-oriented project.

"Our home is in Birmingham; our business is in the city. We knew something had to change. Members of the older neighborhoods asked Elias to run because they wanted change.

"The business community was giving up and they didn't see the potential for growth. Elias had already done a lot of work in the community. He is a smart guy and I felt he really had something to offer."

The Hendricks work as a team.

"He has always been very supportive. He has always pushed and encouraged me. There are things I am good at and he is a visionary, he can see the dream. I'm more of an implementer. Together we make things work."

But Mrs. Hendricks' life is about much more than just the business.

"Wee Care being successful and being owned and operated by an African American woman is important. It's a tremendous responsibility that goes along with it. There is a sense of pride to know we can be a part of future growth.

"I'm a very spiritual person. My faith is a source of comfort and strength. I pray about everything I do. God has given me abilities and as a result of that, I give back to the community. I think it's important for people to say that and not be ashamed to say that. My faith in God and the life I try to lead is what it's about.

"It's important to give God the credit for what we do."

CORY WATSON CROWDER & DeGARIS, P.C.

Helping People From All Walks of Life Is a Privilege.

The Birmingham law firm of Cory Watson Crowder & DeGaris has become known as one of the region's leading law firms devoted to representing individuals and businesses injured by the wrongful conduct of others. The firm is founded on the belief that the civil jury system is the best means to provide compensation to injured parties and deter wrongdoers from injuring others in the future.

Cory Watson Crowder & DeGaris was founded in 1995, with two of the firm's partners having practiced together for almost 20 years. Ernest Cory and Leila Watson first met as part of a predecessor firm in 1983 and have been together since that time. Charles Crowder and Annesley DeGaris joined them in 1992, and the four lawyers eventually founded the firm as it exists today. Charles Crowder, a former Jefferson County Circuit Court judge for 20 years, is well known and respected in the legal community. Annesley DeGaris joined the group after serving as an attorney with the Eleventh Circuit Court of Appeals. The addition of Rick DiGiorgio and Craig Niedenthal as shareholders in the firm has added decades of collective legal experience.

The firm has grown to a 40-person staff, including 11 attorneys licensed to practice in several Southeastern states. Working with local co-counsel, and with the help of five ambitious associate attorneys, the firm now represents clients in venues across the United States and abroad.

"Our firm is made up of attorneys and staff who are interested in helping people from all walks of life," states Ernest Cory, one of the firm's partners. "We teach our staff that it is a privilege to represent our clients. We represent ordinary people who usually do not have the resources to confront the wealthy corporations that may have injured them or their families."

Cory also points out that the firm is a lawyer's law firm. "We are very proud of the fact that attorneys who don't handle certain types of litigation have enough confidence in our work that they refer their clients to us for representation," he notes.

Cory Watson Crowder & DeGaris handles cases across the legal spectrum. The firm's attorneys are experienced in a number of areas of practice, including:

- pharmaceutical drug litigation
- aviation accidents
- environmental/toxic tort litigation
- business litigation
- highway design and construction
- civil rights cases
- building design and construction
- motor vehicle accidents
- defective products
- nursing home litigation
- defective medical devices
- defective motor vehicles
- product liability
- employment law
- workplace accidents

The firm has represented thousands of people who have sought legal assistance, including victims of on-the-job injuries, motor vehicle accidents, and defective products. Cory Watson Crowder & DeGaris is among a small group of attorneys who have experience and success in representing clients in mass tort litigation. The firm's involvement in mass torts began in the 1980s with the Dalkon Shield cases. Since that time, the firm has also represented large numbers of individuals injured by silicone breast implants, diet drugs, phenylpropanolamine, and other drugs and defective implantable medical devices.

The firm has represented large numbers of clients injured by silicone breast implants, diet drugs and defective medical devices.

The firm's offices were renovated from existing space and turned into a law firm showcase of design and efficiency.

The firm's office is located on the corner of Magnolia Avenue and 22nd Street South, across from Brother Bryan Park. Leila Watson's husband, Robert, a local architect, worked with the firm to renovate an existing building into a showcase law office. Watson's design balances aesthetics with the functional demands of a practice that serves the needs of thousands of clients.

"As a new and growing firm, we had defined our identity and philosophy for our practice," Leila Watson relates, "and wanted to create a physical presence in the area as well. Robert assisted in the spatial design to give us an elegant work space without sacrificing efficiency."

The law firm has made a concerted effort to bring in artwork and sculpture from Alabama artists for display in the office. "This is just another way that we can support and recognize Alabama's talent," Watson relates.

Employing the latest electronic technology has been an important part of building the firm's reputation for excellence. Cory Watson Crowder & DeGaris was among the first firms to create an in-house computer database to monitor and handle client cases. In the silicone breast implant litigation involving claims for over 2,300 women, database technology enabled the firm to monitor all aspects of these cases including the status of litigation, detailed medical records, statistics, and other information.

The firm's philosophy of service to its clients extends to the service its attorneys offer the community at large. A number of civic and charitable organizations benefit from this philanthropy.

"Community service is an integral part of our firm's philosophy," Ernest Cory relates. "We support the Susan B. Komen Breast Cancer Foundation, Magic Moments, the Rotary Club, and the United Way, to name a few." Charles Crowder has served as a past Potentate of the Shriners Association which helps injured and disabled children all over America. Other firm members donate money and time to community service initiatives that improve the quality of life for people across Alabama.

The firm is also committed to sharing its knowledge and expertise with other lawyers, law students, and the general public. Members of the firm regularly speak to various business and professional groups, conduct seminars, contribute articles to legal publications, and serve on national, state, and local bar committees and associations. Annesley DeGaris is currently a professor of Constitutional Law, and has served as an adjunct professor at Emory Law School and the University of Alabama at Birmingham. Leila Watson was selected by the American Trial

Lawyers Association to co-chair the national Baycol Litigation Group.

The attorneys and staff at Cory Watson Crowder & DeGaris are proud to be a Birmingham-based law firm. Ernest Cory observes, "Ten years ago, I would have never considered that a firm from Birmingham, Alabama would be representing clients in over 30 states. We are blessed and aware of the enormity of this responsibility."

Cory, Watson, Crowder and DeGaris has become one of the region's leading law firms in representing individuals and businesses harmed by the wrongful conduct of others.

The firm has grown to a 40-person staff, including 11 attorneys licensed to practice in several Southeastern states. Working with local co-counsel, the firm now represents clients in venues across the United States and abroad.

Honda Odyssey minivans roll off the assembly line at the rate of more than 650 per day at the automaker's plant in Lincoln, about 40 miles east of Birmingham. When Honda completes its expansion in 2004, the $1 billion Alabama facility will employ more than 4,300 associates and have the capacity to produce 300,000 vehicles and V-6 engines a year.

HONDA MANUFACTURING OF ALABAMA, LLC

A Premier Automotive Manufacturing Facility

It didn't take long for Honda Manufacturing of Alabama, LLC (HMA) to establish a strong foundation in Alabama. Since Honda first announced plans in May, 1999 to build a vehicle and engine factory near Lincoln, the company has quickly grown to become one of the premier automotive manufacturing facilities in the world.

Just 18 months from the company's ceremonial groundbreaking in the Spring of 2000, Honda's Alabama team produced its first Odyssey minivan on November 14, 2001. Today, the company employs more than 2,400 associates, most of whom live within a 50-mile radius of the $580 million state-of-the-art manufacturing facility. Annual production at the facility, which is just 40 miles east of Birmingham, now totals more than 150,000 Odyssey minivans and V-6 engines each year.

But that's just the beginning of the Honda story in Alabama. In July, 2002, Honda announced it would expand its operations with the addition of a $425 million assembly line that will employ another 2,000 associates, and eventually double production capacity to 300,000 engines and vehicles per year.

"With demand continuing to increase for Honda products, the dedication and commitment of our associates to build quality products for our customers made further expansion in Alabama the right choice for Honda," said HMA president and CEO Masaaki Kato, who lives in Birmingham. "We have forged a strong bond with our Alabama community, and we are excited that this bond will now grow even stronger."

Construction of a second production line raises Honda's investment in Alabama to $1 billion and increases total employment to 4,300 associates. In all, Honda's Alabama operation will include 2.8 million square feet of manufacturing space at the company's 1,350-acre complex near Lincoln. More than 90 percent of HMA associates, including engineers, process associates, and administrative personnel, were born and raised in Alabama.

Both manufacturing lines incorporate Honda's New Manufacturing System, which allows for production flexibility based on customer demand. Unique to Alabama is Honda's capability to produce both engines and vehicles under one roof—a first for Honda operations in North America. With this production system, HMA can easily build a variety of vehicles in the Alabama plant without a costly overhaul or retooling of the facility. But the Odyssey minivan is HMA's primary focus due to continued strong customer demand.

Though many of Honda's Alabama associates were new to the automotive industry, they have been the key to HMA's early success in getting the company established and into full production in such a short time period. All have exhibited a commitment to efficiency and flexibility, and share Honda's unique approach to teamwork.

"Our associates have certainly embodied Honda's 'challenging spirit' in the many milestones we have already achieved in Alabama," Kato said. "Our strong team at HMA has made many dreams come true."

Honda's continued investment in Alabama is part of the company's North American production strategy unveiled by Honda, which has added flexible capacity in the manufacturing of vehicles and powertrains. Honda's production capacity in North America will stand at more than 1.4 million units by late 2004. At that time, Honda's capital investment in North America will stand at more than $7 billion, with North American employment at more than 26,000 associates.

Honda began operations in North America in 1959 with the establishment of American Honda Motor Co., Inc., Honda's first overseas subsidiary. Using domestic and globally sourced parts, Honda began assembling motorcycles in America in 1979, with U.S. automobile manufacturing starting in 1982. Honda designs, manufactures, and markets its products in North America and worldwide. Honda currently builds products in 11 manufacturing plants in North America, with three major R&D centers in the U.S.

Honda is also the world's preeminent engine maker, and builds more than 15 million engines globally each year for its diverse line-up of automobiles, motorcycles, and power products.

CVTRAVEL, INC.

Designing Unique Travel Experiences.

Growing up on a horse farm in rural Queenstown, Alabama, Norma Borella succumbed at an early age to the irresistible siren song of enchanting, mystical places beckoning to her from around the globe. Not content to merely fantasize about someday visiting the world's wonders, she resolved to create a business built on assisting wide-eyed travelers to experience for themselves the thrill of exploration and discovery. In 1983, she launched CVTravel. It proved to be the most exciting road on which she has ever ventured.

As a custom tour operator and destination management expert, CVTravel excels in designing unique travel experiences around specific requests and requirements of each of their clients. Why would a national, multi-station broadcast company based in Baltimore depend on a travel professional in Birmingham to plan and execute a trip to Europe for their top advertisers from across the U.S.? Why would a mission organization from California consistently submit their travel needs to this same tour company? Because they have all learned to depend on the unsurpassed knowledge and dedication of the CVTravel staff, confident that the company's professionals will attend to every detail. Art museums and botanical societies look to them to create custom itineraries for their patrons to destinations throughout the world. The newly created division of CVTravel, the Kingdom Company, provides mission travel for churches and mission-sending organizations nationwide. Last year, over 15,000 people turned to CVTravel for extraordinary travel programs.

CVTravel's reputation for excellence and the company's volume of international travel have led to advantageous contracts with industry giants such as Delta Air Lines, Swiss, Northwest Airlines/KLM, British Airways, and Cathay Pacific. Working relationships with hotel brokers, land operators, and suppliers translate into the best airfares and most competitive tour costs for the company's clients.

CVTravel's original staff of two has mushroomed to more than 20 today. Each is a well-trained, experienced professional offering personalized service and meticulous attention to detail. Aware that they are in the business of making dreams come true, they understand that there can be no compromise on quality or service.

"I learned that the only way to get what I want in life is to help others get what they want," Borella notes. "I feel that travel is the ultimate form of education because it enlightens a person culturally, exposing them to that place in every way. Travel teaches tolerance and understanding as well as the obvious history, art, cuisine, language, politics, and geography. I love being able to help people experience all this."

The travel industry, probably more than any other, is extremely sensitive to a host of factors that can dramatically impact individual destinations. An ever-changing global political climate, internet travel bookings, and commission restructuring by suppliers have resulted in many agencies closing their doors in recent years. CVTravel, on the other hand, has over its two decade existence weathered a number of world crises, and continues to sustain a successful pattern of growth. Taking a broad view of the market and maximizing its advantage as a wholesale operator has helped the company grow from annual sales of $200,000 in 1983 to over $20 million today.

While she has now officially retired and turned over the operation of the company to executive vice-president and chief operating officer Diane Lee, Borella remains available for consultations. "I still want to see Kathmandu and climb Kilimanjaro," Borella smiles. "My travels have taken me to every continent several times and to locations too expansive for any photograph to capture. I want people to realize that every journey is a very personal experience that each traveler can claim as their own."

"I learned that the only way to get what I want in life is to help others get what they want," Borella notes. "I feel that travel is the ultimate form of education because it enlightens a person culturally, exposing them to that place in every way. Travel teaches tolerance and understanding as well as the obvious history, art, cuisine, language, politics, and geography.

CHRISTIAN & SMALL LLP

Preeminent Legal Experience with a Personal Touch.

When it comes to performance and service, Christian & Small offers the best of both worlds. Just ask the clients of Christian & Small, the successor firm to Rives & Peterson. Established in July 2000 by Thomas W. Christian and Clarence M. Small, Jr., Christian & Small is a full-service law practice successfully representing a diverse clientele throughout Alabama and across the nation from its Birmingham based offices. Collectively, the firm's attorneys have over 500 years of experience and comprise a formidable team of skilled professionals both in and out of the courtroom.

Christian & Small provides a comprehensive range of services, demonstrating breadth and versatility impressive for a firm of its size. The firm represents individuals and businesses, including several Fortune 500 companies. As a result, its attorneys have garnered a wealth of experience in various industries, including banking and financial services, health care, construction, labor and employment, technology, transportation, insurance, retail, and manufacturing. The firm also offers expertise in the areas of criminal defense, bankruptcy, family law, wills, trusts and estate planning. Christian & Small is committed to alternate dispute resolution, recognizing that mediation often provides an efficient and cost-effective strategy for minimizing litigation.

Several of the attorneys serve as mediators and arbitrators. With a keen knowledge of industry-specific regulatory matters, Christian & Small attorneys consider every contingency to provide the best possible counsel.

Christian & Small resolves legal issues using local, regional and national resources. "With our state-of-the-art research and technological capabilities, we have the tools we need to provide successful solutions to the legal problems of our clients," explains Duncan Y. Manley, one of the firm's senior partners. "We know our clients and their legal needs, and provide personal care and attention to protect their interests."

Whether clients need guidance or action, Christian & Small commands the know-how to deliver positive results. Its attorneys carefully assess the demands of each challenge and approach their work with thoroughness, ingenuity and skill. Clients involved in litigation can be confident that Christian & Small will deliver a solid performance in the courtroom, both at the state and federal level. Recognized for its strong business practice, Christian & Small also routinely advises its clients on a full spectrum of business law issues, such as acquisitions, mergers, tax planning, financial structures and products, and business operations.

Additionally, the firm's appellate practice provides superior representation for matters which the firm handles at the trial level as well as for clients seeking assistance specifically on appeal.

In recognition of their superior skills and dedication to legal practice, several Christian & Small attorneys have been selected as fellows of the American College of Trial Lawyers, the International Academy of Trial Lawyers, the American Board of Trial Advocates and the American Bar Foundation. A number of the firm's attorneys have served as president of the Birmingham Bar Association and the Alabama State Bar Association, while others devote their time and energy working in various capacities on local, state and national bar committees. Not only do the people involved with Christian & Small excel in their work, but they also provide leadership in the community. The firm is a Trustee of the Birmingham Regional Chamber of Commerce and encourages civic service and participation in numerous cultural and charitable activities.

Christian & Small endeavors to provide the knowledge, excellence and integrity that its clients expect and deserve. These guiding principles have earned the firm a distinguished reputation among Alabama's elite law firms.

Partners Thomas W. Christian, Duncan Y. Manley and Clarence M. Small.

Lawton Higgs

The storefront is bathed in sunlight, obscuring through the plate glass the activities inside. A small but steady stream of people passes through the weathered door to enter the Church of the Redeemer.

Inside arranged in three semi-circles around a table, lectern, and gold cross are mismatched chairs, anchored on cracked tile, supporting the bodies of people Lawton Higgs would call the children of God.

Higgs stands in the center. In a white, short-sleeved dress shirt and blue pants—a thick man with shining white hair—Higgs is speaking to a congregation that is startling in its contrasts, especially in a city where worship is arguably the most ethnically and economically homogenous of activities.

A young couple sits on the front row, college-age, in shorts and Birkenstocks. A blond family from the suburbs sits among a young black woman and her children. Homeless men. Young children whose mothers have sent them to church on their own. An elderly white woman sits next to a young black woman bouncing a toddler on her lap. The woman reaches out with a finger bent with age and caresses the face of the child. They both smile.

Behind the lectern and often bouncing on tip-toes in front of it, Lawton Higgs is talking about God's grace and the condition of the human heart.

For more than twenty-five years, Higgs has been on a journey, of which this place of grace on a Sunday morning in the city, is a culmination of sorts. He was thirty-seven back in 1977 when he was ordained a minister in the United Methodist Church, but his real journey began much earlier than that, as a member of a church who heard a call it took him a while to answer.

Higgs moved to Birmingham with his wife Nancy in 1966, joining West End United Methodist Church, in the heart of a white neighborhood in the midst of historic change. "All of the discussions in the white community's experience was to diminish and discount and negate everything that took place in the Civil Rights Movement. There were all kinds of stories and efforts to diminish Martin Luther King, Jr. That was a part of the world I swam in, and I accepted all of that as authentic and true.

"When I entered ordained ministry... I started reading John Wesley's forty-four standard sermons. I would read one of them every morning. And it transformed my life. I discovered the expression of God's grace and the articulation of faith that enabled me to commit to that grace and experience God's spirit, forgiveness, love and hope and expanded my whole view of what the Christian faith was about and what God was about.

"When I got to seminary, I was given the opportunity to read Martin Luther King, Jr. Well, Martin Luther King, Jr. wrote and preached the same thing that John Wesley wrote and preached.

"And so when I read his "Letter from the Birmingham City Jail," I wept for days, because I recognized that I had lived and bought into a system that was in opposition to God.

"And that began the journey of what I call a recovering racist. And it began a struggle, a hard struggle, to come to self-consciousness."

Higgs was appointed pastor of McCoy Methodist Church, near Birmingham-Southern College, a dying white church in a black neighborhood. He and others tried to build a congregation that was both black and white, a living neighborhood church. They failed.

In response to the loss, Higgs tried again; this time in downtown Birmingham. "We were led to this unbelievable place. It's right on the corner of the historic black business district and the historic white business district. And all of the city center dysfunction exists around it; economic depression, homelessness, addiction and everything else was piled on this corner."

Today the Church of the Redeemer is about 70 percent black and 30 percent white. Sunday services average about 75. They've outgrown the old store and are renovating a building for a new church not far away.

So the vision is succeeding: a neighborhood church that serves both black and white. Higgs guards against the notion that this downtown church should be viewed as a church for the homeless or some other kind of social experiment.

"Or that I'm some kind of special person, some kind of urban myth. 'Nobody could do this but you, Lawton.' That's not true. You just have to not be afraid to love your neighbor. It's pretty simple. Just because it's simple, doesn't make it's easy. But anybody can do it."

Bobby Horton

Bobby Horton's home music studio is a jumble, a junk-yard-like pile of antique banjoes and trumpets and guitars and fiddles and sheet music and tape decks and keyboards with a seat right in the middle just big enough for his slight body.

This excitable man who can't keep his long fingers off any musical instrument within reach has been instrumental in telling America's story to millions. Horton's love of history—specifically the Civil War—and music has propelled him into a unique partnership with Ken Burns, maker of public television documentaries on such subjects as The Civil War, Lewis & Clark, Mark Twain, baseball and Frank Lloyd Wright.

"I've only been around Ken two times," Horton says in his soft, yet quick-paced Southern accent. "I've talked to him scads of times on the phone. It's really an unusual relationship."

Horton, with his graying hair and neatly trimmed beard of the same color, looks as if he could be at home around a Confederate Army campfire or in his house in Vestavia Hills. He says he has been fascinated with music and with history since he was a child.

"My mother says that when I was eight I asked Santa Claus for pictures of Confederate generals. I got hooked on history from listening to the males in my family. They were all World War II guys."

Horton has played with the popular Birmingham-area band Three On A String for 30 years. But it was his interest in history and his drive to research old instruments and sheet music that led to his career in television working on Ken Burns' documentaries.

In 1984 he began researching and recording Civil War music. The cassettes were selling in federal parks and other specialty outlets. Then in the late '80s the editor of *American Heritage* mentioned to Burns that he should listen to some of Horton's Civil War recordings.

"They called and asked permission to pull some stuff from my Civil War volume," Horton says. "I didn't actually record anything for that (documentary). They used what was there. A year later, about '91 or so, Burns called me and asked if I would do classical guitar arrangements to 'Take Me Out to the Ball Game.' I told him I could work in all kinds of music, that I cut the tracks right here and play everything myself.

"It's been working ever since. I recorded five or six hours of stuff for Baseball. I did 86 cuts of 'Take Me Out to the Ball Game' in all different styles—Italian, Jewish, Big Band. I got to record a lot of tunes from all time periods."

Horton, sitting on his couch in a crowded living room amid framed pictures of Confederate soldiers and shelves crammed with war tomes, said he has always been curious about the use of instruments in songs written and played before recordings.

"I've always listened to what is unique about tunes. That's served me well with Ken. There is a lot of intuitive work that goes into this thing. You have distinctive eras in American music. Thomas Jefferson was next after Baseball. I knew the sounds and the instruments they used. Lewis & Clark was the same story. The harmonica was invented in 1860 and the banjo in 1830, so they couldn't be used in the music (for those documentaries).

"You take some liberties because you can't actually hear the music performed as they did it then. But there are clues in sheet music like chord progression that help you determine what instruments they used."

Horton, a man who enjoys good company and conversation at least as much as playing music, said his notoriety has placed him in some interesting situations.

"When I was working on *Lewis & Clark* a British couple knocked on my door. They had come to find the 'studio' that produced the historical music. They stayed until the next day. I was literally standing in the yard waving goodbye to Ann and Malcom when a German couple pulled up. They went to (his daughter) Rachel's volleyball game."

"I was sending recordings behind the Iron Curtain," Horton said. "They would send letters saying that they couldn't get dollars, but would I send them something.

"The Civil War is an amazing bond between people."

CARRAWAY-DAVIE HOUSE AND CONFERENCE CENTER

n a wooded hilltop overlooking the lazily flowing Cahaba River, the former home of a noted Birmingham neurosurgeon is now recognized as one of the Birmingham area's premier venues for social events, business meetings, and conferences. In 1979, Dr. Clayton Davie donated his remarkable home to the Carraway Methodist Medical Center to host events ranging from wedding receptions and special events to corporate conferences. A talented trio of partners with an eclectic mix of backgrounds has acquired the property and further enhanced the facilities and the gracious setting.

Rebecca Corretti, Ken Effinger, and Warren Bailey, operating as Prestige Hospitality Services, obtained the home and conference center in May, 2002, and immediately launched a marketing campaign touting the facility. They had much to brag about.

The three-story, 10,000 square foot house is the centerpiece of the facility. The beautifully furnished 28 rooms include a library, den, formal dining room, card room, and six bedrooms, two of which have marble fireplace sitting areas and French doors opening onto a terrace. There is also a garden, beautifully landscaped terrace, patio, and swimming pool.

Among the home's most remarkable features are the architectural elements salvaged from long vanished Alabama historic landmarks. The front door, with its hand-crafted lavender glass, originally was the north entrance of Birmingham's old Terminal Station. A two-ton, cast iron chandelier that once lit the storied train station now hangs in the den, and the handsome fireplace in the library warmed travelers in the station's waiting room.

The brass and crystal chandelier in the foyer originally graced Birmingham's Temple Theater, and an elaborate, gilt-trimmed mirror hung in the Tutwiler Hotel. Exterior brick dating from the turn of the century came from the old Birmingham Paper Company, and the six columns on the portico are hand-hewn cypress logs dating back to 1850.

"The house is an ideal setting for a variety of functions," states Ken Effinger, who brings years of experience in restaurant management to the team. "Our goal in acquiring the facility was to restore it to its former grandeur and expand our marketing efforts to introduce more people to what we have here. We now host an average of 20 functions each month. People from throughout the Southeast and as far away as New York have booked everything from weddings, proms, receptions, Christmas parties, and other events. And they've also discovered that the conference center is the perfect meeting facility."

The conference center, located adjacent to the house, can accommodate groups as large as 300 people. A tastefully decorated reception area leads into 8,000 square feet of meeting space that can be partitioned into three smaller rooms. Complete audio-visual facilities area available as well as a large, fully equipped kitchen. A lovely patio is ideal for entertaining or simply enjoying scenic views of the Cahaba River.

Another goal of the management team was to make the facility known for its innovative food catering services. Rather than the standard rubber chicken meals served during breaks at many meeting venues, the food and

service at the Carraway facility have come to be recognized as a quality dining experience. Breakfast, lunch, and dinner meals, ranging from light snacks to complete multi-course dinners, are available.

Rebecca Corretti brought her culinary skills and extensive background in imaginative food preparation and presentation to her role as coordinator of the catering services at the center. Her impressive credentials include training and working as a chef at restaurants in the Ritz Carlton Hotel in New York City and the Four Seasons in San Francisco. "I later operated Corretti Catering for a number of years," she notes, "and enjoyed the opportunities to be creative in providing fine food to the people we served. We have an entire menu from which event planners can choose, and we have the ability to custom create almost anything our clients want. I

probably most enjoy what we can do with meats and seafood items. The most important thing for me is for people to leave a function here talking about the exceptional quality of the food and service that we provide. It's especially gratifying when people tell me that our food perfectly complements our facilities here, and has become a magnet drawing people back."

That magnet has become particularly strong since Prestige Hospitality Services acquired the center. The house and conference center are now booked 18 months in advance for special events. The facility's events coordinator, reports that word-of-mouth referrals from satisfied clients continue to account for a large percentage of the bookings at the center.

"People really appreciate our ability to handle all the details of their function" she explains. "We're available to assist in everything from ideas for a theme party to ordering the flowers for a wedding. We focus on making each function a truly unique experience with attention to every detail."

The ability to attend to the myriad details involved in ensuring a successful event are what attracted Warren Bailey, the management team's third partner, to the operation. A former surgeon at St. Vincent's Hospital, Bailey opted for a complete career change to help launch Prestige Hospitality Services.

"I had been in practice for about ten years, and was looking to branch out into something different," Bailey relates. "I have always been intrigued by the entertainment business. The opportunity to assist people in planning a special event, and the satisfaction in making it a reality were exactly what I was looking for. My strengths are in the planning and execution of the function and coordinating all aspects to bring it off without a glitch. Making that happen is my greatest satisfaction."

Whether it's a seated dinner or a casual lawn party, the talented professionals at the Carraway-Davie House and Conference Center have the energy, expertise, and the commitment to provide the finest in food, service, and facilities to ensure a memorable function.

BALCH & BINGHAM LLP

Balch & Bingham LLP partnering with Banks Middle School since 1991.

Balch & Bingham LLP is a full-service firm that strives to be a proactive partner in its clients' businesses rather than a reactive legal advisor. The firm's 180 attorneys, as well as its support staff, realize that today's consumer of legal services needs more than just outstanding legal results. Clients expect and deserve outstanding service as well, including prompt responses and efficient and cost-effective legal services delivered with courtesy. The firm's individual attorneys strive to meet these expectations and promote this policy collectively.

The founder of Balch & Bingham LLP, William Logan Martin, joined his brother in opening a law practice in Montgomery before serving as the State's Attorney General and as Judge of the 15th Judicial Circuit. In 1922, he moved to Birmingham and established the law firm that is today Balch & Bingham LLP. The tradition of integrity and unparalleled service to its clients, which Judge Martin infused into the law firm he established over 80 years ago, continues today at Balch & Bingham LLP.

Balch & Bingham LLP is known for its deep involvement with the various industries it serves. The firm's attorneys view their roles as counselors who assist clients not only in times of crisis, but play significant roles in a planning and preventive capacity to help them avoid potential legal problems. The firm is active in writing and lobbying for key legislation, and actively participating in trade associations. The firm provides newsletters, updates, and seminars to keep clients apprised of changes in laws that could affect their businesses, their industries, and their legal well-being. Periodic reviews soliciting client feedback assist the firm's attorneys in monitoring their clients' level of satisfaction with the service they receive.

The firm currently maintains offices in Birmingham, Huntsville, and Montgomery, Alabama; Gulfport and Jackson, Mississippi; and Washington, D.C. From these centers, Balch & Bingham attorneys serve a varied and diverse range of clients throughout the U.S. and abroad. Businesses and individuals from the private and public sectors, including profit and non-profit corporations; partnerships; limited liability companies; federal, state, and local governments; and quasi-governmental entities have turned to Balch & Bingham professionals for their expertise and service-oriented philosophy. The firm represents many companies who are included on the Fortune 500, Forbes 500, and other nationally recognized listings.

Balch & Bingham LLP is committed to employing the latest technology to enhance the legal services it delivers to its clients. Primary focus is on providing highly reliable, cost-effective solutions that facilitate easy access, while, at the same time, meeting stringent security standards.

The company has made substantial investments in several areas to make its communications capabilities second to none, deploying new technologies as they become available and as they add value for the firm's clients.

The firm's commitment to serving its clients also extends to serving the communities in which Balch & Bingham LLP maintains offices.

(Above): Balch & Bingham LLP's Explorer Post Attorneys with Ronnie Holmes, Scout Executive.
(Top right): Mr. Glen Sears, Band Director of Banks Middle School trying out new instrument with student. (Bottom right): Banks Middle School Band.

Attorneys and staff members are involved in a broad range of community projects individually and as a firm. Those projects range from serving meals at area homeless shelters to serving on the boards of directors for many non-profit and charitable organizations. A number of the firm's attorneys have participated in both Leadership Birmingham and Leadership Alabama.

For over a decade, Balch & Bingham has participated in the Birmingham City School's Partners in Education program (formerly known as Adopt-A-School). The entire staff in the Birmingham office is proud of its partnership with Banks Middle School and the many successful initiatives it has helped create and implement there:

- Teacher of the Month program
- Honor Roll system
- Celebration of African/American History Month
- Women of Distinction Month
- Men of Distinction Month
- Annual athletics banquet
- Field trips to area schools, businesses, and attractions
- Annual art contest
- Career Day
- Mentoring program

The firm's community involvement is not limited to education initiatives.

In 1991, Balch & Bingham joined Samford University's Cumberland School of Law in sponsoring an Explorer post through the Boy Scouts of America. The firm continues this program today, providing scholarship information pertaining to a career in the legal profession by the Boy Scouts for inclusion in its master scholarship database.

Balch & Bingham also provides legal assistance to Birmingham's Partnership Assistance to the Homeless (PATH), a non-profit organization that serves homeless women and children in domestic violence situations by providing food, shelter, temporary and permanent housing, and employment training. The firm's attorneys coordinate projects with PATH's executive director; participate in credit, family law, and housing matters; present educational programs to PATH's employment training classes; and serve on the PATH board of directors.

The lawyers and staff at Balch & Bingham LLP view themselves as responsible citizens in the areas they serve and as an integral and vital part of the business communities in those regions. Accordingly, the firm's involvement inures to the benefit of all of its clients, as well as its members, and this effort will continue and increase as the firm grows.

Vaughn Randall

Vaughn Randall spends his days covered with sweat and grit, working with his hands amidst the flying sparks and intense heat of blast furnaces and sparking slag and red molten iron.

On this cold, overcast day in a cavernous brick power house at Sloss Furnace, Randall, coordinator of the Sloss Furnaces Metal Arts Program, is working. His blackened fingers move quickly to build a mold, the nail gun at home in his grasp as he fits joints together with a journeyman's economy of movement. In fact, Randall is a journeyman caster. He went to work in his father's fabrication shop after high school and then moved to Intertool in Hampton, Georgia, making wood patterns for castings.

Randall lived in an extra room in a wood shop at Intertool for two years while he earned his bachelor of fine arts degree from Georgia State.

"This is about half and half art and trade," Randall says while sitting on a stool amid a jumble of tools and work tables. "A lot of the art part is sitting there scratching your head. Once you get a plan, you build. They're inseparable.

"Part of the reason I work in iron is that the art work I do is about how to construct things. A lot of times I use industrial imagery to reference emotion.

"I think what sets us apart from other animals is that we are builders of tools. Figuring out a tool to help you realize your concept. Art and craftsmanship are inseparable."

Randall, a tall, lean man with a mass of tight brown curls atop his head, is thoughtful and smiles a lot when he talks. On this day he is building a wood positive image in a mold that is covered with a sandy mixture that will set up. When the mold is removed, a negative image is created and later molten iron will be poured into the space to create a piece for a sculpture. One of the companion pieces, smooth and gray and heavy, rests atop a table in one of the foundries at Sloss.

After earning his masters of fine arts degree from the University of Washington, Randall returned to the South. Two years ago he started volunteering at Sloss' Metal Arts Program.

"We do vessels to sell for Sloss, historical reproductions, one-of-a-kind short runs and commissions," Randall says. "I do a lot of commissions. We give 30 percent of that to Sloss. We also do a lot of outreach stuff; build products with summer youth so we can sell them and take some strain off the grant writer."

Sloss' Metal Arts Program offers workshops, classes, open studios and residencies. It also has an emerging artist program that allows successful candidates to earn a stipend of $1,000 a month while working with Sloss staff artists 30 hours a week. Randall remembers a time when $1,000 a month would have been nice.

"I made $8,000 my first year and that sucked," he says. "I lived with a friend and ate a lot of rice and chicken. I'm a little bit more comfortable now. Not any happier, but better paid."

"I'm dedicated to staying here," Randall says, adjusting his glasses. "Because I've been helping out, nurturing the site to make it what it is. The last couple of years the Metal Arts Program has come to the point where it's one of the best places in the world to do this. Other universities come here and learn from us."

Sitting under an oval shape that is a recurring theme in Randall's sculpture, he says he is inspired by the huge blast furnaces and complex at Sloss. And he thinks he knows why the massive, rusty tangle of rivets and valves and pipes is interesting to passersby.

"The furnaces are so complex that your mind can't understand it at one glance," he says. "Everything around here is riveted. It's the amount of craftsmanship and hard-ass work."

Working in iron is a challenge for many reasons, not the least of which is the weight of the final product. Randall says he builds heavy pieces and has plans to build a cast-iron sculptural gazebo.

A sign in the foundry where the artist works remains from the days when the furnaces melted tons of iron ore every day. It reminds workers to be safe and protect their hands, which it calls their "wage earners." The sign adds: "You owe it to your family."

Randall says of his art: "Lately I've been kind of questioning the industrial revolution, the pros and cons."

It would be a heavy piece in deed to represent the burden of the men who built Birmingham with fire and iron oar and sweat. And too often their lives.

ALTEC, Inc.

"Helping Crews Work Safer & Smarter"

ltec Industries, Inc., founded in Birmingham in 1929 by Lee Styslinger, is a privately-held company led today by the third generation of the family. With 2,500 associates worldwide, 800 of whom are employed locally, Altec specializes in the manufacture, sale, and service of aerial devices, digger derricks, and specialty equipment for the electric utility, telecommunications, tree care, and light and sign maintenance industries in over 120 countries.

At Altec, advanced technology efforts are aimed, without exception, at helping customers work "Safer & Smarter." Smarter in the sense that Altec sees itself in the productivity business—enhancing productivity for customers. This translates into developing technologies that dramatically increase uptime and dramatically decrease lifecycle costs. Altec invests more resources than any other manufacturer in advancements for reliability, uptime, and low cost of ownership. Safer translates into the rugged construction of its equipment as well as training for all customers to ensure safe and effective work practices using Altec equipment.

In addition to the design, manufacture and sale of highly specialized mobile equipment, Altec works directly with its customers to create solutions that meet their customers' ever-changing needs. The New Product Development Center meets a customer's need for a totally customized product, from chassis, to body, to aerial device requirements. If used equipment is more suitable, Altec also offers a used equipment solution (National Used Equipment Company) providing previously owned units. And a financing department (Altec Capital) is available to assist in custom-tailoring financing options designed to help customers acquire their equipment. If a customer isn't prepared to add additional units to its fleet permanently, but could use extra equipment for a specific job, or while another piece of equipment is being serviced, Altec provides a rental option as well, Global Rental Company, Inc.

The values on which the present owner's grandfather founded Altec over seven decades ago remain at the heart of the company's core philosophy. "My grandfather started this company with the idea that the customer comes first, and that people are our greatest strength," says Lee Styslinger, III, Altec's President and CEO. "My father ran the company using the same basic principles, and over the years, the initial ideas my grandfather had have helped us earn the trust and confidence of our customers worldwide. Listening to our customers and creating solutions is key to our commitment to total customer satisfaction in all that we do."

Altec's vision is to be recognized by its customers as the preferred supplier in all the markets it serves. The company's values play an important role in sustaining that vision and achieving its goal of total

The latest manufacturing techniques and rigorous prototype testing guarantees every piece of Altec equipment meets the standards of quality its customers have come to expect.

customer satisfaction. Every Team Altec associate strives toward these values: (listed alphabetically)
- customer first
- enjoyment at work
- family
- financial stability
- integrity
- people are our greatest strength
- quality
- spiritual development
- teamwork

Altec's long-term stability allows for resources to invest in research and development. The company remains at the forefront of providing solutions and innovations in information support services allowing its customers to fully integrate their businesses and streamline processes for increased efficiency and cost savings. The latest manufacturing techniques and rigorous prototype testing guarantees every piece of Altec equipment meets the standards of quality its customers have come to expect. This commitment to quality and safety has led to an unsurpassed warranty in the industry. In addition, the company has both

ISO 9001 and Class A certifications.

From its headquarters in Birmingham, Alabama, to service and manufacturing divisions in Georgia, Florida, Kentucky, North Carolina, Indiana, Minnesota, Missouri, Texas, Colorado, California, Oregon, Pennsylvania, Massachusetts, and Ontario, Manitoba, and British Columbia in Canada, Altec offers:
- most complete line of equipment
- lowest cost of ownership
- financial services
- rental
- used
- direct channels of distribution
- most comprehensive after-the-sale support
- most comprehensive road service network
- tools and accessories

In short, Altec invests in making crews' lives easier through safe, reliable equipment. Altec is not simply a vendor, but rather a business partner and consultant to assist its customers and ensure their crews work "Safer & Smarter."

William Gilchrist

There are just a couple of windows in the City Hall office of William Gilchrist, but then again for a man who understands the vision of what a city at the start of a new millennium in America should look like, windows may be a superfluous gesture. Gilchrist has the city committed to memory, to a vision of what a city should be.

According to Gilchrist, when people come to Birmingham and view the urban experience here, they find more character than they imagined they would see: A city with character in a setting of splendid natural beauty.

"We don't have block after block of anonymity. We have a lot to work with," Gilchrist says.

He sees a city that is and should be cautious of mistakes—of sprawl, of adding roads and the sprawl that accompanies them as the only solution to transportation needs. "Transportation and land use must be linked," Gilchrist says.

Unlike in some Southern cities, Atlanta for instance, the historic architecture of Birmingham is intact. A fabric of authenticity weaves through the city's residential neighborhoods and commercial centers.

Building on the authenticity and sense of design that has survived in modern Birmingham is the greater city's great challenge. Planning means more than deciding where to put the next subdivision.

In the modern city that works, things are interconnected. Land use is tied to transit, which is connected to economics, which then impacts the way we live. dream and prosper.

Born in New York and schooled in Boston, William Gilchrist is the director of the City of Birmingham Department of Planning, Engineering and Permits, responsible for regulating development of public and private construction in the city. He works with a staff of more than 220 people, overseeing the administration of land use, zoning, historic preservation, commercial revitaliza-

tion, special design districts, soil and erosion controls, engineering, building permits and inspections, transportation planning, and the city's capital program.

In short, Bill Gilchrist watches over the things that make a city a city.

An alumnus of Harvard University's Kennedy School of Government and the Massachusetts Institute of Technology (MIT), Gilchrist holds a master of architecture degree from MIT and a master's in management from MIT's Alfred P. Sloan School. He is a licensed architect with national certification.

A member of the American Institute of Architects, he has been a local director and served on the AIA's national Urban Design Committee and the board of directors of AIA's Rural/Urban Design Assistance Team. He also belongs to the American Planning Association and the American Public Works Association.

He is a founding member of Birmingham's Chapter of the National Organization of Minority Architects. He also belongs to the Urban Land Institute and the Construction Specification Institute. He is a member of the resource team for the Mayor's Institute on City Design sponsored by the U.S. Conference of Mayors, the National Endowment for the Arts and the American Architectural Foundation.

Gilchrist is a member of the Engineering Foundation Council for the University of Alabama at Birmingham. He also serves on the Visiting Committee to MIT's Department of Architecture and on Auburn University's Advisory Committee for Architecture and Urban Studies.

Vonetta Flowers

Imagine a cold corridor of ice.

The bob sled run is among the most exciting events in all of winter sports. In 2002 it was made all the more exciting because of the athlete whose nimble feet and strong legs set the sled careening down the icy mountain slide.

It was a long trip from Birmingham, Alabama to this Olympic venue in the mountains of Utah. For Vonetta Flowers it was an unusual and unexpected trip, too.

Born in 1973, Flowers had been an athlete from the time she was a very young child. She began running track at age 9. At Jonesboro Elementary School, Coach Dewitt Thomas watched Vonetta develop her God-given talent as an athlete. By the time she graduated from UAB, where she ran track and field and played volleyball and basketball, Vonetta Flowers has become one of that university's most decorated athletes; seven times she was named an NCAA All-American.

She competed in the Olympic Trials in both 1996 and 2000 in track and field events, pursuing a dream she first imagined as a young girl. With injuries and disappointments mounting by 2000 it looked as if her dream of competing as an Olympian might never be realized.

Shortly after the 2000 Trials, her husband, Johnny, also an Olympic hopeful athlete, saw a flyer soliciting athletes to try out for the U.S. Bobsled team. Johnny wanted to try out for the team and Vonetta accompanied him. An injury caused Johnny to pull out of the competition, but Vonetta tried out in his place.

From that unlikely scenario, Flower's career as an Olympian began. It culminated at the Salt Lake City Games where she and bobsled partner Jill Bakken completed their history-making bobsled run. Vonetta Flowers had fulfilled her Olympic dreams and became the first African American to win a gold medal in the Winter Games.

What happened after was no less extraordinary. Flowers became an instant celebrity, even making People magazine's list of the 50 Most Beautiful People. She won her gold medal in February 2002. In August she became a mother for the first time, as she gave birth to twin boys, Jaden and Jorden.

Today Flowers is an assistant track and field coach at UAB in training for another icy run at Olympic glory.

235

CITY OF FAIRFIELD, ALABAMA

The sprawling U.S. Steel works in the western section of Jefferson County evokes images of the early days of the 20th century when the giant furnaces that produced iron and steel also gave birth to the City of Fairfield. Most of those heavy manufacturing operations that were the backbone of the city, founded in 1910, are silent now, but Fairfield is alive and well.

The city experienced a renaissance under the leadership of its former mayor, Larry P. Langford, and the civic and business leaders in the area who, working together, made Fairfield a model for economic diversification and planned growth.

"We are the most densely populated city in Alabama," Mayor Langford relates, "with more than 13,000 people in about four square miles. Our focus has been to improve the quality of life for all citizens through the expansion of economic opportunities here and the provision of adequate

housing. We used to say that Fairfield was one of the best kept secrets in Alabama, but we can't say that any more. A great number of people are now aware of what Fairfield has to offer."

A community-wide effort was spearheaded in touting the city through a variety of successful initiatives. Expanding the city's economic base has been a major focus. No longer known only as a steel town, Fairfield boasts a healthy mix of business and industrial operations providing employment and a sound tax base.

Residents of Fairfield and visitors to the city need not travel outside the city limits to find banks, restaurants, home improvement stores, hotels, professional services, and a variety of other businesses.

Fairfield operates its own school system that has become known for the small average number of students per classroom and its above average per student spending. The city also points with pride to its community facilities. A sparkling civic center, an Olympic-size swim complex, a soccer field, softball fields, public parks, and a ten-

Right: Habitat for Humanity of Greater Birmingham, headquartered in downtown Fairfield, ranks among the top 40 of more than 1,620 Habitat affiliates in the nation in the production of housing. The organization builds homes through partnerships with volunteers, Habitat staff, and financial contributors. A total of 51 Habitat homes have been built in Fairfield.

Below: The sprawling U.S. Steel works evoke images of the early days of the 20th century when the giant furnaces that produced iron and steel also gave birth to the City of Fairfield.

nis center offer recreational opportunities rarely found in a city of this size.

City services are other points of pride. The city's police force, headed by one of the few female police chiefs in the nation, is known for its get-tough policy on criminal offenders, even to the point of using a Lexus confiscated from drug dealers as a police vehicle. The personnel and equipment of the full-time fire department have resulted in an excellent insurance rating for the city, and quality development of the city's neighborhoods is ensured through a zoning ordinance and subdivision regulations.

Fairfield is served by the former Lloyd Noland Hospital, now a 264-bed HealthSouth Medical Center, a name that has become synonymous around the country with quality healthcare. In addition, UAB Medical West, a regional medical facility, is located only minutes away.

The provision of adequate housing has been the cornerstone of the initiatives that have resulted in the successful revitalization of Fairfield. The city ranks among the cities with the lowest

The city points with pride to its community facilities. A sparkling civic center, an Olympic-size swim complex, a soccer field, baseball/softball fields, public parks and a tennis center.

Fairfield operates its own school system that has become known for the small average per student spending.

number of dilapidated houses. The goal has been to take people off the welfare rolls and out of public housing. Putting people into their own homes leads to pride in ownership. That pride translates into better citizens and a better community."

To achieve those goals, Fairfield turned to an innovative housing construction program that has transformed the city as well as developed it into a major player on the national and international stages. Habitat for Humanity of Greater Birmingham, headquartered

TRAINING SITE FOR 1996 OLYMPICS

in downtown Fairfield, ranks among the top 40 of the more than 1,620 Habitat affiliates in the nation in the production of housing. The organization builds homes through partnerships with volunteers, Habitat staff, and financial contributors. Building and renovating homes for people who would normally be excluded from the home ownership market helps provide decent housing and break the cycle of need, restores hope, and gives families an opportunity to enhance their quality of life. By literally investing

themselves in the building process, homeowners gain self-confidence, self-esteem, and skills.

Habitat families contribute 300 hours of sweat equity in the form of volunteer labor on their future homes as well as others' homes, office work, and various other duties. They complete ten educational workshops on subjects ranging from budgeting to home repairs. They also pay closing costs and make monthly mortgage payments. Homes are sold at no profit and with no interest. A selection com-

mittee evaluates prospective homeowners based on need for decent, affordable shelter; willingness to partner with Habitat; and ability to repay a zero percent interest mortgage.

The organization's work in Fairfield has been significant. According to Mayor Langford, an area of the city once identified by vacant, trash-filled lots was transformed into Habitat Court, a model neighborhood.

"There are 20 homes there now," says Cassie Sanford, Habitat's director of development. "A total of 51

Habitat homes have been built in Fairfield. That's 51 families that now live in decent, affordable housing, and have pride in home ownership."

That pride is evident throughout Fairfield, Alabama as the city focuses on even greater accomplishments in the future. Many hands joined together to make the city a vibrant, dynamic center of commercial activity and a quality residential area. Their voices join together in echoing the city's motto of "To God Be The Glory."

J.O. RODGERS & ASSOCIATES, INC.

A management consulting firm based in Decatur, Georgia, just outside Atlanta, has become a leader in the field of diversity management. J.O. Rodgers & Associates has been educating business leaders and conducting diversity training for some of the largest and most successful businesses and organizations in the world for over a decade.

Managing diversity in the workplace is one of the most important issues currently facing businesses. Reports from the Bureau of the Census and the Department of Labor indicate that the U.S. workplace today is becoming increasingly characterized by a shortage of skilled workers, a rise in the average age of workers, more women in the workplace, a larger percentage of workers who are minorities, more diverse markets, and global competition. American business leaders are recognizing the fact that diversity is a fact of life and must be an integral part of management thinking.

Certified Management Consultant (CMC) James O. Rodgers was among the first to recognize those needs and establish a firm committed to developing diversity management strategies to respond to the changes in the workplace. He and his associates bring their unique talents and skillsets to this critically important process. The firm's experienced consultants and faculty have been lead consultants on diversity management initiatives for companies such as IBM, Texaco, Hewlett-Packard, Coca-Cola, and Georgia Power.

Rodgers' strategic approach includes several key points. First, the firm's consultants meet with the client's senior leaders to review what, if anything, they know about the value of an effective diversity management strategy. Next, they assist in setting clear expectations (vision) of what the client hopes to gain or achieve through the strategy. Defining the target of the initiative is crucial.

A clear, concise statement of commitment is then drafted, and leaders go on record in support of the corporate change required to achieve the objective. Communication among the client company's leaders and staff is stressed as the key to whether the strategy is effectively implemented or will remain on the shelf as a static document. Engagement and learning activities are implemented to make everyone in the company feel a sense of involvement in the diversity strategy process.

Finally, J.O. Rodgers & Associates monitors the progress of its clients in achieving their goals. Results are measured and reviewed regularly to determine if the company is moving in the right direction.

Rodgers' clients have found numerous benefits from the training:

- access to emerging markets
- access to more top talent
- better resources to apply in a global economy
- more productive and efficient work teams
- improved customer relations
- a better work environment and enjoyment in the workplace
- progress in creating a culture of inclusion

"My experience with companies that approach diversity as a strategy is that most people want to be a part of the solution — they simply lack the awareness and skills to do so," James Rodgers states. "One positive by-product of this approach is that diversity is a natural umbrella for addressing issues of teamwork, management skills, quality, empowerment, and customer satisfaction."

Diversity represents both a challenge and an opportunity. J.O. Rodgers & Associates has accepted that challenge and built a successful business on seizing the opportunity to bring consulting and services to the hundreds of clients who seek to effectively deal with our differences in gender, age, ethnic culture, physical ability, religion, and personality traits.

Jim Rodgers, the founder, is a former Birmingham resident and graduate of UAB's MBA program.

THE ALTAMONT SCHOOL

Since its founding in 1975, the mission of The Altamont School has been to improve the fabric of society by graduating compassionate, educated individuals capable of independent thinking and innovative ideas. Students in grades five through twelve are prepared for a high level of performance in the most rigorous post-secondary institutions by equipping them with the intellectual tools required in the most demanding sectors of the adult world.

The 34-acre campus includes the main building, perched along the crest of Red Mountain, and the nearby Comer athletic facility. The 410 students attending the college preparatory independent school are an ethnically and racially diverse student population from Birmingham, the suburbs, and the surrounding communities. Candidates for admission are evaluated from personal interviews, test scores from the Independent School Entrance Examination, and previous school grades.

Approximately 72 percent of the 39 teachers at the school hold Masters degrees or higher diplomas. The favorable student/teacher ratio of approximately 10:1 permits an advisor system in which every student chooses a faculty member who will be a personal and scholastic advisor.

These professionals are obviously doing an exceptional job in preparing their students for post-secondary education. The Class of 2003 scored a 27 in its Mean ACT Composite Score. The National Composite was 21.8, and the Alabama Composite was 20.1.

The prescribed one-track honors curriculum for grades five through eight includes English; foreign languages (French, Spanish, and Latin); social studies; mathematics; science; and physical education. The curriculum for grades nine through 12 includes English; social science, science, mathematics, foreign languages, speech, health, and physical education. Electives include music, orchestra, art, drama, computer science, math team, and creative writing. The school's athletics programs for boys and girls feature competitive teams in swimming and diving, soccer, softball, baseball, basketball, tennis, golf, volleyball, cross country, and indoor and outdoor track.

The school's alumni association lists 1,800 graduates hailing from as far away as China and as near as Forest Park. The group sponsors an alumni scholarship, book fair, career day, and other activities.

"The relationship of the teacher and the individual student is the most important element of the Altamont education. While academic success is an important goal, the personal growth of an ethical young person is just as significant. Teachers model their passion for learning and ethical citizenship; students seek to learn in the classroom, on the stage, and on the court and field from those models," says Headmaster Thomas Wheelock. "Our small size and rigorous curriculum enable us to know each child's capacity to learn and to provide a college preparatory liberal arts curriculum that promises success in college and beyond. We feel Altamont is a resource for the city of Birmingham and the state of Alabama."

Headmaster Thomas Wheelock with Altamont students. Above, the main campus building.

SOMERBY AT UNIVERSITY PARK—HOMEWOOD
SOMERBY AT JONES FARM—HUNTSVILLE

Since its founding in 1964 as the real estate management arm of the international engineering and construction firm, Daniel International Corporation, the Daniel Corporation has broadened its scope of services to include the acquisition and development of investment properties. Locally owned and privately held since 1986, Daniel Corporation is headquartered in Birmingham, Alabama, and maintains offices in Raleigh, North Carolina and Richmond, Virginia.

The explosive growth in demand for high quality retirement alternatives led Daniel to further expand its existing senior living portfolio through the development and operation of innovative campus senior living communities. The firm's resume in this market ranges from a 128-bed skilled nursing care facility to freestanding independent living apartments to large scale campuses of continuing care retirement communities. In 1999, Daniel completed the first develop-

ments in a series of high quality senior living facilities ventured with Dr. David Bronner on behalf of the Retirement Systems of Alabama.

Somerby at University Park, off Lakeshore Drive in Homewood, and Somerby at Jones Farm in the Jones Valley area of Huntsville, Alabama, provide a continuum of care for senior residents enabling them to gracefully age in place through an array of shel-

ter and service options, all provided within a large-scale care community.

Somerby at University Park

Located across from Samford University on Lakeshore Drive in Homewood, one of Birmingham, Alabama's premier suburban communities, Somerby at University Park is set along a wooded area buffering the banks of Shades Creek and its exercise paths and trails. This campus style senior residential community covers 40 acres and consists of 240 independent living apartments, 84 assisted living apartments, 28 Alzheimer care apartments, and 48 fee simple garden homes. Amenities include a full service dining facility, exercise facilities, 24-hour security and emergency response systems, library, beauty shop, community center, living room, convenience store, mail delivery, a Compass Bank branch, and courtesy transportation. Each floor features a large activity room, quiet room/den, and laundry facility.

Somerby at Jones Farm

Somerby at Jones Farm is located on Carl T. Jones Drive in Huntsville, Alabama. This campus style senior

residential community is situated on 23 acres of land and features 138 independent living apartments, 48 assisted living apartments, and 47 fee simple garden homes. Residents have access to a full service dining facility, library, beauty shop, community center, living room, convenience store, mail delivery, ATM, and courtesy transportation. Similar to Somerby at University Park, each floor features a large activity room, quiet room/den, and laundry facility.

In keeping with its commitment to excellence, Daniel enlisted a premier name in the senior property management industry to professionally market and manage both developments. American Retirement Corporation, headquartered in Nashville, Tennessee, is one of the country's oldest and largest providers of senior health care services and housing in the nation. The company owns and operates 65 retirement and assisted living communities in 14 states across the U.S.

According to Bill Sheriff, Chairman and CEO of American Retirement Corporation, "Daniel Corporation has done a wonderful job of developing two premier communi-

ties in Birmingham and Huntsville, and our company is proud to be associated with them in these ventures. In the Somerby concept, Daniel Corporation has succeeded in creating a rental retirement model that places these two retirement centers among the most desirable senior living communities anywhere and underscores the inherent quality of the entire Daniel organization."

The Daniel Corporation has begun construction on a third Somerby development in the western section of Mobile, Alabama adjoining the Providence Hospital campus. Construction is expected to be completed in mid-2005 on this community, which will offer the same continuum of care as the Somerby communities in Birmingham and Huntsville.

John Gorecki, the Senior Vice President of Daniel's senior living group, reflects on the success of its Somerby communities. "We were most fortunate to collaborate with two great partners on our Somerby communities. Dr. Bronner's vision for, and financial commitment to, the State of Alabama was the first and most important step in our mutual success. American Retirement Corporation's experience and leadership, along with our 30-plus year involvement in the senior living and residential development sectors, allowed us to bring quality housing and services to the fastest growing segment of our population—

those over 55 years of age. We at Daniel Corporation view ourselves as a service company, and the Somerby communities are examples of our desire to match our real estate knowledge and experience with the needs of the people and communities we seek to serve."

For almost four decades, Daniel Corporation has pursued an unwavering commitment to excellence in its expanded role as a full service real

estate organization. Daniel's diverse real estate portfolio, built through long-term relationships with prominent institutional and investment partners, currently focuses on commercial and residential properties and land development in select markets in the Southeastern and Mid-Atlantic states.

Daniel's commercial ownership and development portfolio includes some 8.5 million square feet of Class A office buildings and award-winning

suburban office parks in Birmingham, Atlanta, Charlotte, Raleigh, and Richmond. In the Birmingham area, the list includes such landmarks as Meadow Brook, Grandview, University Park, Oxmoor Corporate Center, Lakeshore Park Plaza and Ross Bridge.

The firm's imprint on residential development is equally impressive, with signature neighborhoods such as Greystone, Meadow Brook and Brook Highland. All of Daniel's developments share a commitment to the communities of which they are a part, from advanced design concepts to preservation of the natural environment. In its residential communities, Daniel has utilized innovative construction technology and design with environmentally sensitive site planning to create spaces in which people reside harmoniously with nature.

WARREN & ASSOCIATES LLC
ATTORNEYS AT LAW

John Warren

Innovation and renovation. John Warren relied on generous helpings of each to establish his legal practice and restore the historic building in Jasper, Alabama that now serves as his headquarters.

Warren & Associates is a full-service law firm representing and advising clients in areas of practice including personal injury, product liability, workers' compensation, wrongful death, motor vehicle accidents, nursing home litigation, medical malpractice, railroad litigation, consumer fraud, insurance fraud, social security disability, business torts, and civil litigation law. His dedication to quality, a thorough understanding of the law, and respect are the foundations on which he has built long-standing relationships with his clients in the Jasper community and across north-central Alabama.

John Warren has based his practice of law on integrity, honesty, and compassion, the same principles by which he lives. He offers a personalized and specialized approach in his commitment to aggressive advocacy and representation of the people of Walker County. "I chose the less traveled road in pursuing the best results for my clients," Warren states.

"That road of integrity, honesty, and compassion combined with hard work and dedication enables me to offer the kind of representation that each of my clients deserves. Keeping current with the most recent legal issues and knowing how to apply them to each individual are what differentiate great attorneys from good ones."

Warren has an unparalleled track record of success having recovered millions of dollars for clients over the years. Whether litigating personal injury cases, product liability cases, nursing home abuse allegations or worker's compensation claims, Warren & Associates takes a proactive approach to each client's case.

Consequently, the firm has earned a reputation as being thorough and vigorous advocates for its clients.

In addition to his academic credentials, the firm utilized state-of-the-art technology to provide superior legal services to its clients. Attorneys and staff have access to voice mail, electronic mail, the internet, presentation software, audiovisual technology, and computer-aided presentation graphics. Warren was among the first lawyers to employ video graphics presentations in the mediation process, and he produces a videotape presentation of his clients' cases in almost every settlement mediation process. Electronic services for legal research

are also utilized in order to provide needed information in the most efficient, economical manner possible.

In addition to actively practicing throughout most counties in the north-central section of the state, Warren & Associates also practices in federal court in Alabama and the Eleventh Circuit Court of Appeals.

John Warren found his penchant for innovation in the provision of legal services to his clients had a counterpart in a certain talent he possessed for building renovation. When searching for a location in Jasper to serve as his headquarters, he found a historic structure in the heart of the downtown area that he felt fit his needs exactly.

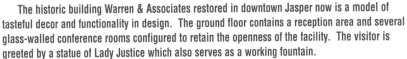

The historic building Warren & Associates restored in downtown Jasper now is a model of tasteful decor and functionality in design. The ground floor contains a reception area and several glass-walled conference rooms configured to retain the openness of the facility. The visitor is greeted by a statue of Lady Justice which also serves as a working fountain.

The three story building had been constructed in 1931, and formerly served as a bus station on the Miss/Ala bus line between Alabama and Mississippi. In the 1940s, it became one of only two hotels in operation in Jasper before closing its doors. The building was in good structural condition, but would need a great deal of work before it could serve as a legal office.

"It was a challenge, but one we enjoyed accepting," explains Leesa Warren, John's wife who had always been interested in interior design, and spearheaded the renovation effort. "A number of very talented people in Jasper offered their help in the transformation of the building. Many did it in appreciation of the services that John had rendered to the community in the past."

The building now is a model of tasteful decor and functionality in design. The ground floor contains a reception area and several glass-walled conference rooms configured to retain the openness of the facility. The visitor is greeted by a statue of Lady Justice which also serves as a working fountain.

The second level is a mezzanine that serves as a lounge area with an eclectic mix of furnishings and equipment that underscores the diversity of interest of Warren. Exercise equipment, a ping-pong table, and a billiards table offer pleasant diversions, while a complete set of drums caters to Warren's musical bent. Walls are lined with Auburn memorabilia that Warren collects as an alumni of the university.

The third floor work area houses the attorney's offices, audio-visual room, investigation offices, complete shower facilities, and a break room. A play room for the children of employees is also provided. The entire facility is designed to reflect the firm's move to become more family oriented.

Even though the firm sports a new look and the latest in legal resources, Warren's basic business tenet remains the same. John Warren looks forward to offering the highest quality legal services to each client who comes through his door.

The following is required by Rule 7.2 of the Alabama State Bar Rules of Professional Conduct: "No representation is made that the quality of legal services to be performed is greater than the quality of legal services performed by other lawyers."

Authors, Photographer

Bill Caton

Bill Caton is a native of Alabama, raised in Birmingham. He graduated from Auburn University in 1980 with a bachelor's degree in journalism. Caton has worked for more than 20 years as an editor and writer for newspapers and magazines. He now serves as director of membership and public relations for the Alabama AGC, which has won three national public relations excellence awards in the past five years. Caton is the author of several books, including *Fighting Words: Words on Writing from 21 of the Heart of Dixie's Best Contemporary Authors*, *Josh and the Flat Cows* and *Vulcan: Rekindling the Flame*.

Caton lives in Birmingham with his wife Ann and their son Josh.

Niki Sepsas

Song of the Gypsy is the first novel by Birmingham-based freelance writer Niki Sepsas, who swerved into the writing life after being bitten by the travel bug at an early age. Following college at West Point and UAB and serving in the Army, he worked on offshore oil drilling rigs in Southeast Asia. Deciding that a pen and a passport were preferable to hard hats and oil derricks, he opted for a career as a tour guide and travel writer. For the next 25 years, he pointed out the wonders in over 100 countries around the globe to wide-eyed pilgrims on tours and cruises. He drew on his travel adventures to publish more than 600 articles in over three dozen national, regional, and local magazines and newspapers. Readers have followed him climbing Africa's Mount Kilimanjaro, kayaking in Iceland, canoeing the Amazon, ballooning over the Serengeti, rafting the Grand Canyon, trekking the Himalayas, cruising around the world, and countless other adventures. He is also a contributing author to the Chicken Soup for the Soul series of books, where one of his stories was adapted into a short film that aired on PAX Television.

Sepsas' romance novel, his first venture into fiction, is set in the spectacular mountains of Greece's Peloponnesos region which was home to his grandparents before immigrating to the U.S. He has made over 30 trips to Greece and the tiny village in which the story takes place.

The book is available through the local bookstores and at Amazon.com.

Beau Gustafson

Beau Gustafson is the primary photographer of Birmingham magazine. He also does photography work for advertising agencies and magazines throughout the country. Beau moved here about nine years ago from the city of smog and traffic jams (Los Angeles) and now makes Birmingham his home with his wife, Audrey, and their son, Darby Jack. He spends his free time with his family, and teaching Northern Shaolin Kung-Fu at Blue Dragon Academy in Hoover.